Analysing Change

Analysing Change

Measurement and Explanation Using Longitudinal Data

Ian Plewis
Thomas Coram Research Unit
University of London Institute of Education

JOHN WILEY & SONS
Chichester · New York · Brisbane · Toronto · Singapore

Library of Congress Cataloging in Publication Data:
Plewis, Ian.
  Analysing change.

  Bibliography: p.
  Includes indexes.
  1. Social sciences—Statistical methods.   2. Social change—Mathematical models.   I. Title.
  HA29.P6244   1985   300′.72   84–22044
  ISBN 0   471   10444   2

British Library Cataloguing in Publication Data:
Plewis, Ian
  Analysing change: measurement and explanation using longitudinal data
  1. Social sciences—Longitudinal studies
  I. Title
  300′.722   H61

  ISBN 0   471   10444   2

Phototypeset by Macmillan India Ltd, Bangalore
Printed in Great Britain at The Pitman Press, Bath

If the abysm
Could vomit forth its secrets—but a voice
Is wanting, the deep truth is imageless;
For what would it avail to bid thee gaze
On the revolving world? what to bid speak
Fate, Time, Occasion, Chance and Change? To these
All things are subject but eternal Love.

P. B. Shelley, *Prometheus Unbound*, Act II, Scene IV

Contents

Preface

I started thinking systematically about how to analyse the different kinds of change data collected by social scientists some years ago, when I was awarded a Fellowship by the Social Science Research Council (as it then was) to think about the statistical problems of longitudinal studies. This book has grown out of the work I did then and is an expanded version of the report I submitted to the SSRC towards the end of 1981.

I have written the book primarily for social scientists who want to learn how to analyse quantitative longitudinal data. However, I hope that postgraduate students in the social sciences, social statistics students, and even statisticians working with social science data will also find it useful. I have tried to keep the technical content of the material at a fairly elementary level, relegating some of the more difficult ideas to appendices and giving references to more theoretical expositions, and I have deliberately avoided presenting the statistical ideas in a wholly rigorous way. Instead, I have chosen to show how to analyse longitudinal data and, most importantly, how to interpret the results, using a number of examples taken from actual research projects. This has meant sacrificing some generality in places, but this loss will, I believe, be outweighed by the gain in accessibility which this approach gives.

Nevertheless, it would be wrong to pretend that only the most straightforward statistical methods are needed to answer all the interesting questions for which longitudinal data are well suited. Consequently, readers will need to be familiar with basic statistical ideas and methods up to the level of, say, Blalock (1981) and perhaps supplemented with some of the material on multiple regression from Draper and Smith (1981) or Weisberg (1980). With this background, the material in the first five chapters should not pose any problems. However, Chapters 6 to 9 present methods for categorical data—these are still relatively new and readers might find it helpful to look at, say, Fienberg (1980) before tackling them.

I have used examples from a wide range of contexts within the social sciences, and they are typical of the kinds of data collected by educationalists, social and developmental psychologists, social administrators, sociologists, and political scientists. The two areas which are not covered are experimental psychology, where the problems are much more akin to those faced in human growth studies, which in turn are well covered by Goldstein (1979a); and economics. Most analyses of change in economics use time series data, and time series analysis is well covered in other books. However, recently economists, particularly labour economists, have become much more interested in longitudinal data, and I allude to their interests in Chapter 9 ('Models for transition and duration').

This book could not have been written without the help of a number of people. I would like to thank George Smith for letting me have the Educational Priority Area data, Dougal Hutchison for the data on progress in secondary schools from the National Child Development Study, Theo Cox for the data used in Chapter 9, and colleagues at the Thomas Coram Reseach Unit who worked on the Pre-School project. The ESRC Data Archive provided me with the British Election Study data.

Russell Ecob, Dougal Hutchison, Bianca De Stavola, and Barbara Tizard made useful comments on individual chapters, and Maria Harrison used the flexibility of the word processor to cope with my many drafts with great skill and patience. Charlie Owen read through my final draft and came up with a number of timely suggestions. I am grateful to all of them, but especially to Harvey Goldstein who read and commented on all the chapters and whose own work in this area provided an indispensable framework for my forays. All of these friends and colleagues eliminated some of my mistakes, but none bears any responsibility for those that remain.

IAN PLEWIS
London
August 1984

CHAPTER 1

The Concept of Change

1.1 INTRODUCTION

Many of the interesting questions in the social sciences are about change and process and cause, questions about dynamics, and they cannot be answered with static descriptions and associations. To give some examples, it is useful to know the distribution of reading ability for children of a certain age, but more useful to know how reading skills develop as children grow. An observed relationship between drug taking and criminal behaviour in adolescence is suggestive, but it is much more valuable to find out whether taking drugs leads to criminal behaviour or whether such behaviour leads to drug taking. It is disturbing to find that working class children leave school with fewer educational qualifications than middle class children, but more important, from the point of view of formulating policies to reduce inequality, to understand the processes which lead to this situation.

In other words, we often need to take an explicitly dynamic approach to empirical research in the social sciences, and this means collecting data over time rather than, or as well as, collecting data about a particular point in time. This has long been recognized by students of physical growth and by developmental psychologists, but only relatively recently in the other disciplines that make up the social sciences. One of the earliest examples is the study carried out by the sociologist Paul Lazarsfeld, who looked at the voting intentions of a *panel* of voters before the 1940 US Presidential election and who recognized that 'the repeated interview technique allows us to establish a time sequence and therefore greatly facilitates causal analysis' (Lazarsfeld, Berelson, and Gaudet, 1944).

Since 1945, the need for dynamic or *longitudinal* data has been more widely appreciated, although progress in collecting and using data of this kind has been inhibited by cost, by data processing difficulties and by uncertainties about how to analyse them. As long as funding for social science research remains scarce, it will continue to be difficult to find money for these kinds of studies, but developments in computers and computer packages have eliminated most of the data processing problems. The main aim of this book is to show how modern statistical methods can be used to analyse longitudinal data of various kinds in order better to understand how and why individuals and groups change. It is not the purpose of this book to give a complete discussion of all the methodological issues involved in organizing and carrying out longitudinal studies or, more generally, studies of change. These are discussed in Wall and Williams (1970),

1

Janson (1978), Goldstein (1979a) and Robins (1980). However, this chapter sets the scene and gives a brief general introduction to the concept of change and to designs for measuring it.

1.2 WAYS OF THINKING ABOUT CHANGE

The concept of change can be examined from a number of angles. Perhaps the most common of these is to see change in a variable in terms of growth or development, in other words, change as a function of age. Developmental psychologists usually take as their domain of interest the time between birth and the beginning of adulthood and, within that period, change would normally be regarded as continuous with age. It could be regarded as a linear function of age, as in Figure 1.1, but psychological variables are more likely to show a non-linear but never decreasing relationship with age (Figure 1.2), just as human growth does. However, we shall see that the problems of studying psychological and indeed all social science variables in the same way as height are formidable, not least because these variables often cannot be measured on the same scale at different ages.

It is also possible to think of development in terms of passing through a series of stages—first learning to walk and then learning to hop, for example—and this could be represented as a discontinuous set of steps, as in Figure 1.3. Singer and Spilerman (1979) discuss this perspective on development and show how it might be modelled mathematically.

Developmental change, both for a population and for all the individuals within it, normally takes place in just one direction, but many variables do, of course, change in a more haphazard way over time. Individuals' attitude towards

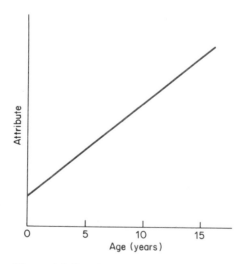

Figure 1.1 Development as a linear function of age

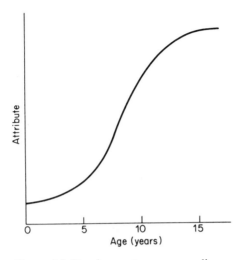

Figure 1.2 Development as a non-linear
and non-decreasing function of age

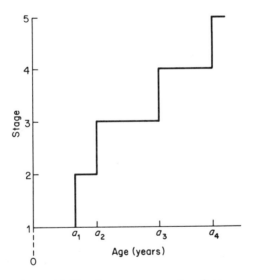

Figure 1.3 Development as a series of stages

a political party can show marked fluctuations over time, for example, and even a steady increase or decline in party support over time can mask considerable fluctuations in attitude at the individual level. Other fluctuations over time can be more regular and this is particularly true of economic measures such as the unemployment and inflation rates which often show both seasonal and long-term cyclical variation.

Change can sometimes be brought about by altering an environment from the outside. This manipulation can take place at the group level, as in the Head Start interventions in the United States (Zigler and Valentine, 1979), which can be seen as an attempt to speed up the educational development of disadvantaged pre-school children by providing extra educational experience in a group setting. It can also take place at the individual level, as in the application of techniques of behaviour modification. Evidence about the effects of these kinds of intervention is usually obtained by applying them in some sort of experimental context.

Change, then, can refer either to change over age or to change over time (or period), or to both. In fact, a third effect—cohort—has also been proposed as a 'dimension' of change. Cohort, or generation, effects are usually defined as those effects due to differing dates of birth, although the term is more general and can be applied to the start of any experience such as secondary school or a spell in the army. Period effects are those which can be attributed to different times of measurement: they are the changes which are observed over time and are often referred to as secular trends, although this term could also be applied to cohort effects. Although each of the three effects can be interpreted *on their own*, it is important to realize that when taken together the three effects are logically dependent. This dependence can be expressed quite simply as:

$$\text{Cohort} = \text{Period} - \text{Age} \qquad (1.1)$$

Considerable controversy has surrounded estimation of age, period, and cohort effects (see, for example, Fienberg and Mason (1978) and Goldstein (1979b)), and we return to this theme in Section 1.6.

We can think about change both at the *individual* level (gross change) and at the *aggregate* level (net or mean change), and these are defined algebraically in the next chapter (Section 2.2). It is important to realize that a particular pattern of net change can coexist with different patterns of individual change; this is illustrated by Figure 1.4, which is taken from Merrell (1931). It shows net change having one kind of relationship with age which is quite different from the symmetrical relationship exhibited by the two individuals.

Rather than looking at change, it is sometimes useful to look at stability over time. Stability is usually defined as the correlation between measures on a variable taken on the same individuals at separate occasions. A high positive correlation implies high stability, which in turn implies that the rank order, or relative position, of individuals on the variable changes little over time, as in Figure 1.5(a). Correlations which are close to zero are usually taken to indicate low stability (Figure 1.5(b)), but this might be misleading if there is a markedly non-linear relationship between the measures on the variable over time. High negative correlations rarely occur, but would indicate high instability, as in Figure 1.5(c). High stability does not imply that there can be no change at the individual level, merely that whatever change there is, it is highly predictable, just as it is when there is high instability. Similarly, data on stability, when defined in this way, cannot be used to make inferences about change at the aggregate level.

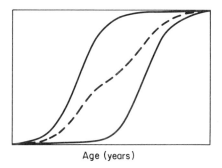

Age (years)

Figure 1.4 Net (average) and individual change
Legend: ——Individual logistic
– – –Average curve
(Reprinted from 'The relationship of individual growth to average growth', *Human Biology*, Vol. 3, No. 1, 1931 by Margaret Merrell by permission of the Wayne State University Press. © 1931 Wayne State University Press)

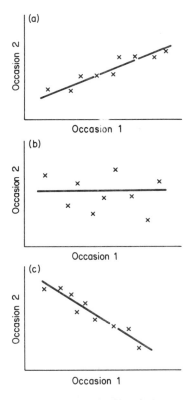

Figure 1.5 (a) High stability
(b) Low stability
(c) High instability

So far in this section we have implicitly assumed that change can refer only to variables which have some sort of ordering, that is, they are measured at least on an ordinal scale. However, this is not so, and it is perfectly sensible to see change in terms of movement between categories of an unordered variable. For example, researchers working on the Negative Income Tax experiments in the United States were particularly interested in the effects of cash supplements on rates of marital formation and dissolution (Tuma, Hannan, and Groeneveld, 1979), and so they looked at change over time in individuals' marital status. Marital status can be treated as an unordered variable with several categories—single, married, divorced, and widowed, for instance.

It is usual to think of change as occurring all the time—in continuous time—although the measurement of change normally takes place in discrete time. In other words, repeated measurement takes place at occasions which are often widely spaced in time, and cannot always take account of what happens between these occasions. To formulate change in discrete time is clearly reasonable for some variables; for example, children move between types of school, and governments change at time points which could reasonably be regarded as fixed, while the effects of various kinds of interventions are usually only required for a specific time span. On the other hand, attitudes and developmental variables such as cognitive abilities and skills are changing all the time. A third group of variables, such as hours per week worked and marital status, while not changing all the time, do not change at fixed time points and so would perhaps be dealt with better in continuous time. These issues are raised again in Chapter 2 and in Chapter 9.

1.3 DESIGNS FOR MEASURING CHANGE

There are a number of research designs which can be used to collect change data, each with its methodological advantages and disadvantages.

Perhaps the easiest way to collect change data is within the context of a simple *cross-sectional* study when data are obtained at just one point in time. Although there is only one measurement occasion in a cross-sectional study, it is possible to get data which refer not only to that occasion but also to previous occasions by asking retrospective questions or by using official records. Indeed, nearly all cross-sectional studies incorporate a certain amount of retrospective data collection, but the need to get more accurate data prevents its widespread adoption. Retrospective interview data suffer from reporting errors of various kinds— respondents may forget an event altogether, or they may forget when it happened, or they may change their account of an event or an attitude so that it fits more easily into their present situation—and these errors can lead both to bias and to increased variability of the estimates (means, correlations, etc.) of interest. Sometimes it is just not practicable to collect retrospective data—clearly one cannot get retrospective measures of IQ, for example. Moss and Goldstein

(1979) deal with the advantages and disadvantages of retrospective (recall) data.

A second way of getting at least some data on change is to measure individuals from a series of independent samples, or cross-sections, over time. In other words, samples from the same population are measured at each occasion, but individuals are only measured once. If it is combined with retrospective data collection methods, this design will provide change data at the individual level but otherwise it can only provide information on aggregate or net change and, as we shall see in Section 1.5, may not be the most efficient way of collecting this information.

The most convincing, and most popular, way of collecting change data is to use a *longitudinal* design, a design in which more than one member of a set of cases is measured on more than one occasion. A distinction is drawn in this book between a longitudinal study, which uses a longitudinal design, and longitudinal data which refer to *any* data collected at the individual level about more than one occasion, and so include retrospectively collected data. The term 'longitudinal study' is very general: it encompasses the terms 'pure' and 'mixed' longitudinal studies, 'cohort' studies, 'panel' studies, 'prospective' studies, 'follow-up' studies and even 'repeated measures experiments'. However, it excludes the studies of a single case that are sometimes found in the medical sciences (including early studies of growth) and in psychology. The definition is also intended to exclude economic and other time series, although it is not easy to draw a boundary between longitudinal and time series data. Time series data tend to consist of one or few variables, commonly measured on just one case (for example, a country), on at least ten and often many more occasions, whereas longitudinal data in the social sciences rarely contain ten observations per case, but consist of many cases, often thousands, and many variables. The analysis of time series data is not discussed here, and interested readers are referred to Chatfield (1980). Hersen and Barlow (1976) and Kratochwill (1978) deal with the analysis of single subject data. Longitudinal studies do not have to be studies of individual people over time, although they often are. It is perfectly possible to study social groups and institutions such as communities, schools, and hospitals with a longitudinal design.

In most longitudinal studies in the social sciences, measurements are taken at fixed occasions which are often regularly spaced, such as every year. But in some, times of measurement are not predetermined, but depend instead on the occurrence of events such as births, deaths, and job changes. The Office of Population Censuses and Surveys Longitudinal Study (Goldblatt and Fox, 1978) is an example of the second kind which is more common in the medical sciences and so receives less attention than the fixed occasion studies in this book (but see Chapter 9).

In the previous section, three dimensions of change—age, period, and cohort—were explained. (Cohort effects are only meaningful at the aggregate level, but the other two can be used both at the individual and at the aggregate level.) It is possible to design a study to estimate any two of age, period, and cohort, although it is common to find longitudinal designs which follow a particular birth, or other, cohort over time. This enables only one of the two remaining effects to be estimated because age and period cannot then be separated. (They can never be separated at the individual level, only at the aggregate level.) The usual response to this design has been to think in terms of individual age effects. This is mainly because the substantive concerns of these cohort studies have been medical, psychological, and educational where age is a key variable, but perhaps also because they have been strongly influenced by the use of the design in the study of growth. Clearly the effects of age are different not only for different variables but also at different stages of the life cycle—dramatic changes are observed in the first five years of life, but are not usually found between 30 and 35. Thus, many longitudinal studies of adults are concerned less with age effects and more with period effects, and this has influenced design in the sense that the initial population is often defined by a wide age range, rather than by a single birth cohort. However, the longer studies of adults last, the more useful is the idea of individual age effects.

Baltes (1968) considers the problem of designing studies to estimate dimensions of change and Figure 1.6 is adapted from figures 2 and 4 in his article. Each row of Figure 1.6 represents the design discussed previously—a birth cohort measured, in this case, every year for ten years with the possibility of relating change at the individual level to age or to period but not to both, and with all inferences restricted to the particular cohort chosen. The diagonal slices represent the usual cross-sectional studies with period constant, no possibility of measuring individual change (except retrospectively), and both cohort and age affecting aggregate change in a way which cannot be disentangled. The individual columns have been defined by Schaie (1965) as time-lag designs and allow net change to be related just to cohort for a particular age, but time-lag designs are really just a series of cross-sectional studies on a restricted population. However, by judicious selection of sampling units, it is possible to obtain longitudinal information from time-lag designs. The most convenient way of getting a sample of children, for example, is first to select a sample of schools (the primary sampling units) and then to select children from within schools. If children of a certain age are selected from the *same* schools at different times then longitudinal data become available for schools.

The horizontal and diagonal boxes marked in Figure 1.6 have been called longitudinal and cross-sectional sequences respectively by Baltes. A longitudinal sequence enables a period or cohort effect for net change to be estimated as well as individual and net age (or period) effects. A cross-sectional sequence allows the separation of cohort and age effects on net change.

An approximation to the longitudinal sequence design illustrated in Figure 1.6 is provided by putting together the three national birth cohort studies conducted in Britain (see Figure 1.7). The 1946 cohort—the National Survey of Health and Development—is a stratified sample of births in the first week of March that year; the 1958 cohort—the National Child Development Study—consists of all births in the first week of March; while the 1970 cohort—Child Health and

Cohort \ Age	0	1	2	3	4	5	6	7	8	9
1970	1970	71	72	73	74	75	76	77	78	79
71						76	77			80
72					76	77				81
73				76	77					82
74			76	77						83
75		76	77							84
76	76	77								85
77	77									86
78	78	79	80	81	82	83	84	85	86	87
79	79	80	81	82	83	84	85	86	87	88

Figure 1.6 The age–cohort plane with period given in the body of the figure. (Reproduced by permission of S. Karger AG, Basel)

Education in the Seventies—consists of all births from the first week of April. (There have been more contacts with the 1946 cohort than with the other two, but the information obtained at each occasion gives only a partial picture of the children's health and development, whereas the follow-ups of the 1958 and 1970 cohorts have been more complete. Further data were collected from members of the 1946 cohort at nearly every age up to 26 and wide-ranging interviews were conducted with them when they were 26 and 36. Children of cohort members are also being followed in a second-generation study. There was another follow-up of the 1958 cohort in 1981, and follow-ups of samples from the 1970 cohort took place in 1972 and 1973.)

It can be seen from Figure 1.7 that it is possible to compare across cohorts (or periods) for some ages, although changes in the measuring instruments used by

Cohort \ Age	0	1	2	3	4	5	6	7	8	9	10	11	12	13	14	15	16
1946	1946		48		50		52	53	54	55	56	57		59		61	62
1958	1958							65			69						74
1970	1970				75					80							

Figure 1.7 Age–period–cohort representation of the British birth cohort studies

the different studies mean that any results must be interpreted with caution. It would also be possible to use the three cohorts to see whether a longitudinal relationship observed for one cohort also holds for the others. For example, does the gap in school attainment between the social classes widen over age for the 1970 cohort in the same way as it does for the earlier cohorts, or have educational policies designed to reduce the gap had any effect?

1.4 DEFINING THE POPULATION IN STUDIES OF CHANGE

It is not difficult to define the population of interest for a cross-sectional study. It is, essentially, a predefined group of interest (for example, families with a child under 5 and income less than £100 per week) living in a predefined geographical area at a particular time, although a precise definition of time is usually neither practical nor necessary. However, the population for longitudinal studies must be defined not for a particular time but over time, and this can lead to difficulties; for example, children are born, families break up, firms go bankrupt, characteristics such as income are not fixed, and there is movement into and out of the area of interest. The way in which these difficulties are resolved will vary according to the aims of the study.

Individuals and households moving within the chosen geographical area (or at least a sample of them) will normally be traced, but it is more difficult to know how many resources should be spent on tracing those who move to a different area. If the initial population is based on a small area, then there will be much more movement out (and in) than for a national population. The costs of tracing the small proportion who emigrate to other countries will almost always be too high, but this is less true for those moving to, say, another region. It is important to realize that those who move and those who stay are likely to have different characteristics. Research on families with a child under 5 living in small areas of Inner London (Moss, Plewis, and Bax, 1979) which provides the data for several of the examples in this book, shows that between 25 % and 50 % of the families moved out of the areas over a period of one year. These families were more likely to have been badly housed and to have been in the area for a shorter time than those who did not move; moreover, families moving into the areas did not have the same characteristics as those moving out. However, because a major aim of the research was to evaluate the effects of interventions (Children's Centres) assigned to two of the areas, it was decided not to trace those families who moved out because they could no longer be influenced by the intervention, but those eligible families who moved in were included in the study. The definition of the longitudinal population for this study is shown in Figure 1.8, and this illustrates that some families became eligible and others ineligible over time, and that some moved out and others moved in.

It is perhaps more usual to design longitudinal studies so that those who move out of an area are retained in the study but those who move in are not added to it. If this strategy is followed for a longitudinal study then it is likely that populations will differ depending on whether change data are obtained by

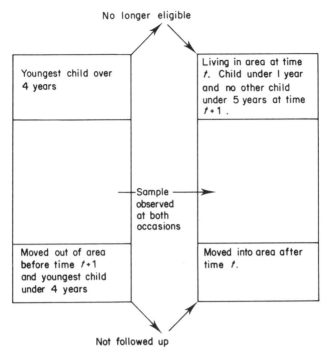

Figure 1.8 Longitudinal population as defined in Moss, Plewis, and Bax (1979)

retrospective questioning within a cross-sectional study, by a series of cross-sections, or with a longitudinal design. Suppose data are required for just two occasions. If data for the first occasion are collected retrospectively in a survey carried out at the second occasion, and if the population is defined in the usual cross-sectional way, then measures of individual change will be available for those who have come into the area since the first occasion, but not for those who moved out. Hence results from the two designs could differ, not because of any biases in the retrospectively or prospectively collected data, but because the *populations* are defined differently. In the same way, problems of eligibility are likely to be tackled differently by the two designs—the retrospective design would include those who became eligible after occasion 1 but exclude those initially eligible who were no longer eligible at occasion 2, whereas the longitudinal design would probably do just the reverse.

Each of the three designs is likely to produce estimates of aggregate change for different populations. Like a retrospective study, two cross-sections will also exclude those who move out and include those who move in, after the first occasion. But that design will also estimate a mean for the first occasion which differs from the retrospective study because this mean will be based only on those living in the area at occasion 1, whereas the data from the retrospective study will not be restricted by area at occasion 1. These points are illustrated by Figure 1.9.

Design	Moved in after T I		Moved out after T I		Did not move	
	T 1 data	T 2 data	T 1 data	T 2 data	T 1 data	T 2 data
Cross - section and retrospective data collection	/	/	X	X	/	/
Series of cross-sections	X	/	/	X	/	/
Longitudinal	X	X	/	/	/	/

Figure 1.9 Data obtained from different designs
Legend: × not likely to be collected
/likely to be collected

Problems of this kind are discussed by Morris, Newhouse, and Archibald (1980) in the context of a social experiment. They are likely to be less severe for studies which define their populations in national terms unless there is substantial immigration and emigration. The issues are, however, particularly germane to research on rapidly changing populations such as one might find when studying small firms, for example.

The national birth cohort studies described in the previous section all defined their population in terms of one week's births. However, this is not ideal in that they are unable to examine the effects of season of birth on later development and there is some unpublished evidence which shows that these effects can be important. Those who design studies of this kind in the future might consider spreading the sample over, say, four separate periods at different times of the year, even though this is administratively less convenient.

1.5 SAMPLING ON SUCCESSIVE OCCASIONS

We saw in Section 1.3 that net or mean change for a variable can be estimated either with a longitudinal design or with a series of cross-sections or time-lag designs. Are the two designs equally efficient in the sense of producing estimates of net change with the same sampling variances for the same cost? If the cost of measuring and re-measuring sample cases in a longitudinal study is the same then a longitudinal design will always be more efficient (see Cochran, 1977). However, it is sometimes argued that one of the disadvantages of longitudinal studies is their cost, which is high because it is expensive to trace individuals over time in order to make follow-up visits. If the average cost of following-up and re-measuring individuals is K times the average cost of measuring for the first time, then there will be occasions when two cross-sectional studies estimate net change more efficiently than a longitudinal study. Table 1.1 shows that the values of K, which mark the border for choosing between the two designs, vary with r, the product moment correlation between values of the variable on successive occasions.

Table 1.1 Optimum strategies for estimating net change

r	0.1	0.2	0.3	0.4	0.5	0.6	0.7	0.8	0.9
K	1.22	1.50	1.86	2.33	3.00	4.00	5.67	9.00	19.0

Thus, if the correlation is 0.5 then it has to be at least 3 times more expensive to follow up individuals in a longitudinal study before it would be more efficient to use two independent samples. And when r is greater than 0.7, it is unlikely that independent samples will ever be more efficient. It is possible to extend this argument by allowing for the likelihood that re-measuring individuals who do not move will be cheaper than tracing and re-measuring movers; further results along these lines are given in Plewis (1981a).

1.6 WAYS OF EXPLAINING CHANGE

It is clearly important to be able to measure change and hence to describe it. But it is perhaps even more important to go beyond description to try to explain change; in other words, to reach a causal understanding of change.

We have seen that one way of thinking about change is in terms of age, period, and cohort effects. However, these variables are often merely surrogates for variables of more fundamental interest and cannot themselves provide satisfactory explanations of change. As Markus and Converse (1979) put it, the age–period–cohort representation is an accounting model, and not an explanatory model that adequately reflects the processes which generate the observed data. Their concern is with models of political attitudes such as partisan strength and for such a variable, age is just a crude indicator of 'the accumulation of electoral and other partisan experience over the life cycle', while cohort stands for different types of socialization. One might also argue that age is not the variable of ultimate concern in developmental psychology—for example, one might prefer to replace age by an index of cognitive experiences when studying cognitive development.

Let us consider the explanation of change in three ways. First, there are those situations for which explanations of relative group change are sought. Usually this means relating change to a background characteristic having the form of a categorical variable, and, where a specific intervention is being evaluated, these categories often label groups referred to as 'treatment' and 'control'. Second, one may wish to explain change in the dependent variable by other variables which are also changing. It is assumed that there is sufficient theoretical knowledge to be able to state that the causal direction is from the changing explanatory variables to the changing dependent variable, and one wants to know the strength of this relationship. The third way, and the one which poses most problems for analysis, occurs when, at a single point in time, two variables are related but the relative causal direction is unknown. Thus, a change in variable A could cause a change in variable B or vice versa, and only longitudinal data can resolve this difficulty, although they will not always do so. These three approaches provide a framework for much of what follows.

The idea of cause figures prominently in this book, but it does present a number of philosophical difficulties, particularly for the social sciences. It is usually assumed that a necessary but not a sufficient condition for variables A and B to be causally related is that there is concomitant variation in A and B, in other words, A and B vary together. In addition, it is widely thought that A can only be a cause of B if changes in A precede, and lead to, changes in B. It is this need for temporal ordering to establish cause which was recognized by Lazarsfeld and which makes longitudinal data so attractive for causal analysis. However, Zellner (1979) has challenged the need for temporal asymmetry by pointing out that there are laws in 'psychological' time which will not necessarily fulfil the requirement that cause precedes effect in chronological time. Suppose prices rise after interest rates have gone up. If temporal asymmetry is a necessary condition for a causal sequence, then clearly the only causal inference that might be drawn from these data is that changes in interest rates lead to price changes. But an economic theory based on expectations would predict the opposite: it could have been the expectation of rising prices which caused interest rates to rise. Zellner's argument does appear to make it difficult to include the condition of temporal asymmetry when defining cause. One way round this difficulty is to argue that theories couched in terms of expectations (or aspirations or motivations) can only be tested if these variables are measured. If expectations about prices are measured then, by observing whether changes in these expectations are followed by changes in interest rates, the condition of temporal asymmetry can be re-introduced. The condition is retained in this book.

Other assumptions about cause are also made. It is assumed that changes in B can come about without A changing, so that A is not the sole cause of B. The causal relationship is assumed to be probabilistic in the sense that, with a particular probability, a given change in A will lead to a given change in B for a randomly chosen case. It is usually accepted that A can be a cause of B without it being the basic or direct cause of B in the sense that A can be at the beginning or in the middle of a chain of causes which lead to a change in B, with many links in the chain being unknown at the time of study. Finally, it is assumed that A is a cause of B only under certain conditions, but these conditions can be clearly specified.

These ideas about cause are similar to those given by Cook and Campbell (1979), except that they choose to limit causal inferences to situations in which the explanatory or causal variables can be manipulated, as they are in experiments of various kinds. There is much to be said for this position, which is not dissimilar to Zellner's dictum that 'predictability without theory is not causation'. However, it does mean that the third way of explaining change given above, which includes questions such as the one about drug taking and criminal behaviour posed in the Introduction, cannot be attempted. This would perhaps be too restrictive. But it is fair to say that causal inferences from the analysis of these 'passive observational approaches', as Cook and Campbell call them, will always be made less confidently than those made from deliberately manipulating the environment.

1.7 OVERVIEW OF THE BOOK

It would be possible to write at greater length about the concept of change and its relationship to social science theories, as Wohlwill (1973) and Baltes and Nesselroade (1979) have done for developmental psychology. This book is, however, much more concerned with the problems of statistical analysis, although Chapter 2 does extend the discussion about the meaning of change by presenting the merits of various ways of measuring it. Chapters 3 to 8 focus, in various ways, on methods of analysis for explaining change: Chapter 3 on the causal analysis of relative change, Chapter 4 on causal models and how to tackle the problem of determining causal direction, Chapter 5 on the effects of measurement error, and Chapters 6 and 7 on causal analysis for categorical data. Each of Chapters 3 to 7 presents methods of analysis for data collected on just two occasions, but extensions to more than two occasions are given in Chapter 8. Chapter 9 is rather different; it draws on a less familiar part of statistical theory and shows how to model both movements between categories of a variable and durations in those categories. The book ends with some comments on the ubiquitous problem of missing data followed by some concluding remarks.

1.8 SUMMARY

This chapter takes a broad look at change, at designs for measuring it and at ways of explaining it. Only very limited inferences about change can be made without longitudinal data and good longitudinal data can usually be obtained only with an explicitly longitudinal design (Section 1.3). However, it is sometimes difficult to know exactly how the population should be defined for a longitudinal study and various options are presented in Section 1.4. Statements about change in the social sciences are bound up with ideas about cause and some of the ideas are discussed in the final major section of the chapter. The chapter ends with an overview of the book.

CHAPTER 2

Ways of Measuring Change

2.1 INTRODUCTION

The focus of this chapter is on the measurement of change. It deals mainly with measurements for two occasions, partly for convenience, but partly because the problems of measuring change typically do not alter in nature as the number of occasions increases. In other words, if an adequate method for measuring change can be found for data about two occasions, the method can generally be extended in a straightforward way.

Sections 2.2 to 2.6 aim to show that 'change' as it is usually understood, which is as an observed difference between two measurements, is often misleading and can profitably be replaced by other formulations. One alternative is to use latent variable models, and these are discussed in Section 2.7. Another, not necessarily competitive, alternative is to frame questions about change in terms of conditional linear models (Section 2.8). A further issue is whether change should be measured in discrete or in continuous time, and this is taken up in Section 2.9. The final section looks at the measurement of change when the data are categorical.

2.2 INDIVIDUAL AND NET CHANGE

The notions of individual and net change were first introduced in the previous chapter (Section 1.2). Let us now define net or aggregate or mean change, $\bar{d}$, as the difference between the observed means of a variable x at two occasions, i.e.

$$\bar{d} = \bar{x}_2 - \bar{x}_1 \tag{2.1}$$

where $\bar{x}_t$ is the mean of x at occasion t ($t = 1, 2$).

Clearly it is possible to estimate $\bar{d}$, and to compare $\bar{d}$ across subgroups, either with a pair of cross-sectional studies, that is, independent samples for the two occasions, or with longitudinal data. The first of these two methods will not usually be efficient in the sense of minimizing the sampling variance of $\bar{d}$, a point which was discussed in the previous chapter (Section 1.5). However, there could be advantages in using independent samples if it was thought that collecting data from the same people about two occasions would result either in repeated measurement bias, or in biases due to faulty recall. Repeated measurement bias is a threat to the validity of data collected using a longitudinal design if people's subsequent attitudes and behaviour are affected by the measurement process.

It is the notion of individual, or gross, change which accounts for much of the attraction of longitudinal data. Yet this notion is hard to nail down; one way of defining change for an individual, i, is as a simple difference or gain or loss, i.e.

$$d_i = x_{2i} - x_{1i} \qquad (2.2)$$

Net change, $\bar{d}$, can then be derived from individual change, d_i, but the reverse is not true. However, this definition of individual change is often unsatisfactory. There are four reasons for this: there is the problem of operationalization, the problem of scale, the difficulties arising from measurement error, and there is the rationale for measuring change. Hence this book has a fundamentally different view of change from that of Kessler and Greenberg (1981) who assert that d_i is a 'natural measure' of change.

2.3 OPERATIONALIZING INDIVIDUAL CHANGE

If individual change is operationalized as a difference between two observed variables then this would seem to imply that the same variable must be measured on the two occasions. An economist interested in income dynamics would see no problem about this—clearly the difference between measures of real income at two occasions is a reasonable measure of income change. On the other hand, an educationalist might be less happy about interpreting a difference between two measures on a reading test, for example, even if the same test is used each time. Leaving aside questions of age standardization and so working with raw test scores, the educationalist may not be prepared to accept that the individual items of the test which are answered on the first occasion are necessarily measuring the same thing as those answered when the child is older. The problem becomes more severe if different tests are used at the two occasions, even if the tests have been standardized to have the same distribution at each occasion. The question is essentially one of validity—how reasonable is it to assume that a difference between the same or different tests (or any other measures) on two occasions will give a valid measure of change?

Bereiter (1963) argues that, rather than measure change indirectly as a simple difference, or some other function such as a ratio of measures on two occasions, we should be looking for direct measures. One possibility would be to devise a test in which all the items ask about change since the first measurement, and respondents provide their own assessment of change for each item. Alternatively, outside observers of some kind could rate each subject for change on the variable or dimension of interest. Bereiter's suggestion does not seem to have been taken up, presumably because the obvious biases of subjectivism, as he calls it, are thought to outweigh the possibility of getting a valid measure of the underlying process.

2.4 CHANGE AND SCALE

Some variables in the social sciences are measured on ratio scales, variables like income, age, and hours per week worked. This means that we can talk about an individual working twice as much as another individual or being paid three times as much as someone else, but such statements can only be made for the given scale. Both linear and non-linear transformations of the scale will invalidate them, so if x stands for income then neither y, when $y = a + bx$ ($a \neq 0$), nor z where, for example, $z = \log x$, would have the same scale properties as x.

However, for many other variables, the scale is more arbitrary. For instance, the scale for IQ is constructed from a set of items so that the scores of a chosen population, usually of the same age, are normally distributed, with a mean of 100 and a standard deviation of 15. Scales like this have many convenient features, but a scale defined to have a constant mean and variance is not very useful if one wishes to use differences to study change or, more particularly, growth. If the problems of operationalization could be forgotten, then a difference on the same or separate tests, where the tests are standardized to have a constant mean for all ages, would give a measure of relative individual change rather than absolute growth. In some situations, it might be justifiable to use the differences between raw scores on the same test and one might then be getting a little closer to the notion of growth. However, neither of these approaches is entirely satisfactory because, in order to rank differences between scores (i.e. the d_i of equation (2.2)), one has to assume that the measures have interval scale properties. In other words, they must be arbitrary only up to a linear transformation so that a difference of, say, 10 points has the same meaning wherever it occurs on the scale. Yet there is often no reason to suppose that an order-preserving but non-linear transformation of the scale would be any less valid a measure and it is easily shown that this can change the rank order of the *differences*, d_i. (An order-preserving, or monotonic, transformation of a scale means that the rank order of individuals on the new scale is the same as the rank order on the original scale.)

Suppose child A has a score of 120 on a standardized test at the first occasion and 135 at the second, while child B scores 68 and 80 at the two occasions. Child A has gained 3 points more than child B on this scale, but if a new scale is created by taking the square root of all the scores (a non-linear transformation), then child B gains 0.034 points more than child A and a similar reversal is found if logarithms (to base e) of the scores are taken. It could be argued that this is a long-winded way of saying that differences on ordinal, as opposed to interval, scales are uninterpretable. Perhaps it is, but the assumption of an interval scale goes by default so often that the implications for change need to be spelled out.

Even for variables with interval scale properties, the measurement of relative net change (RC) between groups can present problems where

$$RC = (\bar{x}_{12} - \bar{x}_{11}) - (\bar{x}_{22} - \bar{x}_{21}) \tag{2.3}$$

and $\bar{x}_{it}$ is the mean of variable x for group i ($i = 1, 2$) at occasion t ($t = 1, 2$).

Consider the following set of group–occasion means:

Occasion \ Group	1	2	
1	A	$A+c$	$b, c > 0$
2	$A+b$	$A+b+c$	

Applying equation (2.3) to these data leads to the conclusion of no relative change, each group having gained b units. Suppose, however, that the pooled within-group (or population) standard deviation at occasion 1 is s_1, while at occasion 2 it is ks_1. Standardizing the measures at each occasion to give constant variance over time (just a linear transformation) and then using equation (2.3) gives a relative change of

$$\left(\frac{A+b}{ks_1} - \frac{A}{s_1}\right) - \left(\frac{A+b+c}{ks_1} - \frac{A+c}{s_1}\right) = \frac{c(k-1)}{ks_1} \tag{2.4}$$

which is > 0 or < 0 depending on whether $k > 1$ or $k < 1$ respectively.

Similarly, 'positive' change can be transformed to 'negative' change if $k < 1$, and vice versa for $k > 1$. Suppose group 1 had gained $2b$ units. Then, ignoring the change in variance, the relative change is b units, which is positive, but standardizing gives a relative change of $[c(k-1)+b]/ks_1$ which would be negative if, for example, $b = 4$, $c = 10$, and $k = 0.5$.

This general point is relevant both to group comparisons, where the variances of the measure may not be equal at the two occasions, and to comparisons where the measures may be standardized to have equal variances at all ages (e.g. IQ), but where the variance of the underlying variable of interest (i.e. intelligence) may not be constant. A method for measuring relative change which overcomes these problems of scale is given in the next chapter.

2.5 MEASUREMENT ERROR AND CHANGE

Turning now to the third of the reasons for avoiding difference scores, it is generally agreed that variables in the social sciences are measured with more error than are variables in the physical sciences. This often has serious implications for the analysis of change. Indeed, the criticisms voiced most often about simple differences are that an observed individual change does not equal 'true' individual change, and that difference scores are unreliable. (The question of what is meant by true change is considered in the next section and in Chapter 5.)

Suppose that for each individual, i, observed and true scores are related in the following way:

$$x_i = X_i + u_i \qquad (2.5)$$

where x_i is the observed score, X_i is the true score (which, by definition, is unobservable), and u_i is the measurement error. Suppose also that the measurement error (u_i) has a mean of zero, that true score (X_i) and measurement error are uncorrelated, and that individuals' measurement errors are uncorrelated. These conditions define a particular kind of measurement model which is known in psychometrics as the classical test theory model, but which is widely used in all the social sciences. It can be seen, by substituting equation (2.5) into equation (2.2), that

$$d_i = D_i + (u_{2i} - u_{1i}) \qquad (2.6)$$

and so observed (d_i) and true (D_i) individual differences are not equal. Also, the rank orders of d_i and D_i are not, in general, the same, and so the procedure of defining 'gainers' and 'losers' on the basis of observed differences is fraught with danger. Methods have been proposed to estimate D_i (see Lord and Novick, 1968), but there is disagreement about the best method of doing this.

Researchers are sometimes interested in the relationship between change and initial score and this is often measured by correlating x_1 and d (r_{xd}). However, given the above measurement model, it is easy to show that r_{xd} will be less than the correlation between the true initial score and true change (r_{XD}). This well-established result (Thorndike, 1924) still tends to be forgotten.

Nevertheless, if x is perfectly measured (i.e. $u = 0$) and has constant variance over time, and if the correlation (ρ) between x_2 and x_1 is positive but less than one, then the correlation of initial score and difference $(r_{xd}$ or $r_{XD})$ is bound to be negative:

$$r_{XD} = \frac{\rho - 1}{\sqrt{2(1 - \rho)}} < 0 \qquad (2.7)$$

Thus, if $\rho = 0.3$, then $r_{XD} = -0.59$, and if $\rho = 0.7$ then $r_{XD} = -0.39$.

If the variance of x_2 is λ^2 times as great as the variance of x_1 and the other conditions hold, then

$$r_{XD} = \frac{\lambda \rho - 1}{\sqrt{1 - \lambda(2\rho - \lambda)}} \qquad (2.8)$$

and $r_{XD} > 0$ if $\lambda > 1/\rho$ and $\rho > 0$.

Correlations between change and initial score are at worst misleading and at best little more than reflections of underlying mathematical equivalences. They should be avoided, particularly when the measurement scale for x is arbitrary.

2.6 WHY MEASURE INDIVIDUAL CHANGE?

What is the rationale for measuring individual change? If the sole aim of a study is to determine the distribution of individual change in a population, and if the difficulties already mentioned can be avoided, then using simple differences might be acceptable. However, most studies of change aim to go further, at least to the measurement of relative change and often to seek an explanation of individual change. Putting this another way, as social scientists we are not interested in whether Fatima makes more educational progress than Delroy or whether examination results in Middletown school change more than in Upriver school. Rather, we want to know whether individuals like Fatima (say, girls) make more progress, on average, than individuals like Delroy (boys), and whether change in schools is related to, say, change in pupil numbers so that schools like Middletown (with falling numbers) might change more than schools like Upriver (with constant numbers).

For these more sophisticated aims, we shall see that an approach based on one of the major techniques of applied statistics—the conditional regression model—is usually more appropriate and although difference scores can be incorporated into these linear models, there is generally no advantage in doing so. In a paper concerned with ways of measuring change in psychology, Cronbach and Furby (1970) conclude that 'investigators who ask questions regarding gain scores would ordinarily be better advised to frame their questions in other ways'. This statement could be applied to the analysis of change in all the social sciences, although it does perhaps have less force in economics, where many of the variables are measured on the fixed scales of time and money, and these present fewer problems. It has been challenged by Rogosa, Brandt, and Zimowski (1982), who put the case for using individual difference scores mainly in the context of using individual growth curves for data collected on more than two occasions. They assume that the problems of operationalization have been overcome, which is perhaps unrealistic, and they rather beg the question of why one should want to measure individual change. Further discussion of growth curves can be found in Chapter 8.

There is a great need, certainly in developmental psychology and in education, for new measures which are tailored to answer important questions about growth and change. The existing measures may be good for providing pictures of a particular point in time, but it is clear that they have serious drawbacks when thinking dynamically. But it is not only psychologists and educationalists who have these problems; sociologists and political scientists who study attitude change, for example, would seem to face rather similar difficulties.

Given that there are a number of problems connected with 'commonsense' definitions of change, we need to ask whether there are alternatives. Let us now consider three possibilities—latent variable theory, conditional linear models, and models in continuous time.

2.7 LATENT VARIABLE THEORY

Many of the concepts used by social scientists can only be measured imperfectly. For instance, children can be given a score on a reading test, but this is not a totally reliable way of measuring their reading ability. Economists cannot measure permanent income directly, and sociologists have the same problem with alienation and racial prejudice. Political scientists would like to measure partisan strength, some social psychologists are interested in life satisfaction, while a good deal of research is concerned with early childhood stimulation at home, and all these underlying variables are imperfectly measured by various indicators and scales. These underlying variables are often called *latent variables*, or *latent traits*.

There are two links in the chain which connects observed and latent variables. The first link is between observed and true scores, as in equation (2.5). The second is between true scores with what is presumed to be a single latent variable, τ, and one way of formulating this link is as follows:

$$X_j = \alpha_j + \lambda_j \tau \tag{2.9}$$

where α_j is the origin and λ_j is the scale of each observed x_j ($j = 1, 2, \ldots, m$). Combining equations (2.5) and (2.9) gives

$$x_j = \alpha_j + \lambda_j \tau + u_j \tag{2.10}$$

and *if* equation (2.10) can be shown to represent the data adequately then the x_j are known as a set of m 'congeneric' measures for the single latent variable, τ (Jöreskog, 1971). It is assumed that τ has interval scale properties. If equation (2.10) does not fit the data well, then one has to consider whether there is more than one underlying variable or, putting it another way, whether the latent variable has more than one dimension. This raises difficult questions about the relationship between theory and measurement, which is not explored here.

Suppose there are sound substantive grounds for believing that the same latent variable is measured on two occasions, either by the same set of m tests, scales, questions, etc., on both occasions with α_j and λ_j constant over time, or by the same set, but with α_j or λ_j or both different at the two occasions, or by a set of m_1 measures at the first occasion and by a different set of m_2 measures at the second. Then it is possible to compare differences between individuals on the latent variable by calculating $\tau_2 - \tau_1$, even though these differences may have little meaning for any one individual.

Latent variable theory cannot completely solve the operationalization problem, but it does reduce its severity by providing a way of combining measures and by allowing different measures to be used at different occasions. Nor does it necessarily eliminate the problem of scale because if equation (2.9) is used (and it is just one of many possible models), then the scales of the true scores and the latent variable differ only by a linear transformation, so the true scores (and the observed scores) must have interval scale properties. However, the approach does provide one way of dealing with the difficulties posed by measurement error. The rationale for using differences as measures of change may still be questioned even if a scale for the latent variable has been determined. However, the usefulness of latent variables is not affected by this because, as we shall see in Chapter 5, linear models can be built round them, and these are often called *structural models*.

Latent variable models have had an undeniable and often a beneficial influence on quantitative theoretical developments in the social sciences. However, one might question whether the assumptions of the models and the requirements they impose on data collection are always appropriate, especially for more applied areas of social research. Perhaps one of the keys for deciding on the usefulness of latent variable theory is provided by examining what is meant by imperfect measurement. In other words, what are the components of u in equation (2.5)? Should it include short-term, transitory variation (usually measured by test–retest coefficients); should it include variations arising from the use of different testers or interviewers (known as interviewer variance in survey research); what about variation arising from the sampling of test items? It is likely that different definitions of error will be needed for different situations. Consider, for example, a test of mathematics. If, given an imperfect measure at the first occasion, the best predictor of the observed measure at the second occasion is required, then there is no need to eliminate the measurement error from the predictive equation. Goldstein (1979a) discusses occasions in education when this might be the most appropriate procedure. Also, there may be times when the true score for the particular test is needed. That is, one may wish to know or estimate the error associated with transitory fluctuations and different testers, but not that associated with sampling test items. However, the latent variable itself is mathematical ability and anything else that the test might measure, such as reading ability, is then treated as error. More detailed discussion of these points can be found in Cronbach, Gleser, Nanda, and Rajaratnam (1972).

Another problem with the latent variable approach is that it requires more than one measure at each occasion in order to determine a scale. However, in many situations it will not be possible, and perhaps not even ethical, to obtain multiple measures (for example, when testing young children) and, even if it were possible, such measures might be distorted by differential practice or fatigue effects, or both. Also, the statistical complexities of dealing with several measures of one latent variable may deter potential users of research (which is not to say that complexities should be avoided when simple alternatives would be misleading).

Perhaps a more serious objection is that the approach tends to emphasize reliability rather than validity; in other words, although it is accepted that the observed variables are imperfect measures of the underlying variable, it is assumed that, apart from these imperfections, they do measure it. Consider, for example, the researcher who wants to measure reading ability and who is willing to accept that only one latent variable is involved. He or she might be tempted to administer several reading tests and combine them to determine a scale for the latent variable (more technical details of how to do this can be found in Chapter 5). However, such a procedure would be biased for those children who do not perform well in the test situation, or because the tests are not related to the children's school curriculum. One might, therefore, get a more valid measure of reading ability by combining test scores with teachers' assessments, and observations at home and at school. The latent variable method does not preclude such an approach, but neither does it encourage it. It is not difficult to think of situations, particularly when data are collected by surveys, in which one might be forced to choose between getting several rather poor indicators of the underlying variable or asking a series of more sensitive questions, answers to which might be considered together and coded on a single scale.

And so latent variable theory is not necessarily the best way of dealing with the inevitable imperfections of measurement in the social sciences, although it can make a valuable contribution to some analyses of change. This contribution is examined in more detail in Chapter 5.

2.8 CONDITIONAL MODELS FOR THE ANALYSIS OF CHANGE

There is a statistical model lying behind the analysis of change defined as individual and net differences, and this model is known as a *time-related*, or *unconditional*, model. Goldstein (1979c) distinguishes this model from *conditional* models for the analysis of change. A conditional model for measures on two occasions treats the measure at the first occasion (x_1) as fixed and so works with the distribution of the measure at the second occasion, which we now call y, for *fixed* values of x_1. The most convenient way of doing this is to find a linear regression equation which models adequately the relationship between y and x_1. Suppose the relationship can be expressed quite simply as:

$$y = \alpha + \beta x_1 + \varepsilon \tag{2.11}$$

where β is the slope of the straight line, α is the intercept on the y-axis, and ε is an error term representing the fact that variables other than x_1 will affect y. If $\beta = 1$ then equation (2.11) would appear to give the same result as an analysis of individual difference scores (because $y_i - x_{1i} = \alpha + \varepsilon_i$), but in fact equation (2.11) implies a quite different approach to the measurement of change.

If the method of least squares is used to estimate α and β then, for a given value of x_1 at the first occasion, say x_1^*, the best predicted value of the variable at the second occasion, $\hat{y}$, is then

$$\hat{y} = \hat{\alpha} + \hat{\beta} x_1^* \tag{2.12}$$

Clearly, the $\hat{y}$ from equation (2.12) can say nothing about whether one individual changed more than another because they are just linear transformations of the value at the first occasion. A more useful measure in this context would be the difference between the observed and predicted values of the measure at the second occasion, i.e. $(y_i - \hat{y}_i)$. These are just the residuals $(\hat{\varepsilon}_i)$ when equation (2.11) is estimated and give an indication of whether an individual changed more or less than expected, given the score at the first occasion, and by how much. Using these residuals creates its own problems and there is often no strong reason for preferring them to the observed differences, d_i. However, most research is interested less in that question than in the question of what kinds of individual gain more or less, and what causes change. As we shall see in the next two chapters, conditional models are usually very much better suited than unconditional models to answer these questions.

Although the advantages of the conditional approach should become much more apparent in subsequent chapters, let us make some brief comparisons with the time-related approach in terms of the themes of Sections 2.3 to 2.6.

Consider first the problem of operationalization; there is no need for x_1 and y to be measuring the same thing for a model such as (2.11) to be interpretable. On the other hand, the interpretation of the conditional model as a description of change would seem to require that x_1 and y are measuring 'similar' variables. And so, the conditional model does perhaps allow more latitude when dealing with the issue of operationalization. Certainly it does free researchers from thinking that they have to use the *same* measures over time in order to analyse change even though these measures are not appropriate for all occasions. But it would clearly be unreasonable to suppose that there is a technical solution to this substantive problem.

Conditional models are also more logical than the time-related models because they take account of the direction in time; they put questions such as: 'knowing what happened in the past, what do we expect to happen now or in the future?' It is, of course, possible to estimate a 'time-reversed' conditional model,

$$x_1 = \gamma + \delta y + \varepsilon \qquad (2.13)$$

and, in general, $\gamma \neq \alpha$ and $\delta \neq \beta$. However, the reversal of time does lead to problems when wishing to produce conclusions of a causal nature about change if one assumes that a necessary condition for A to cause B is that A precedes B (see Section 1.6). An analysis of individual changes will not be affected by considering $x_1 - y$ rather than $y - x_1$ and so the unconditional approach is ignoring important information about the direction of change. In some situations, and if x_1 and y are known to be measuring the same thing, a model such as

$$y - x_1 = \alpha^* + \beta^* x_1 + \varepsilon^* \qquad (2.14)$$

might be appropriate. However, equation (2.14) reduces to

$$y = \alpha^* + (\beta^* + 1)x_1 + \varepsilon^* \qquad (2.15)$$

which has the same form as equation (2.11) and so $\alpha^* = \alpha$ and $\beta^* = \beta - 1$ and no new ideas are introduced.

Turning now to scale, equation (2.11) will not always fit the data well, but an order-preserving transformation of the measure at the first occasion to, say, $\log x_1$ or to x_1^2 might lead to a much better fit. The results from the conditional model will remain essentially unaffected by *any* order-preserving transformation of x_1 in the sense that the rank order of the predicted values at the second occasion will not be changed. A plot of y against x_1 should reveal an appropriate transformation. There may be sound statistical reasons for transforming the measure at the second occasion either to achieve a normal distribution or because the variance of y is not constant for all x_1. If the scale for y is arbitrary, then these statistical considerations will carry more weight than if the scale were fixed, because interpretation could be difficult if a fixed scale were transformed. On the whole, then, the conditional model is more flexible when it comes to dealing with issues of scale.

However, the problem of measurement error is just as serious for the conditional model as it is for the time-related model. If x_1 is measured with error, as in equation (2.5), then the least squares estimates of α and β in equation (2.11) are biased estimates of the parameters in a model linking the true scores on the two occasions and this, in turn, affects $\hat{y}$ and the residuals. There are ways of correcting for measurement error, one of which is the latent variable approach described in the previous section, and all the methods are discussed in more detail in Chapter 5.

The parameters of equation (2.11) can also be used to give information about the stability of a variable (see Section 1.2). If the correlation between x_1 and y is 1, then the rank order of individuals does not change between the two measurement occasions and $\hat{\beta}$ shows how much y changes when x_1 changes by one unit. If x_1 and y are perfectly correlated and if $\hat{\alpha} = 0$ and $\hat{\beta} = 1$, then there is no individual change over time. If $\hat{\alpha} = (1 - \hat{\beta})\bar{x}_1$ then there is no net change. However, any estimate of the correlation between x_1 and y needs to take account of the measurement error in both these variables, since otherwise it is a biased estimate.

2.9 CHANGE IN CONTINUOUS TIME

(Readers need some elementary knowledge of calculus to understand this section properly.)

All the discussion so far has been of change in discrete time, whereas one might argue that change occurs all the time. Although the argument is not easily dismissed, there are good reasons for analysing change in discrete time, some of which were given in Chapter 1 (Section 1.2). Hence the usual methods of the physical sciences (i.e. continuous time models written as differential equations) are not necessarily the most appropriate for the social sciences. Nevertheless, Coleman (1968) argues cogently for the representation of change as a dynamic process in continuous time, and he distinguishes between two types of processes. If x is the variable of interest and t is time (or age), then Coleman considers the rate of change of x as a function of time or

$$\frac{dx}{dt} = f(t) \tag{2.16}$$

If $f(t) = b + ct$, say, then equation (2.16), when integrated, becomes

$$x = a + bt + \tfrac{1}{2}ct^2 \tag{2.17}$$

which is a quadratic equation in t. This is a particular instance of an unconditional, or time-related, model and the disadvantages of such models for two occasions have already been discussed. To estimate equation (2.17) requires data for at least three occasions and the assumptions needed to make the time-related model appropriate in the social sciences becomes more tenuous as the number of occasions increases. Models like (2.17) are presented in more detail in Chapter 8.

Coleman also proposes that the rate of change of x is modelled as a function of x itself, i.e.

$$\frac{dx}{dt} = f(x) \tag{2.18}$$

and, if $f(x) = bx$, then integrating equation (2.18) gives

$$x = ae^{bt} \qquad (2.19)$$

so that x is related to t in an exponential fashion, where a is a starting value for x. It is possible to estimate b in equation (2.19) from

$$x_t = \beta x_0 + \varepsilon_t \qquad (2.20)$$

where x is measured at two points in time, t units apart, as deviations from its mean, and then $b = (\log \beta)/t$. However, it is unlikely that variables in the social sciences change exponentially with time as equation (2.19) suggests. It will only be true if b is constant over time and if dx/dt depends only on the current value of x and not on earlier values. These assumptions will often not be reasonable, but some progress can be made in testing them when there are measures on more than two occasions (see Chapter 8).

The problems of constructing and interpreting models in continuous time for social science data are so serious that most of the rest of this book is concerned only with models in discrete time. However, in Chapter 9 observed transitions between states of a categorical variable in discrete time are used to suggest models in continuous time.

2.10 MEASURING CHANGE WHEN THE DATA ARE CATEGORICAL

So far, we have focused only on variables measured on continuous scales, but many of the variables used by social scientists are in fact categorical—either dichotomous (0–1) variables, such as marital status (married/unmarried) and employment status (employed/unemployed), or polytomous (with categories $1, 2, \ldots, K$ where K is usually small) such as social class when defined by a classification of occupations. Although it is true that some categorical variables, particularly those for which the categories are ordered, are just rather coarse representations of underlying variables which are continuous, nevertheless there is a need for techniques which deal with categorical variables as they stand.

A definition of net change for dichotomous variables corresponding to equation (2.1) is straightforward—it is just the difference between the two proportions. But a succinct definition for polytomous variables is more difficult unless the categories are ordered and are allocated scores, when net change can be measured in the same way as it is for continuous variables. However, these scale values are nearly always arbitrary. It is possible to test for the statistical significance of net change for all categorical variables; this is known as a test of marginal homogeneity and is discussed in more detail in Chapter 6.

The notion of individual change is perhaps less problematic for categorical variables than it is for continuous variables. It can be defined by the cells of the 2×2 or $K \times K$ contingency tables linking the measurements on the two occasions with the diagonal cells possibly combined to form a 'no change' category. For example, a 2×2 table linking marital status at two occasions can be transformed, as in Figure 2.1, but for $K > 2$, the definition can become rather cumbersome.

Occasion 2 Occasion I	Married	Unmarried
Married	a	b
Unmarried	c	d

OR

Became married	Became unmarried	No change
c	b	$a + d$

Figure 2.1 Alternative perspectives on change in marital status

Nevertheless, problems of scale disappear (unless scores are assigned to the categories), measurement error is often, but perhaps wrongly, assumed to be less important for categorical data, and there are likely to be fewer problems of operationalization because it will often be reasonable to assume that the same variable is being measured on the two occasions.

Unconditional models for the analysis of change for categorical data are defined in terms of individual and net change as above. Conditional models focus on conditional probabilities, that is the probability of being in a particular category at the second occasion given the position at the first occasion. In Figure 2.1 these are $a/(a + b)$ and $c/(c + d)$ and their complements, $b/(a + b)$ and $d/(c + d)$. These can be written more generally as p_{ij} where i and j both run from 1 to K and i refers to the first occasion and j to the second, and $\sum_j p_{ij} = 1$. Each of Chapters 6, 7, 8, and 9 considers models for the explanation of change when the data are categorical.

2.11 SUMMARY

This chapter sets out to come to terms with the rather difficult problems posed by the measurement of change in the social sciences. In Sections 2.3 to 2.6, the use of simple differences to define change is shown to be unsatisfactory for most situations: they may not be valid measures of change, they are bedevilled by problems of scale and measurement error, and they are rarely suited to answer the questions social scientists ask of their longitudinal data. One alternative is to use latent variable models (Section 2.7): they provide a way of combining different measures and of dealing with measurement error and can therefore be used to deflect some of the criticisms which are levelled at difference scores. However, latent variable theory does make assumptions about scale, and its requirement of multiple measures of a variable is often difficult to satisfy in practice.

Another way of looking at change is with the help of conditional linear models (Section 2.8). These models cannot eliminate all the problems of difference scores, especially measurement error, but they are more logical and they can be extended to deal with most of the interesting questions about change, both for continuous and for categorical data (Section 2.10) and for latent variables. Models in continuous time are considered briefly (Section 2.9), but they have drawbacks which make them difficult to use for most social science data. The foundations of an approach based on conditional linear models for all types of data in discrete time have been put down and succeeding chapters will aim to build on these foundations.

CHAPTER 3

Models for the Description and Explanation of Relative Change

3.1 INTRODUCTION

In the previous chapter, we started to make out a case for approaching the measurement and explanation of change by conditional (i.e. regression) models. Let us now extend those ideas and focus on the problems of specifying models for the description and explanation of relative change between groups. At this stage, the models will be confined to variables which are measured without error on just two occasions, and the dependent variable is measured on at least an interval scale. Each of these assumptions is relaxed in later chapters.

The kinds of studies which look at relative change are described in Section 3.2, and this is followed by a simple introduction to the specification and interpretation of conditional models. After a rather deprecating discussion of unconditional models for relative change which extends the criticisms made in Section 2.4, an attempt is made in Section 3.5 to neutralize some of the difficulties raised by what is often known as 'Lord's paradox'. An example using data from one of the British birth cohort studies—the National Child Development Study—is introduced in Section 3.6, and a more extensive analysis of these data is presented in Section 3.7, together with a more detailed look at model specification for the explanation of relative change. Section 3.8 looks at strategies for dealing with 'nonparallel regressions'.

The final three sections of the chapter look at alternatives to regression models for getting valid causal estimates of relative change. In Section 3.9, a technique known as 'value-added analysis' is described and illustrated, and in Section 3.10 some of the ideas which have surfaced in the econometric literature for analysing relative change are considered. The chapter ends with a brief review of matching; this is the most popular alternative to regression for comparing groups, but it is more an issue in design than in analysis. Readers interested in a more complete discussion of matching are referred to Anderson *et al.* (1980).

3.2 A CLASSIFICATION OF STUDIES OF RELATIVE CHANGE

Studies which seek to measure and explain relative change can usefully be grouped into three categories—experiments, quasi-experiments, and observational studies. The second and third of these are often known collectively as non-randomized studies. Although it is true that many studies which compare groups rely solely on cross-sectional data collected at just one point in time, the more convincing of these studies in the social sciences do collect data for two, and sometimes several, occasions.

For the purposes of this chapter, a study will be called *experimental* if:

(i) it contains at least two groups, with the elements of at least one of these groups subject, after assignment, to some kind of intervention; and
(ii) all the groups are formed solely on the basis of a random procedure, that is, units from the population of interest are randomly assigned to the groups.

A *quasi-experimental* study differs from an experiment in two ways:

(i) the formation of the groups is not completely determined by a random procedure; and
(ii) there is usually a pre-treatment measure either of the outcome variable or of a variable closely related to it.

Quasi-experiments and *observational studies* are sometimes regarded as synonymous, and indeed have many similarities, but they will be distinguished here by the fact that groups in observational studies are less easily labelled 'treatment' or 'control' and there is no deliberate attempt to obtain 'pre-treatment' measures for all the elements. This is particularly true when the groups are defined by background variables such as social class and marital status. It could be argued that quasi-experiments might, in some sense, have been experiments, whereas this is not true of observational studies. In other words, the differences between the groups in an observational study are much more fundamental. Campbell and Stanley (1966) discuss several quasi-experimental designs, but our attention will be confined to the most popular of these, the nonequivalent control group design, in which non-randomly formed treatment and control groups are measured both before and after the treatment is applied.

The distinction between observational studies and quasi-experiments also has implications for analysis. In certain circumstances, the *measurement* of group differences will be the only requirement of an observational study, whereas the rationale of quasi-experiments (and experiments) is the *causal explanation* of group differences. The essential question that experimental and quasi-experimental studies attempt to answer, therefore, is whether the treatment had an effect or whether one treatment was more effective than another. In many cases, this can be rephrased as 'was the change in the treatment group significantly greater than in the control group, and could that change have been caused by the treatment?' These questions can be answered by experiments without any need for pre-treatment measures providing the experimental groups are of sufficient size. Indeed, it can be argued that pre-testing in experiments is positively harmful in that it makes the study groups different from the population from which they are selected, and this reduces what Campbell and Stanley call the 'external validity' of the experiment. On the other hand, using the pre-treatment measures in the analysis can lead to a more powerful experiment (i.e. more precise comparisons) by using the analysis of covariance (ANCOVA) to adjust for 'random' pre-treatment differences. Winer (1971), and many other texts, give details of a technique originally introduced by Fisher (1932) for this purpose.

It is often said, for many situations in the social sciences, that experiments are impossible, and researchers are forced to rely at best on quasi-experiments. Gilbert, Light, and Mosteller (1975) present a powerfully argued alternative to this position by discussing a number of experiments carried out in the United States, such as the Negative Income Tax experiments, and by arguing that many of the objections to randomization are specious. Nevertheless, there will always be some cases where randomization is not feasible. Moreover, rates of attrition which vary between the groups in experiments can result in studies which should be regarded more realistically as quasi-experiments, because those who leave the experimental group sometimes have characteristics which differ from those leaving the control group.

There is one design, known as the *regression discontinuity* design, which straddles the quasi-experimental/experimental boundary. In this design, subjects are assigned to the treatment and control groups solely on the basis of the values of a continuous pre-treatment variable or variables (which can be measured with error), possibly combined with some randomization of subjects who score around the median of the pre-treatment variable (see Figure 3.1). Berk and Rauma (1983) describe the use of such a design in the evaluation of a crime-control programme. Prisoners who had completed a certain number of hours of prison work were eligible for unemployment benefit on release (the treatment group), whereas the control group consisted of released prisoners who had not done enough prison work to receive benefit. The advantage of this design, which it shares with experiments, is that the process which assigns subjects to groups—completed hours of prison work, in this example—is known. But it differs from an experiment in that this assignment process must be explicitly introduced into the analysis by carrying out an adjustment to eliminate the *known* confounding

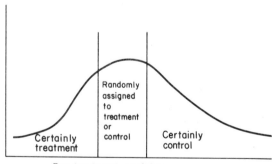

Pre-treatment variable

Figure 3.1 Using a hypothetical distribution of a pre-treatment variable to determine group assignment in a regression discontinuity design

between selection and treatment, and so to give an unbiased estimate of the treatment effect; see Rubin (1977). On the other hand, unbiased estimates can usually only be obtained by *assuming* that certain functional (usually linear) relationships hold between the pre-treatment variable(s) and the outcome variable in the two groups.

However, for most quasi-experimental designs, the assignment process is not known. Conditional models (which are sometimes known as regression adjustment models and sometimes, confusingly, as analyses of covariance) cannot then be relied upon for unbiased estimates of the treatment effect. This important point is discussed in more detail in Section 3.7.

3.3 SPECIFYING SIMPLE CONDITIONAL MODELS

In the previous chapter (Section 2.8), change was modelled as a linear relationship between a variable at occasion 2 and the same or a similar variable at occasion 1. This was equation (2.11), which we repeat here:

$$y = \alpha + \beta x_1 + \varepsilon \tag{3.1}$$

It is the interpretation given to β in equation (3.1) which is crucial to a proper understanding of change obtained from a conditional model. Either β can be considered as a parameter linking x_1 to y in a model which is used solely to measure change, or it can be given a causal interpretation—if x_1 changes or is changed by one unit, then y will change by β units. However, the causal interpretation will only be valid if equations like (3.1) are correctly specified. In other words, there should be no other variables which are related to x_1 and which are related to y for fixed values of x_1. Suppose that, rather than equation (3.1), the 'correct' model is:

$$y = \theta_0 + \theta_1 x_1 + \theta_2 z + \varepsilon^* \tag{3.2}$$

so that there are two explanatory variables, x_1 and z, which help to explain the variation in y. If x_1 and z are uncorrelated then the expected value of $\hat{\theta}_1$, the estimate of θ_1, in equation (3.2), and the expected value of $\hat{\beta}$, the estimate of β, in equation (3.1), will be the same. However, it is common in non-experimental research for x_1 and z to be correlated and, if that is so, then θ_1 and β will differ and it would not be valid to give β a causal interpretation. The greater the correlation between x_1 and z, the more θ_1 and β will differ.

Let us consider the implications of these ideas for the description and explanation of relative change. Suppose data are obtained for members of two groups about two occasions. Then equation (3.1) can be expanded to

$$y = \alpha + \beta_0 x_0 + \beta_1 x_1 + \varepsilon \tag{3.3}$$

where x_0 is a 'dummy' variable taking two values, 0 and 1, corresponding to the two groups. (Dummy variables are treated in the same way as continuous variables when estimating regression models.) The least squares estimate of β_0 is

$$\hat{\beta}_0 = (\bar{y}_2 - \bar{y}_1) - \hat{\beta}_1 (\bar{x}_{12} - \bar{x}_{11}) \tag{3.4}$$

where $\hat{\beta}_1$ is the least squares estimate of β_1 and $\bar{y}_t$ and $\bar{x}_{1t}$ are the means of y and x_1 at occasion t ($t = 1, 2$).

In equation (3.3), β_0 could be interpreted as a descriptive measure of relative change between the two groups. However, providing there were no variables like z in equation (3.2), omitted from equation (3.3)—variables correlated both with y and with the variable defining the two groups—then β_0 could take on a causal interpretation. In other words, if equation (3.3) were correctly specified, and if it were possible to change from one group to another, then this would lead to a change of β_0 units in y for all values of x_1. Similarly, if there were no omitted variables correlated both with y and with x_1, then β_1 could also be given the causal interpretation mentioned earlier. Equation (3.3) assumes that the relationship between y and x_1 is the same for both groups, i.e. β_1 is constant across groups. This assumption will be relaxed later in this chapter (Section 3.8). The model is illustrated diagrammatically in Figure 3.2.

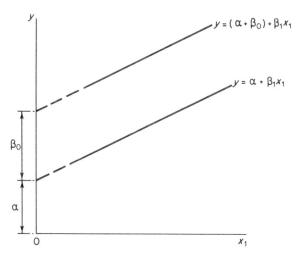

Figure 3.2 Graphical representation of equation (3.3). The lines for the two groups are parallel with slope β_1, and β_0 is the constant difference between the two groups for fixed values of x_1

3.4 UNCONDITIONAL MODELS FOR RELATIVE CHANGE

Before moving on to consider in more detail the specification of conditional models for relative change, let us examine critically unconditional models for the measurement and explanation of relative change. As shown in Section 2.4, a simple unconditional model compares the net changes $\bar{x}_2 - \bar{x}_1$ (i.e. $\bar{y} - \bar{x}_1$) across groups and, for longitudinal data on two groups, a t-test can establish whether or not the difference between these net changes is statistically significant (Blalock, 1981, Ch. 13). (This t-test is equivalent to testing for a group–time interaction in a repeated measures analysis of variance, and this is explained in more detail in Chapter 8.)

However, we have seen in the previous chapter (Section 2.4) that results from this approach can be changed by a simple change of scale such as one gets by standardizing the variance of the measure over time. For example, Goldstein (1979a) points out that there is no relative change in the mean heights of boys and girls between the ages of 4 and 8 using an unstandardized unconditional model, but the sex difference is less at 8 than at 4 if height is standardized to have equal variances at 4 and 8. Kenny (1975a) discusses a similar phenomenon which is postulated to occur with some psychological variables and is known as 'fan spread', that is, increasing raw differences between groups and increasing variance over time. It may be most useful to work with the untransformed scale for variables with a fixed and widely accepted scale such as height. But it is not at all clear, in the absence of theoretical guidelines, which criteria should be used to decide between unstandardized and standardized unconditional models for those variables with arbitrary scales which are common in the social sciences. For example, the use of standardized scores on educational and psychological tests usually gives standardized differences, but the use of raw scores from a test usually does not. Kenny recommends the use of standardized differences when there is 'fan spread', but he does not really justify this choice. Nor does he consider the alternative of a conditional model for which the conclusions are unchanged by these changes of scale. In the conditional model, neither separate linear transformations of x_1 and y nor non-linear but order-preserving transformations of x_1 lead to results which are essentially different from those obtained from equation (3.3); the size of β_0 would change, but its sign would not. (It is possible, although unlikely, to change the sign of β_0 by a non-linear, order-preserving transformation of y.)

3.5 LORD'S PARADOX

The previous section reinforces the idea put forward in Chapter 2 that unconditional models are not usually as satisfactory as conditional models for the measurement of change. However, one might argue that for some observational studies (but not for quasi-experiments), the statistically more straightforward approach of the unconditional model could be as useful as the conditional model. Thus, it might be appropriate for variables having a fixed scale (e.g. income) and constant variance over the period of interest, or for variables which have been measured in the same way in several studies and which are not standardized to have equal variance over time but nevertheless do have constant variances. These conditions are more likely to apply to measurements of adults than to measurements of children. The unconditional model also suffers from fewer problems of measurement error, particularly if the group sizes are reasonably large. The error variance of a net change will then be much smaller than the error variance of an individual change.

Different answers can be obtained according to whether the conditional or unconditional approach is adopted. Consider the following set of group–occasion means:

Occasion \ Group	1	2
1 (x_1)	10	15
2 (y)	20	25

Suppose also that the variances of x_1 and y are both 10 for each group and the within-group covariance of x_1 and y is 6. The groups show no relative change using the unconditional model but, from equation (3.4),

$$\hat{\beta}_0 = (25 - 20) - 0.6(15 - 10)$$
$$= 2 \qquad (3.5)$$

so that, for fixed values of x_1, group 2 gains 2 more points than group 1. This is shown diagrammatically in Figure 3.3 with AB equal to BC. Lord (1967) presents essentially this example in terms of net change in weight for a group of men and a group of women.

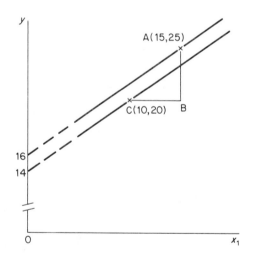

Figure 3.3 Graphical representation of Lord's paradox

The coexistence of these two results has been described as Lord's paradox. But, as Bock (1975) explains, it seems more sensible to accept that both approaches are useful because they each seek to answer rather different questions. For Lord's example, where the variable has a fixed scale and constant variance, the unconditional model does give an unambiguous answer to the reasonable question 'is there a difference in the average gain in weight of men and women?'

The results from a conditional analysis are also reasonable; men and women having the same weight at occasion 1 are, on average, either underweight men (who will gain) or overweight women (who will lose). This is commonly referred to as 'regression to the mean', but the phrase is often used so loosely as to suggest that it should be avoided. Certainly, as Healy and Goldstein (1978) point out, regression to the mean is not necessarily a statistical artefact. It can arise because of measurement error in the explanatory variable and can then lead to artefactual findings (see Chapter 5), but often the phrase is used to cover all kinds of possible, and unstated, specification errors and it is then reasonable to ask 'regression to *which* mean?'.

This example shows that when the correlation between group and pre-test is the same as the correlation between group and post-test, then there is no unconditional relative change. But this is not, as Cook and Campbell (1979, Ch. 7) believe it is, the same thing as no treatment effect. Suppose the group–occasion means had come from a regression discontinuity design so that allocation to groups was based solely on the observed pre-test (see Section 3.2). Then the value of $\hat{\beta}_0$ would be an unbiased estimate of the treatment effect. Suppose x_1 and y are uncorrelated; pre-test differences would then be irrelevant and the treatment effect would be 5. Only if x_1 and y were perfectly correlated ($\text{cov}(x_1\,y) = 10$) would there be no treatment effect with these data.

For quasi-experiments, and indeed for all group comparisons which seek to explain rather than just to describe change, unconditional models are not suitable because it only makes sense to try to talk about the causal explanation of relative change for groups which are either equal at the outset (as in experiments) or are 'made equal' statistically. There is nothing in the comparison of net changes which implies this kind of equality for non-randomized studies, whereas the notion of analysing occasion 2 scores for *fixed* scores at occasion 1 does at least begin to tackle the problem. In essence, the conditional analysis attempts to answer the question: had the groups been alike on all the relevant explanatory variables at occasion 1 (so that all relevant 'z-variables' have been included in equation (3.3)), then what would the difference have been between the groups at occasion 2 (this being, of course, the relative change)? But only if the attempt to eliminate all the relevant initial differences between the groups is successful is there a possibility of giving a valid causal interpretation to the observed change, that is, of obtaining an unbiased estimate of the treatment effect. In this sense, the pre-test has the same status as any other explanatory variable. The justification for its inclusion comes from the fact that it is likely to be the variable which explains the process of assignment to groups and the outcome better than any others.

3.6 AN EXAMPLE

Let us illustrate these ideas with data originally collected for the National Child Development Study and analysed by Steedman (1980). These data refer to the progress made by children between the ages of 11 and 16 in different types of secondary school. This study has a quasi-experimental design and illustrates that quasi-experiments can occur 'naturally', here as a result of political decisions, as well as in a research environment. Only a small subset of the data is analysed here, and it is stressed that the results obtained are purely illustrative. Readers interested in the substantive findings of the study should refer to the report by Steedman.

Random samples were drawn of 100 children whose secondary school education took place in comprehensive schools and 100 children educated in grammar schools. Our attention is confined to progress in mathematics, and the basic data are presented in Table 3.1.

Table 3.1 Mathematics test scores at 11 and 16 by school type

	Comprehensives ($n = 100$)		Grammar ($n = 100$)	
	Mean	s.d.	Mean	s.d.
11-year score (M11)	17.2	10.6	28.6	6.2
16-year score (M16)	12.9	6.7	20.7	5.2

Table 3.1 shows that the mean grammar school score is higher both at 11, just before entry to secondary school, and at 16, but the variation in comprehensive school scores is greater, particularly at 11. Different tests were used at 11 and 16 and that is why the means are lower at 16.

Using equation (2.3) to calculate relative change, we find that comprehensives 'gained' 3.6 points more than grammars and this difference is statistically significant ($t = 4.2, p < 0.001$). However, the variation in 11-year scores is greater than the variation at 16 and this might affect relative change. Indeed, the pooled within-group standard deviation is 8.7 at 11 and 6.0 at 16, and if standardized differences are calculated (as in equation (2.4)), then there is essentially no relative change.

Because different tests were used at the two ages, these unconditional relative changes would be difficult to interpret even if the results had not been ambiguous. More importantly, the unconditional model is not appropriate because the focus of the study was on the *effect* on children's progress of different types of school organization. In other words, the study had a quasi-experimental design with higher-achieving children tending to go to grammar schools, but with quite a lot of overlap in 11-year scores between the two school types (see Figure 3.4).

Estimating the simple conditional model (equation (3.3)) gives the following model:

$$M16 = 6.32 - 2.14ST + 0.50M11 \qquad (3.6)$$
$$(1.05) \quad (0.70) \qquad (0.03)$$

where ST is the variable representing school type (x_0 in equation (3.3)) taking the value 1 for comprehensives and 0 for grammars. The figures in brackets are the standard errors of the regression coefficients and the model explains 67% of

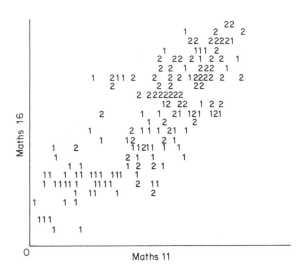

Figure 3.4 Plot of MATHS16 against MATHS11
Legend: 1 = Comprehensive
2 = Grammar

the variation in M16. We see from equation (3.6) that the estimated treatment effect (β_0 in equation (3.3)) is 2.14 points in favour of the grammar schools, and this is statistically significant ($t = 3.08, p < 0.01$). Whether this treatment effect is unbiased is a question we consider again in the next section. However, an examination of Figure 3.4 suggests that the relationship between M16 and M11 is curvilinear and a slightly better fitting model includes a squared term, $M11^2$, rather than M11. Equation (3.6) then becomes

$$M16 = 8.06 - 2.58ST + 0.012M11^2 \qquad (3.7)$$
$$(0.52) \quad (0.68) \qquad (0.001)$$

and the estimated treatment effect is 2.58 points in favour of the grammar schools.

3.7 BUILDING CONDITIONAL MODELS FOR THE EXPLANATION OF RELATIVE CHANGE

In Section 3.3, we saw that β_0 in equation (3.3) was a reasonable measure of relative change, but it could not necessarily be given a causal interpretation. There may be additional variables which need to be included on the right-hand side of a conditional model before one could talk about the groups being equal at occasion 1. However, care is needed when deciding which variables can reasonably be included in the conditional model because there will not always be a logical justification for the inclusion of explanatory variables other than the pre-test. Consider the following hypothetical causal models:

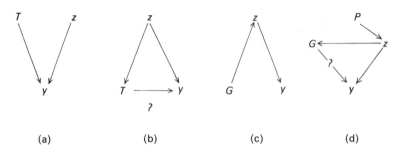

(a)   (b)   (c)   (d)

Diagram (a) illustrates the case of a treatment (T) and an explanatory variable (z, which is not the pre-test) both causally influencing the outcome (y) but without any causal relationship between z and T. This is the causal model behind the use of analysis of covariance in experiments when the inclusion of z leads to a more precise estimate of the effect of T.

It is reasonable to suppose that diagram (b), rather than diagram (c), applies to most quasi-experiments because the intervention occurs 'after' the explanatory variables z and cannot therefore have caused them. However, the fact that groups (G) in observational studies are likely to have existed before they are actually studied means that there will be observational studies for which diagram (c) is at least a possibility. For example, some types of mental illness (G) might determine social class as measured by occupation (z), rather than social class determining mental illness. For diagram (b), it is sensible to control for z in order to establish whether or not an observed association between treatment and outcome is spurious, but to control for z when diagram (c) applies will actually eliminate the indirect causal effect of group on outcome and this will often be unsatisfactory.

In diagram (d), a 'prior' variable (P) is causally related to z and to G via z; using z as an explanatory variable here does not take into account all the facets of the underlying causal system (which is often extremely difficult to specify) and will result in the elimination of that part of the effect of G which is due to P, and this may not always be reasonable. Meehl (1970) discusses this 'causal-arrow ambiguity' and the nature of statistical 'control' in some detail and states that:

> There is no general justification for the routine assumption that demographic and allied variables . . . should be taken as always functioning solely on the input side and therefore as always appropriately 'controlled' by a matching operation or by some similar type of statistical correction.

Suppose, for example, that we want to study the change in reading attainment over a school year for two groups of school children in their final year of primary school, one group defined as 'neurotic' and the other as 'anti-social' according to criteria described by Rutter, Tizard, and Whitmore (1970). Do the neurotic children make more progress in reading than the anti-social children? Rutter *et al.* show that neurotic children are more likely to be found in small families, whereas anti-social children are more likely to be found in large families, and Fogelman and Goldstein (1976) show that family size is associated with changes in reading attainment between the ages of 7 and 11. Thus, family size might reasonably be regarded as a z of diagram (b) and could logically enter a conditional model as an explanatory variable. The decision actually to use family size as an explanatory variable would depend on whether the question posed above was to be answered merely at the descriptive level or whether an answer was sought which might attribute differential progress to the behaviour problems of the child.

Rutter *et al.* also show that girls are slightly over-represented in the neurotic group and boys are over-represented in the anti-social group. Taken with the association between sex and change in attainment found by Fogelman and Goldstein, this suggests that sex could be a z of case (d) with the theoretical possibility of some kind of genetic link corresponding to the prior variable, P, and therefore less justification for the inclusion of sex on the right-hand side of the model.

These various points suggest that a conditional model, possibly with several explanatory variables in addition to the pre-test, will generally be the most appropriate method of analysing a quasi-experiment. For an observational study, a conditional model with just the pre-test will often be the most suitable method of measuring change. Decisions about the inclusion of other variables should be informed by the above considerations and by a clear and precise understanding of the hypotheses guiding the study.

Let us now look in more detail at the kinds of variables, like z, that might be found in equation (3.2). Omitted variables can take two forms: either they can be more complicated functions of the pre-test, such as x_1^2 or e^{x_1}, or they can be variables which the investigator was unaware of or was unable to measure. With samples of reasonable size, a plot of post-test against pre-test should reveal the existence of variables in the first group and the inclusion of these presents no real problem, as the example in the previous section has shown. (Cochran and Rubin, 1973, discuss the extent to which $\hat{\beta}_0$ in equation (3.3) will be biased when e^{ax_1} $(-1 < a < 1)$ and x_1^2 are mistakenly omitted.)

Mis-specification, and thus bias in estimating treatment or group effects, will arise if there are variables omitted from equation (3.3) which remain constant over the period of interest, which are correlated with group formation and which are still related to the post-test after allowing for their effect on the post-test via the pre-test.

Potential explanatory variables (z_j) which change over the period of study present problems both for observational studies and for quasi-experiments. It will be reasonable to include the measure of z_j at the second occasion as an additional explanatory variable when analysing a quasi-experiment only if it is unreasonable to suppose that the intervention would have caused z_j to change. Otherwise, there is a danger of eliminating a treatment effect when in fact such an effect is present but has operated through z_j (as in diagram (c) on the previous page).

An illustration of the dangers of ignoring constant background variables that can arise when estimating treatment effects comes from work by Goldstein

(1979c). By using data from the National Child Development Study, he shows that not only were there social class (as measured by father's occupation) differences in reading and arithmetic at age 7 years, but also, for fixed 7-year scores, there were further social class differences at 11 years. This has implications for educational quasi-experiments of a compensatory nature where social class is often associated with the variable defining treatment, and treatment is spread over, say, a school year. Goldstein's result suggests that social class would be correlated with the pre-test and have a partial correlation with the post-test after controlling for the pre-test. Then any model for British data which did not include a social class term as an explanatory variable, as well as the pre-test, would lead to estimated treatment effects which would be biased downwards, because of this tendency for working-class children to drop further behind in the population. Any design which did not allow considerable overlap between the treatment and control groups on variables such as social class would be irredeemably flawed. However, variables other than a crude measure of social disadvantage such as father's occupation would probably be needed to minimize specification bias and they may not all be available, or the sample size may not be sufficiently large, to include them in the estimation process.

Let us return to the example about school types to develop these ideas in a little more detail. Would the treatment effect be different if a more complete model were specified and estimated? There are a number of additional explanatory variables which could plausibly account for some of the 2.58 points difference between grammar and comprehensive schools found in equation (3.7). The most obvious is social class for the reasons given above; another is a measure of parental interest and encouragement, which is known to affect school attainment. Dichotomous measures of these were available with social class at age 11 years (SC11) divided into middle and working class, and parental interest (PI) divided simply into 'yes/no'. It is also possible that, even for fixed maths attainment at 11, general ability at 11 could affect maths attainment at 16, and so a measure of general ability (GA11) was considered.

Extending equation (3.7) to include social class (SC11) gives

$$M16 = 9.45 - 2.17ST + 0.011\,M11^2 - 1.60\,SC11 \qquad (3.8)$$
$$\quad\; (0.75) \quad (0.69) \qquad (0.001) \qquad\quad (0.64)$$

which shows a reduction (from 2.58 to 2.17) in the difference between grammar and comprehensive schools and also shows that, for fixed 11-year score and within school types, working-class children make less progress (1.60 points) than middle-class children.

If we add parental interest (PI) to equation (3.8) we get:

$$M16 = 10.5 - 2.07ST + 0.011M11^2 - 1.13SC11 + 2.07PI \qquad (3.9)$$
$$\quad\;\; (0.79)\; (0.67) \qquad (0.001) \qquad\;\; (0.64) \qquad (0.59)$$

and this shows another, but smaller, reduction in the school type effect and a substantial effect of parental interest, with children having parents interested in their schooling making more progress.

Finally, let us see whether the inclusion of general ability at 11 (GA11) changes equation (3.9):

$$M16 = 7.11 - 1.57ST + 0.009M11^2 - 1.03SC11 + 1.69PI + 0.09GA11$$
$$\quad (1.32) \quad (0.67) \quad\quad (0.001) \quad\quad (0.62) \quad\quad (0.59) \quad (0.03) \quad\quad (3.10)$$

Indeed it does, with the effect of school type now down to 1.57 points, although this is still statistically significant ($t = 2.34$, $p < 0.025$), and a reduction in the effects of social class and parental interest. Equation (3.10) explains 72% of the variation in M16, 5% more than equation (3.7).

This series of models shows a steady decline in the effect of school type as additional variables are taken into account, and there may be further, unmeasured, variables which, if included, might reduce the effect still more. For example, it is possible that the maths test used at 16 measured aspects of mathematical ability which were not covered in the test used at 11. This raises once again the problem of operationalization first discussed in Section 2.3, which might be solved by having multiple measures at the two occasions.

However, it can be dangerous to keep adding variables, especially when the sample is not large, as here. It is important to have enough observations not only to cover the range of each explanatory variable, but also across the range for fixed values of the other explanatory variables, particularly if some of the explanatory variables are categorical. Otherwise, there is always the possibility of basing conclusions on extrapolations of which the analyst is unaware. For example, there were only 30 observations (out of 200) where the parents were middle class but not interested in their child's education, and only 10 of these 30 were in comprehensive schools. It is possible that there would have been no overlap on general ability at 11 between the school types in this sub-sample, and it would not then have been wise to add GA11 to equation (3.9), even if there had been overlap on GA11 between the school types for the sample as a whole. Fortunately, the plot of M16 against GA11 (Figure 3.5) shows a reasonable degree of overlap between the two school types, but if it had looked like Figure 3.6, different conclusions about the coefficient of ST would have been drawn. The coefficient of ST estimated from Figure 3.6 would be much larger than the one estimated from Figure 3.5, but its validity would rest on extrapolations which might not be supported if more data were available.

Equation (3.10) is a more complete analysis of these data than equation (3.7) and certainly much more appropriate than the unconditional model, equation (2.3). Nevertheless, there are further questions to be considered: one of these, nonparallel regressions, is examined in the next section, and the effects of correcting for measurement error are looked at in Chapter 5.

In certain circumstances which are probably more common in observational studies than in quasi-experiments, the inclusion of an explanatory variable in the model can actually lead to more bias in the estimated treatment effect than if that variable had been omitted. Meehl (1970) calls this 'systematic unmatching'. He illustrates the point by considering the effects on later income of 'dropping out' from school. Those who drop out will, on average, have lower attainment scores

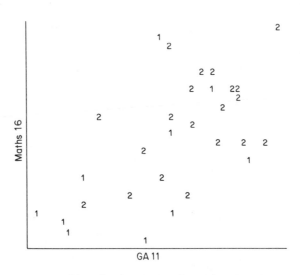

Figure 3.5 Plot of **MATHS**16 against **GA**11 for middle-class parents not interested in their child's education
Legend: 1 = Comprehensive
2 = Grammar

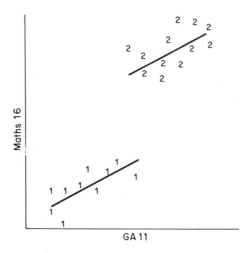

Figure 3.6 Hypothetical plot of **MATHS**16 against **GA**11 for school types 1 and 2. The lines give the within-group regressions

than those who stay, but looking at income differences for fixed attainment score may actually increase the bias in the estimated effect of drop-out by artificially widening the differences between the two groups in parental interest in education, a variable associated with educational success and hence with income. The inclusion of both attainment and parental interest as explanatory variables would, of course, get round this problem. Anderson *et al.* (1980) make a related point when they show how a variable, say z_1, which influences outcome but is not correlated with the group variable (x_0), may become correlated with x_0 for fixed values of another variable, say z_2. The exclusion of z_1 from a conditional model would not then be innocuous, and again both z_1 and z_2 need to be in the model.

The message of this section is that an accurate estimate of the causal effect, β_0, can be obtained only if there is extensive pre-treatment measurement, a clear understanding of how the groups were formed, careful model specification, and detailed analysis. On the other hand, it would be wrong to be too pessimistic. There is a tendency for critics to devalue findings from non-randomized studies by invoking unspecified 'third variables' rather than proposing tenable counter-hypotheses (an argument put forward in more detail by Radical Statistics Education Group, 1982). It would be better to see analyses of this type in the context of ongoing research which is often trying, in various ways, to find answers to important but difficult questions. As our knowledge of the underlying models for both the determination of outcomes and of assignment to groups increases, so will it be possible to reduce specification bias. It is also likely that a stage will be reached when the size of the bias in $\hat{\beta}_0$ will have fewer practical implications than its variance. Nevertheless, it cannot be emphasized too strongly that if experiments are feasible then they must always be preferred to quasi-experiments, and these experiments should be replicated.

3.8 NONPARALLEL REGRESSIONS

Let us now consider the estimation of relative change when we relax the assumption that the relationship between the outcome variable and any of the explanatory variables is unaffected by group membership. This situation is often referred to as a 'group-covariate' interaction, but this term is a little unsatisfactory as it implies that only the relationship between the pre- and post-tests, x_1 and y, is important, whereas in fact the relationships between all relevant explanatory variables and the dependent variable need to be considered. Nevertheless, for simplicity, suppose that the pre-test is the only relevant explanatory variable. We then want to know whether the within-group regression lines are parallel for, if they are not, estimation of group effects becomes problematic. It is straightforward to allow for interactions, and for the simple case, equation (3.3) would become

$$y = \alpha + \beta_0 x_0 + \beta_1 x_1 + \beta_2 x_0 x_1 + \varepsilon \qquad (3.11)$$

The $x_0 x_1$ term represents the interaction so that, for the first group $(x_0 = 0)$, the regression slope would be β_1 but, for the second group $(x_0 = 1)$, it would be $\beta_1 + \beta_2$. Figure 3.7 illustrates two situations: in Figure 3.7(a), β_2 is zero and the treatment effect is therefore constant and positive and equal to β_0 for all values of x_1; but in Figure 3.7(b), β_2 is positive and the difference between the groups varies according to the value of x_1. Indeed, for low values of x_1 in Figure 3.7(b) the treatment effect is actually negative.

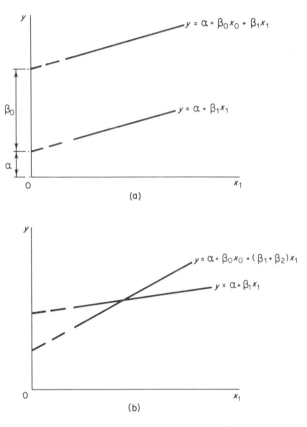

Figure 3.7 (a) Parallel regression lines
(b) Nonparallel regression lines

There are various strategies which one might adopt to deal with nonparallel regressions. The first is to ignore it, and if the regression lines do not show marked differences in slope and do not cross over, this may be reasonable. The second is to look for order-preserving transformations which eliminate the interaction, although these will be difficult to find if the slopes are very different, or if the lines cross. Another solution is to present not just one treatment effect but a range of effects for different values of x_1, although this could make the results of the study unnecessarily difficult to interpret. The Johnson–Neyman technique was developed for this situation and provides a range of values of x_1 for which β_0 is statistically significant and, if the two lines intersect in the observed range of x_1, then the technique gives a confidence interval for the crossover point. Aitkin (1973) discusses two variants of this little-known method. Other useful solutions have been provided by Cochran and Rubin (1973) and Rubin (1977), and we now look at these in a little more detail.

Assume that together, the elements in the two groups form a simple random sample from a population, either by sampling proportionately within the two groups or by taking a simple random sample from the population as a whole, but do not assume that assignment to groups is random. Then Rubin shows that, given linear but nonparallel relationships between y and x_1 in each group, an unbiased estimate for the average group effect over all values of x_1 in the population is

$$\hat{\tau}_1 = (\bar{y}_2 - \bar{y}_1) - \frac{n_2\hat{\beta}_1 + n_1(\hat{\beta}_1 + \hat{\beta}_2)}{n_1 + n_2}(\bar{x}_{12} - \bar{x}_{11}) \qquad (3.12)$$

where n_1 and n_2 are the number of sample elements in each group. It can be shown that if the variance of the pre-test is the same in both groups, and if the two groups are the same size ($n_1 = n_2$), then constraining the regression analysis to fit parallel lines gives an unbiased average group effect.

If the sampling assumption is not satisfied—and often it will not be for quasi-experiments—it is still possible to get an unbiased estimate of the average treatment effect for the treatment group:

$$\hat{\tau}_2 = (\bar{y}_2 - \bar{y}_1) - \hat{\beta}_{11}(\bar{x}_{12} - \bar{x}_{11}) \qquad (3.13)$$

where $\hat{\beta}_{11}$ is the slope for the *control* group. In essence, one is saying that it is possible to estimate the difference between applying and not applying the treatment to the treatment group, but this is not the same as the difference between not applying and applying the treatment to the control group, and this inference is restricted although still useful.

Cochran and Rubin suggest estimating an average group effect over a standard population, i.e.

$$\hat{\tau}_s = (\bar{y}_2 - \bar{y}_1) + (\hat{\beta}_1 + \hat{\beta}_2)(\eta_s - \bar{x}_{12}) - \hat{\beta}_1(\eta_s - \bar{x}_{11}) \qquad (3.14)$$

where η_s is the mean of the standard population which is assumed to be known. They use this result to propose a statistic, R, to act as a guide to the utility of estimating an average group effect, where

$$\hat{R} = \frac{(\bar{y}_2 - \bar{y}_1) + (\hat{\beta}_1 + \hat{\beta}_2)(\bar{x}_1 - \bar{x}_{12}) - \hat{\beta}_1(\bar{x}_1 - \bar{x}_{11})}{\hat{\beta}_1(x_H - x_L)} \qquad (3.15)$$

The denominator of $\hat{R}$ is the estimated difference in the group effects at the extreme values, x_H and x_L, of the range of x_1 of interest (which could be the overlap between the two groups) and $x_1 = (x_H + x_L)/2$. Clearly, if the absolute value of $\hat{R}$ differs very much from unity, then average treatment effects will not be very useful.

Returning to the data of Section 3.6, equation (3.11) is estimated to be

$$M16 = 7.63 - 4.34ST + 0.0128M11^2 + 0.0026M11^2 \cdot ST \qquad (3.16)$$
$$(0.58) \quad (1.26) \qquad (0.001) \qquad (0.0016)$$

The interaction term would not normally be regarded as statistically significant ($p < 0.11$), but if it is included then the difference between the mean maths scores at 16 becomes smaller as the maths score at 11 goes up, as Figure 3.8 shows. The curves do not cross, but they converge at the top of the 11 year scale. The

48

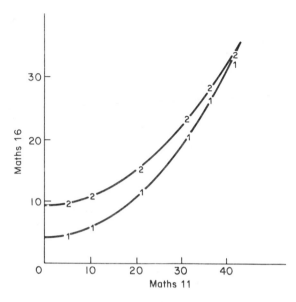

Figure 3.8 Graphical representation of equation
(3.16)
Legend: 1 = Comprehensive
2 = Grammar

difference of 2.58 points found in equation (3,7) is just a little greater than the
mean of the two extreme differences and equal to the difference when the 11 year
score is 26.

Interactions between the group variable and other explanatory variables can
arise because the model is not specified properly, and this is particularly likely if
overlap between the groups on the explanatory variable is small. For example, in
Figure 3.9 there appears to be a much steeper slope for group 2 than for group 1,
but if more data had been available, parallel curvilinear relationships could have
been estimated for both groups. This emphasizes just how important it is to plot
out data of this kind in order to avoid artefactual conclusions, and also how
difficult it can be to obtain unequivocal results when there is little overlap between
the groups.

It would seem that the problems of nonparallel regressions are avoided if an
unconditional model is used, but in fact an unconditional model will provide some
sort of average treatment effect in this situation, although the researcher will not
be aware of this. Moreover, for some studies, an interaction between the pre-test
and treatment could be a hypothesis of interest. For example, if a treatment has to
be given to a complete group such as a school class, but is aimed particularly at
weaker students, then the treatment group slope would be expected to be flatter
than the control group slope, and β_2 in equation (3.11) would be negative. Related
to this is the possibility that the treatment is expected to have a greater effect on

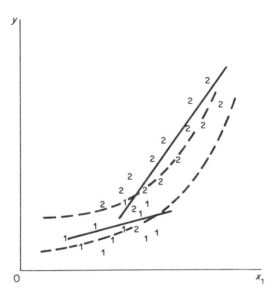

Figure 3.9 Parallel curvilinear relationships mas-
querading as nonparallel linear relationships
Legend: —— within-group regressions for the
sample
— — — within-group regressions for the
population

the proportion of individuals scoring above a cutoff point than it is on the mean.
Methods for analysing non-randomized studies when the outcome is dichotomous or polytomous are given in Chapter 6.

3.9 VALUE-ADDED ANALYSIS

Dissatisfied with regression adjustment for estimating the effects of interventions,
particularly educational interventions, Bryk and Weisberg (1976) propose a
technique called 'value-added analysis'. Essentially, this assumes an underlying
developmental process which can be adequately modelled, and measures a
treatment effect by the difference between the observed mean post-test score and
the predicted mean had there been no intervention, only 'maturation' (see
Figure 3.10). A control group is said not to be necessary for this analysis, although
it could be used to provide a check on the model in that the mean value added, $\bar{V}$,
should be zero for the control group. However, $\bar{V}$ will not be zero if an extraneous
event occurs at the same time as the intervention, and so analyses without control
groups are bound to be suspect.

Let us look at one way of doing value-added analysis with the aid of an example.
These data come from one of the Educational Priority Area (EPA) intervention
studies carried out in England and Scotland in the early 1970s. This particular

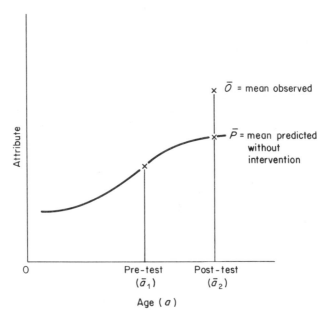

Figure 3.10 Mean value-added: $\overline{V} = \overline{O} - \overline{P}$ where $\overline{P}$ is a function of age

study consisted of three groups of children with data collected on five occasions over four years. The children were originally assigned at random to the three groups, but losses from the study were not random and so the study is better treated as a quasi-experiment; further details can be found in Smith and James (1975). The data for all five occasions are analysed in Chapter 8, but for now, we look just at the data for occasions 1 and 2. For two of the groups (E1 and E2) there was an intervention between these two occasions, while the third group (C) was a control group. At occasion 1, the children were tested with the pre-school version of the English Picture Vocabulary Test (EPVT$_{ps}$).

The developmental process can be modelled by looking at the relationship between the test scores at occasion 1 and age at occasion 1 (a_1). This could be done more precisely by including data from another, similar study to give an overall sample size of 98 with ages varying between 36 and 54 months. Straight lines with different intercepts for the different groups but a common slope, or growth rate, of 0.49 accounted for 26% of the variance of the pre-test (see Table 3.2). There was no evidence that more complicated functions of age would improve the fit.

There were pre-test differences between the three groups and it could be argued that these arose because their mean growth rates were different, but this is only weakly supported for these data (the null hypothesis of equal slopes is rejected only at the 0.09 significance level). An alternative explanation, which finds more support, is that growth on the underlying variable measured by the test did not, on average, start at the same time in each group, so that groups behind on the pre-test started developing later. However, this is speculative because data were not available for very young children.

At occasion 2, some children were again tested with the pre-school version of the EPVT, some were tested with version 1 ($EPVT_1$), while a group of 19 children were tested with both versions. It is only possible to do value-added analysis if there is a scale which is common to both occasions; this was achieved here by first relating $EPVT_{ps}$ to $EPVT_1$ for those children tested on both tests and then using this relationship to transform the scores on $EPVT_1$ to give an estimated score on $EPVT_{ps}$. The estimated transformation was

$$EPVT_{ps} = 15.7 + 1.02\ EPVT_1 \qquad (3.17)$$

with a multiple correlation of 0.74. It was then straightforward to calculate the observed mean at occasion 2 on the pre-school scale (see Table 3.2).

Table 3.2 EPA data: Value-added analysis

Group	Sample size	Predictive equation	Predicted mean	Observed mean	Value added (s.d.)
C	15	$y = -7.8 + 0.49 a_1$	20.3	21.8	1.5 (3.3)
E1	15	$y = -12.8 + 0.49 a_1$	13.6	20.3	6.7 (2.7)
E2	15	$y = -13.9 + 0.49 a_1$	13.5	17.0	3.5 (2.5)

Table 3.2 also gives the results of substituting the mean age at occasion 2 for each group into the predictive equation based on the pre-test ('predicted mean'). It shows that neither C nor E2 have 'value added' which differs significantly from zero, but E1 does appear to have made significantly more progress than expected. (The standard errors for the predicted values, and thus for the value added, are only approximate, being calculated from the standard theory for the variability of predictions made from regression equations (see Weisberg, 1980), together with the assumption that all the observations within a group at occasion 2 were made at the same time, that is at the mean age (but ignoring the error of transformation in equation (3.17)).)

Although the idea of value-added analysis is an attractive one, particularly for developmental psychologists, the method has serious drawbacks and limitations as it stands. It could only be used where the notion of an age-related process is theoretically sensible and also where the measures exist to model it satisfactorily—most standardized tests would not be suitable. The method assumes a reasonable range of ages at pre-test and, crucially, it assumes that it is reasonable to extrapolate the estimated line or curve to age at post-test. The extrapolation is reasonable for the EPA data up to occasion 2, but it would not be wise to go beyond this, and so the method is not suitable for studies which collect data on several occasions after an intervention. Another problem with the method is that it models developmental (or longitudinal) processes from cross-sectional data collected at the first occasion and this can be dangerous if there are 'cohort' effects—effects due to date or season of birth—as well as age effects. There are many similarities between the value-added approach and the time-related models to be discussed in Chapter 8.

3.10 IDEAS FROM ECONOMETRICS

Another way of estimating treatment effects in non-randomized studies can be found in the econometric literature. Here an attempt is made separately to model the process determining the outcome and the process determining assignment to groups (self-selection). There are therefore two equations:

$$y = \alpha + \beta_0 x_0 + \beta_1 x_1 + \sum_{i=1}^{k} \theta_i z_i + \varepsilon_1 \tag{3.18}$$

where x_0 defines the group, x_1 is the pre-test, and the z_i are other variables influencing the outcome, y (equation (3.10) is an estimated version of this equation, except that x_1^2 is used); and

$$t = \alpha_1 x_1 + \sum_{i=1}^{k} \gamma_i z_i + \varepsilon_2 \tag{3.19}$$

for assignment such that $x_0 = 1$ when $t > 0$ and $x_0 = 0$ when $t \leqslant 0$.

In addition, because it is possible that there are unmeasured variables influencing both selection and outcome, it is assumed that the error terms ε_1 and ε_2 are correlated. Thus, equations (3.18) and (3.19) form a simultaneous equation system and must be estimated jointly. One method of doing this is given by Heckman (1979) and elaborated by Barnow, Cain, and Goldberger (1980). They assume that ε_1 and ε_2 come from a bivariate normal distribution and then estimate α_1 and γ_i in equation (3.19) using maximum likelihood probit analysis (Finney, 1971). The $\hat{\alpha}_1 x_1$ and $\hat{\gamma}_i z_i$ are then used to estimate the probability, p, that an individual would be in the treatment group (i.e. the probability that $x_0 = 1$) for the particular values of x_1 and z_i. A revised version of equation (3.18):

$$y = \alpha + \beta_1 x_1 + \sum_{i=1}^{k} \theta_i z_i + \delta p + \varepsilon_3 \tag{3.20}$$

is then estimated using ordinary least squares to give an unbiased estimate, $\hat{\delta}$, of the treatment effect.

The advantage of the method is that, *providing* ε_1 and ε_2 are uncorrelated with x_1 and z_i, and *providing* x_1 and the z_i are measured without error, then it can produce unbiased estimates of the treatment effect. However, the estimates may not be very precise. The correlations between p and x and z_i in equation (3.20) are likely to be high because there is a strong, albeit non-linear, relationship between t and x_1 and z_i in equation (3.19), and a high correlation inevitably leads to regression coefficients with large standard errors. The situation could be eased if data on several explanatory variables were available, especially if some of these variables influenced assignment and others influenced outcome, because the correlations between p and x_1 and z_i in equation (3.20) would then be reduced. On the other hand, if a number of explanatory variables have been measured then the bias in $\hat{\beta}_0$ when equation (3.18) is estimated on its own may well be unimportant; this was, of course, the approach adopted in Section 3.7.

The method should certainly not be applied unthinkingly. Consider the data on secondary schooling first discussed in Section 3.6. It is tempting to suppose that allocation to grammar and comprehensive schools is strongly influenced by general ability at 11, and so estimating equation (3.19) will produce sensible estimates of p which can in turn be substituted into equation (3.20) to produce sensible estimates of the effect of school type. In fact, this is not so; assignment to different types of secondary school is influenced both by general ability and by area of the country, because some children lived in local authority areas which had abolished grammar schools. This means that some children who scored high on the general ability test at 11 and who might have been expected to make substantial progress in mathematics at secondary school were given a high probability of being in a grammar school by equation (3.19) when, in fact, they went to a comprehensive, because they lived in a genuinely comprehensive area. As data on which kind of local authority the children lived in were not available, the assignment model cannot be specified properly and the method breaks down.

This can be explained in another way. Local authorities can be divided into two types: either they are selective (with grammar schools) or non-selective (comprehensives only). This dichotomous variable is included in ε_2 in equation (3.19) and is correlated with general ability because non-selective local authorities do, on average, have children with lower ability than selective authorities. Hence, ε_2 and z_i in equation (3.19) are correlated, and this breaks the first requirement of the model given earlier. It is the assignment model and not the outcome model which is incorrectly specified. Type of local authority area is unlikely to have an independent effect on outcome after allowing for social class, etc., so the estimates of the effect of type of school given in Section 3.7 are probably the best that can be obtained (but see also Chapter 5). Rosenbaum and Rubin (1983) present a similar method which revolves around the calculation of a 'propensity score' for assignment. Again, their method is unlikely to work with these data.

3.11 MATCHING

If matched samples are used, then the treatment effect or the relative change is estimated as the difference between the group means at post-test, that is $\bar{y}_2 - \bar{y}_1$. Various methods of constructing matched samples have been suggested. These methods are normally used at the design stage of a study, but matching can be done at the analysis stage, too. With just one continuous matching variable, say the pre-test, x_1, Cochran and Rubin (1973) describe: (a) 'paired caliper' matching when, for pairs of individuals, the differences on x_1 are predetermined and small;

(b) 'nearest available' matching when, for a fixed treatment group sample, a computer algorithm is used to select an equal number from a large reservoir of potential members of a control group to give pairs close in value on x_1; and (c) 'mean' matching, which focuses solely on making the group means on x_1 the same. However, to match on just one variable suffers from the same disadvantage of potential bias as does regression adjustment with one explanatory variable. In other words, some kind of multivariate matching procedure is often needed, indeed would have been needed for the data on secondary schooling. One method is described by Rubin (1976a).

If the only matching variable is truly dichotomous (e.g. sex), or truly polytomous (e.g. country of origin), then all elements within the sub-classes are the same with respect to that variable, and the aim is then to find the same number in each sub-class for the treatment and control samples. However, a categorical variable is sometimes used to represent an underlying continuous varible as, for example, when age groups are used, and two members of the same sub-class are not then necessarily equal in terms of the underlying variable.

What are the relative merits of matching and regression adjustment? The omission of relevant explanatory variables from a regression model is equivalent to ignoring relevant matching variables in the design, and neither method can completely deal with one of the fundamental problems of comparing groups not formed by randomization. A drawback of paired-caliper matching, particularly if the matching criterion employed is tight, is that the group samples are often no longer random samples of their populations, and this restricts the inferences that can be made. Also, this kind of matching can result in a serious diminution of sample size, especially when there are more than two groups. This problem can be avoided by retaining all the sample elements in the treatment group or groups and finding matches from a larger control group reservoir as in nearest-available matching. But these reservoirs do not normally exist for social science data, although they often do for comparative studies in medicine. A particular disadvantage of mean matching is that it assumes an underlying linear relationship between y and x_1. It would therefore not have been suitable for the data on secondary schooling (see Section 3.6).

It would appear unnecessary, for any form of matching, to check for nonparallel regressions, but this is not the case, and $\bar{y}_2 - \bar{y}_1$ will estimate the average treatment effect only for the treatment population if the regressions are not parallel. Another disadvantage is that it is not possible to take account of *changes* in background variables used for matching, whereas these changes can be specified in a regression model. Also, analyses which extend beyond two occasions (as given in Chapter 8) are very difficult for samples matched only at the first occasion unless they are supplemented by regression models.

Matching on an observed pre-treatment variable which contains errors of measurement leads to just the same kind of biases as occur in regression adjustment, and these are discussed in Chapter 5. However, this practice carries even more dangers because there is no need to write down a statistical model for a matched design and, without one, there is no possibility of adjusting for measurement error in the analysis. This is perhaps the most serious disadvantage of matching.

3.12 SUMMARY

The analysis of relative change in non-randomized, or comparative, studies is undoubtedly a controversial subject; there is no one agreed method of doing it, although there are several contenders. This chapter has looked at those methods which are probably the most widely used. However, it has concentrated on conditional, or regression, models and has paid particular attention to how these models should be specified and how analysis and interpretation will vary according to the aims of the study (Sections 3.3, 3.6, and 3.7). The effects of measurement error on regression models are not considered here; instead they are deferred until Chapter 5, but they can be important and a careful regression analysis of relative change would have to account for them.

The chapter evaluates unconditional models (Sections 3.4 and 3.5), value-added analysis (Section 3.9), modelling assignment and outcome separately (Section 3.10), and matching (Section 3.11) as alternatives to regression. Unconditional models, or comparing net changes, can only be regarded as an alternative when describing relative change, but the other three methods can all be used when trying to explain relative change. They all have drawbacks which make them generally less convincing than a thoughtful regression analysis, although, for each of them, there are circumstances when they will perform well. And so, there will be studies for which the analysis would benefit from applying more than one method. However, the data on secondary schooling which is used throughout the chapter could only be sensibly analysed with the regression model.

CHAPTER 4

Causal Models for Change

4.1 INTRODUCTION

Longitudinal data have great value when we want to make causal inferences from non-experimental data. This was apparent in the previous chapter, although we were only concerned there with causal inferences about relative change where the explanatory variable of interest could be regarded as fixed and where the causal direction was unambiguous. Here we look at models for change when both explanatory and dependent variables can change at any time. First, we consider models for estimating the size of a relationship when there is enough theoretical knowledge to be able to state that a change in a particular direction in one variable will lead to a change in another variable, with enough theory to be able to predict the sign of that change, but not enough to predict its magnitude. These are models for known causal direction and so they have some links with the models presented in Chapter 3.

The other area we explore in this chapter is more problematic and more controversial: at a single point in time, two variables are related, both change over time, and it is thought that they are causally related but the causal direction is uncertain. Several examples can be given—does exposure to television violence lead to aggression in children, or do aggressive children choose to watch the more violent programmes (Lefkowitz, Eron, Walder, and Huesmann, 1977)? Do parents respond to their children's behaviour, or is it the other way round (Clarke-Stewart, 1973)? What inferences can be drawn from a relationship between drug-taking and criminal behaviour? We shall confine our attention to systems with just two causal variables, both of which are measured without error on at least an interval scale, with data collected for just two occasions. Models which allow for measurement error are considered in Chapter 5 and models for categorical data are considered in Chapter 7. Models with more than two causal variables or with data about more than two occasions, or both, are likely to be more realistic; certainly restricting ourselves to just two occasions is limiting. However, even these substantively rather simplistic models are statistically quite involved, and so this restriction is necessary to start with in order to explain how the models can be specified and estimated. More general models are discussed in Chapter 8.

Longitudinal data are not essential for causal modelling. It is possible to construct causal models from cross-sectional data and applications of the technique of path analysis to such data have been popular in recent years (for example, Jencks *et al.*, 1973). However, with cross-sectional data, model specification is more difficult and assumptions about the direction of causality have to be made, assumptions which can often be tested with longitudinal data. Of course, there can be no doubt about the direction of causality for events which are ordered in time (for example, a postulated sequence of nursery school experience leading to better adjustment to infant school, leading in turn to greater academic progress) and information about such events can often be collected by using retrospective questioning within a cross-sectional study.

The sections of the chapter dealing with models for change when the causal direction is unknown are divided into two main parts. The first, comprising Sections 4.3, 4.4, and 4.5, looks at relatively simple models for deciding on causal direction. Section 4.6 looks at more complicated and perhaps more realistic models; this section draws on ideas from the econometric literature which some readers may find unfamiliar.

4.2 MODELS FOR CHANGE WHEN THE CAUSAL DIRECTION IS KNOWN

Consider first a simple cross-sectional relationship at occasion 1 between two variables, x and y, both of which change over time, i.e.

$$y_1 = \alpha^* + \beta^* x_1 + \varepsilon^* \tag{4.1}$$

Rarely will it be possible to give β^* the causal interpretation that a change of one unit in x will lead to y changing by β^* units. Indeed, such a statement will only be justified if the error term, ε^*, does not contain variables which explain an important part of the variation in y and which are correlated with x_1, and if β^* is constant over time.

Suppose that the true model for y at occasion 1 is

$$y_1 = \alpha_1 + \beta x_1 + \sum_k \gamma_k z_k + \varepsilon_1 \tag{4.2}$$

where z_k and γ_k do not change over time, so that z_k are constant background variables, such as country of origin and years of schooling, which may or may not have been measured, and other, possibly unmeasurable, variables such as ability which are often postulated to be constant. We have already discussed this situation in Chapter 3 (equations (3.1) and (3.2)), and we know that $\hat{\beta}^*$ will be a biased estimate of β if some of the z_k are correlated with x_1. If at occasion 2, the true model for y is

$$y_2 = \alpha_2 + \beta x_2 + \sum_k \gamma_k z_k + \varepsilon_2 \tag{4.3}$$

then it is possible to eliminate the effects of z_k, which are often nuisance variables, by subtracting equation (4.3) from equation (4.2) to give

$$y_2 - y_1 = (\alpha_2 - \alpha_1) + \beta(x_2 - x_1) + (\varepsilon_2 - \varepsilon_1) \tag{4.4}$$

Equation (4.4) allows us to get an unbiased estimate of β. This could not be obtained from equation (4.1) because that model is not correctly specified, nor from equations (4.2) and (4.3) because relevant 'z-type' variables may not have been measured. Thus, longitudinal data can give us a result which cross-sectional data cannot, which is that a change of one unit in x will lead to a change of β units in y over the given interval between measurements. However, the result does depend very much on this interval and it is possible that β is an underestimate of the total causal effect of x on y. For example, it is possible for the change in x to take place early in the interval and its full effect on y may have been dissipated by occasion 2. Alternatively, the change in x between occasions 1 and 2 may have further effects on y after occasion 2.

Equation (4.4) depends on the assumption that the value of β does not change between the two occasions. If this is not so, then replacing β by β_1 in equation (4.2) and by β_2 in equation (4.3) gives

$$y_2 - y_1 = (\alpha_2 - \alpha_1) + \beta_2 x_2 - \beta_1 x_1 + (\varepsilon_2 - \varepsilon_1) \tag{4.5}$$

which can also be written as

$$y_2 - y_1 = (\alpha_2 - \alpha_1) + \beta_2 (x_2 - x_1) + (\beta_2 - \beta_1) x_1 + (\varepsilon_2 - \varepsilon_1) \tag{4.6}$$

and this shows that the change in y is not constant, but rather depends on the initial value of x. However, equations (4.5) and (4.6) suffer from the drawback that when x_1 and x_2 are highly correlated, β_2 will be imprecisely estimated.

Equations (4.4) and (4.5) are only correctly specified for change if the background variables, z_k, really are constant and, more importantly, if the relationship of z_k to the dependent variable, y, does not change over time so that all the γ_k are constant. If a background variable (say z_1) is related not only to the value of y at a particular point in time but also to a change in y, then γ_1 will not be constant and β in equation (4.4) will be biased if z_1 is also correlated with the change in x.

These ideas can now be illustrated with some data taken from the longitudinal studies of pre-school children and their families mentioned in Chapter 1 (Section 1.4); see Moss and Plewis (1977) for more details. Information was collected on various worries such as housing, money, and illness, experienced by the mother in the 12 months prior to interview and also on the mother's mental health in the previous 12 months. Indices of worries and mental health were constructed which could be regarded as continuous variables with optimal scores of zero for both indices. (The means, variances, and covariances of these indices are given in Appendix 4.1.) Work on the aetiology of depression in women (Brown, Bhrolchain, and Harris, 1975) suggests that a change in the worries index (x) would lead to a change in the same direction in the health index (y). And so equations (4.1), (4.4), and (4.6) were estimated on a sample of 174 mothers who were interviewed on two occasions 12 months apart. The results are given in Table 4.1. (The assumption about causal direction is tested later in the chapter.)

Models 1 and 2 are based on cross-sectional data and correspond to equation (4.1) and the equivalent equation for occasion 2. Model 3 comes from equation

(4.4). The estimate of β (0.24) for model 3 is lower than the estimates of β^* in models 1 and 2 (both 0.44), which suggests that the cross-sectional estimates—$\hat{\beta}^*$ in equation (4.1)—are biased upwards. Adding x_1 to model 3 to create model 4 (equation (4.6)) does lead to a somewhat better, if not very good, fit, and changes the estimate for $(x_2 - x_1)$ from 0.24 to 0.31 with little change in its standard error. The estimates in model 4 are not, however, convincing. Suppose that $x_1 = 15$ and $x_2 = 12$. Substituting these values into model 4 gives an estimated value for $y_2 - y_1$ of $[-0.83 + 15(0.16) - 3(0.31)] = 0.64$, so lessening worries $(x_2 < x_1)$ leads to worsening health $(y_2 > y_1)$, which is unlikely. But when $x_1 = 3$ and $x_2 = 0$, $y_2 - y_1 = -1.28$, which is reasonable. However, when $x_1 = 0$ and $x_2 = 3$, $y_2 - y_1 = 0.10$, so changes in x which are equal in magnitude and opposite in sign do not produce equal and opposite changes in y, and this does make it difficult to regard equation (4.6) as a genuinely causal model. Equation (4.6) is more vulnerable to mis-specification than equation (4.4) because an omitted variable correlated with a change in y has only to be correlated with the initial value of x, rather than with the change in x, for mis-specification to occur. Thus, model 3 is the most sensible of the four models given in Table 4.1, but it does explain only 6% of the variation in $y_2 - y_1$ ($R^2 = 0.06$).

Table 4.1 Relating worries to health (a): Parameter estimates and standard errors

Model	Dependent variable	Explanatory variables				R^2
		Constant	x_1	x_2	$(x_2 - x_1)$	
1	y_1	3.4 (0.34)	0.44 (0.07)	—	—	0.19
2	y_2	3.1 (0.34)	—	0.44 (0.06)	—	0.21
3	$y_2 - y_1$	−0.21 (0.23)	—	—	0.24 (0.07)	0.06
4	$y_2 - y_1$	−0.83 (0.40)	0.16 (0.08)	—	0.31 (0.08)	0.08

If, for one or more of the reasons given in Chapter 2, $(y_2 - y_1)$ is not regarded as a suitable measure of change, then equation (4.5) could be replaced by the conditional model

$$y_2 = \mu + \delta_1 y_1 + \delta_2 x_1 + \varepsilon \tag{4.7}$$

and δ_2 would then be the parameter of interest. It is the measure of the effect on y at occasion 2 of x at occasion 1 for fixed values of y at occasion 1, or the effect of x_1 on a change in y. The conditions for δ_2 to be unbiased are the same as those for $\hat{\beta}_2$ in equation (4.6)—there should be no omitted variables which are correlated with a change in y and with the initial value of x.

Equation (4.7) might also be preferred to equation (4.5) if it is believed that initial level not only predicts later levels, but also has a causal influence on later levels. For example, one's present income is a good predictor of future income;

moreover, people with high incomes can invest and borrow and so generate future income in a way which people with low incomes cannot.

Equation (4.7) assumes that the partial regression coefficient of x_1 on y_2 will give us a good estimate of the causal influence of a change in x on a change in y. However, it is unlikely that the interval between occasions of measurement will correspond to the 'causal lag' of interest. In longitudinal studies, measurements are often determined by administrative convenience and therefore take place at regular intervals, but it is most unusual for there to be precise knowledge about the likely length of time between a change in one variable and a change in another. Thus, the estimated magnitude of δ_2 in equation (4.7) does not necessarily give us a good estimate of the strength of the causal relationship between x and y because if the time between the two measurements had been either longer or shorter then a different relationship might have been observed.

One way of dealing with the possibility of a short causal lag is to allow x_2 to influence y_2 so that, rather than equation (4.7), we have:

$$y_2 = \mu + \delta_1 y_1 + \delta_2 x_1 + \delta_3 x_2 + \varepsilon \tag{4.8}$$

and now we are interested in δ_3, the measure of the effect on y at occasion 2 of a change in x after occasion 1 for fixed values of x and y at occasion 1. Equation (4.8) also gives a better representation of the idea of x and y both changing than does equation (4.7), which looks more at the effect of variation in x at one occasion on a change in y. The conditions for $\hat{\delta}_3$ to be unbiased are the same as those for $\hat{\beta}$ in equation (4.4)—there should be no omitted variables correlated with the change in y and with the change in x. These conditions are perhaps less severe than the corresponding conditions for $\hat{\delta}_2$ in equation (4.7). It might be argued that equation (4.4) is specified dynamically, or explicitly in terms of change, but equations (4.7) and (4.8) are not. But this argument rests on the assumption that change can only be defined as a difference which, as we have already seen, is an unnecessary assumption. Equation (4.8) is as much specified in terms of change as equation (4.4) is. Equation (4.7) is not as satisfactory, although the effect of a variable at a particular point in time on change in another variable will sometimes be a reasonable measure of causal influence.

The measurement of a social science variable at a particular time does not usually mean that the value of that variable applies only to the instant of measurement; normally one can suppose that the variable does not change round the time of measurement, and sometimes the measurements refer to a particular time period, such as the last week or the last month. Thus, the causal link between x_2 and y_2 in equation (4.8) implies not so much a simultaneous effect as the possibility that a change in x some time after occasion 1 leads to a change in y by occasion 2, although 'some time' is not defined in any precise way. This gives us a way of handling short causal lags, but the only way to deal with causal lags which are longer than the interval between measurements is to collect more data at different times.

The results of estimating equations (4.7) and (4.8) in the usual way are given as models 5 and 6 in Table 4.2.

Table 4.2 Relating worries to health (b): Parameter estimates and standard errors

Model	Dependent variable	Explanatory variables				R^2
		Constant	y_1	x_1	x_2	
5	y_2	1.9	0.39	0.27	—	0.31
		(0.39)	(0.07)	(0.07)		
6	y_2	1.2	0.39	0.11	0.31	0.40
		(0.39)	(0.07)	(0.07)	(0.06)	

We see that the estimates of interest, the coefficient of x_1 in model 5 and the coefficient of x_2 in model 6, are similar (0.27 and 0.31 respectively) and close to the coefficient of $(x_2 - x_1)$ in model 3 given in Table 4.1. And so the different approaches give similar results for these data. The magnitude of the various estimates are not very informative as they stand, because the scales for the indices are arbitrary, but they would become more interesting if the same scales were used and the same analyses carried out, on different populations.

Equation (4.8) does have some disadvantages which are not shared by equation (4.4). The correlations within the three pairs of explanatory variables, but especially the correlation between x_1 and x_2, will usually be high and this will lead to imprecise estimates of the regression coefficients, particularly for small samples. Second, the inclusion of y_1 on the right-hand side of the equation can lead to problems if the error terms, ε, are correlated over time, but discussion of this is deferred until models for more than two occasions are considered in Chapter 8. Finally, the model implies that a change in x will not only affect y_2 but might also affect y_3 (via its effect on y_2), y_4, etc., if δ_1 is large, and this will not always be realistic.

4.3 SIMPLE MODELS FOR TWO-WAVE, TWO-VARIABLE (2W2V) DATA

When the causal direction is unknown, the case of two changing variables measured on two occasions is often referred to in the literature as two-wave, two-variable, or 2W2V, data. The simplest model for these data is illustrated by Figure 4.1. Diagrams like Figure 4.1 are often called 'path' diagrams and the data analysed by path analysis. But path analysis is really just a form of multiple regression analysis and it is not treated as a separate technique here.

The arrows from x_1 to y_2 and y_1 to x_2 show that the causal relationship between x and y is uncertain before data are collected, and these arrows represent the 'cross-lagged' relationships. (There would be no arrow from y_1 to x_2 for the models considered in the previous section, because it was assumed there that x causes y.) The arrows from x_1 to x_2 and y_1 to y_2 represent what are often called 'auto' relationships. The curved line without an arrow between x_1 and y_1 indicates that they may be correlated, but that such a correlation is of no causal interest. This simple model assumes that there is no causal link between x_2 and y_2, that is,

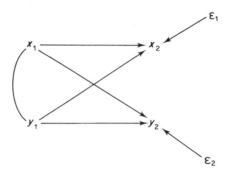

Figure 4.1 Causal diagram for a simple 2W2V model

no 'simultaneous effect'. As we have seen in the previous section, this assumption will not always be justified for social science data. It will be relaxed later, but at the cost of considerably more complex models. Figure 4.1 recognizes that x_1 and y_1 do not account for all the variation in either x_2 or y_2, and so ε_1 and ε_2 are included as error terms.

One method of analysing this model was proposed by Campbell (1963). He suggested comparing the correlation of x_1 and y_2 $(r_{x_1 y_2})$ with the correlation of y_1 and x_2 $(r_{y_1 x_2})$, which are usually known as the 'cross-lagged panel correlations'. Campbell argued that if $r_{x_1 y_2}$ is greater than $r_{y_1 x_2}$, then it is reasonable to conclude that x causes y; but if $r_{y_1 x_2}$ is greater than $r_{x_1 y_2}$, then y causes x. Developments of the method have resulted in the imposition of restrictions before such an interpretation could be considered reasonable (see, for example, Rozelle and Campbell, 1969, and Kenny, 1975b), with opposition to the method coming from Goldberger (1971), Rogosa (1979), and others. These opponents argue that it is misleading to focus on the correlations, and they consider regression analysis to be more appropriate.

Although it cannot be denied that the regression approach imposes various assumptions, these assumptions are made more explicit when a statistical model is written down, and the model can be linked with the mainstream of statistical methods. Also, it is possible to estimate the parameters of a causal model using regression and so to find out by how much y changes when x changes by one unit, for example; the correlational approach is merely a rather unsatisfactory way of testing for causal influence. The popularity of comparing cross-lagged correlations cannot be denied, but it is a dangerous popularity which depends too much on a simplistic recipe and not enough on careful model specification.

The equations corresponding to Figure 4.1 are:

$$x_2 = \alpha_0 + \alpha_1 x_1 + \alpha_2 y_1 + \varepsilon_1 \tag{4.9a}$$

$$y_2 = \beta_0 + \beta_1 y_1 + \beta_2 x_1 + \varepsilon_2 \tag{4.9b}$$

Equations (4.9), together with the important assumption that the error terms, ε_1 and ε_2, are uncorrelated, form a 'recursive' system of simultaneous equations.

(Equation (4.9b) is the same as equation (4.7).) This means that unbiased and efficient estimates of α_i and β_i ($i = 0, 1, 2$) can be obtained by applying ordinary least squares (OLS) to each equation separately, provided the usual conditions are satisfied.

It is not possible to formulate a model for Figure 4.1 in terms of difference scores. We could write down

$$y_2 - y_1 = \gamma + \delta(x_2 - x_1) + \varepsilon_1 \tag{4.10a}$$

$$x_2 - x_1 = \psi + \theta(y_2 - y_1) + \varepsilon_2 \tag{4.10b}$$

but differences between δ and θ will depend only on the relative variances of $(y_2 - y_1)$ and $(x_2 - x_1)$ and so can tell us nothing about causal direction.

It is the relative value of $\hat{\alpha}_2$ and $\hat{\beta}_2$ which determines whether and how the causal inferences of interest can be drawn from equations (4.9), although the actual values of all the $\hat{\alpha}_i$ and $\hat{\beta}_i$ are important when the causal system is being estimated. A decision has to be made about whether to compare the raw coefficients $\hat{\alpha}_2$ and $\hat{\beta}_2$ or whether to standardize and compare $\hat{\alpha}_2^{(s)}$ and $\hat{\beta}_2^{(s)}$, which are known as the 'path' or 'beta' coefficients (they are *not* equivalent to partial correlation coefficients), where

$$\hat{\alpha}_2^{(s)} = \hat{\alpha}_2 \frac{\text{s.d.} (y_1)}{\text{s.d.} (x_2)} \tag{4.11a}$$

$$\hat{\beta}_2^{(s)} = \hat{\beta}_2 \frac{\text{s.d.} (x_1)}{\text{s.d.} (y_2)} \tag{4.11b}$$

There is some disagreement in the literature about which coefficients should be used. Standardized coefficients would usually be preferred both for arbitrary scales and for fixed scales when the only comparison of interest is for the sampled population. However, if the scales in question are fixed and one is looking for causal 'laws' which extend to other populations and to other time periods, then there is less justification for eliminating any effect which is the result of differing variabilities in the dependent variables (x_2 and y_2) between populations. (Obviously it would be foolish to compare the raw coefficients if x_1 had been measured in, say, pounds and y_1 in pence, but differences of this kind should be eliminated beforehand.)

If the absolute values of $\alpha_2^{(s)}$ (or α_2) are positive and $\beta_2^{(s)}$ and $\beta_2 = 0$ and *if* the model is a reasonable one then, because a change in y (or, more precisely, variation in y_1) leads to a change in x but a change in x does not lead to a change in y, the data suggest that y causes x. If $\alpha_2^{(s)} = 0$ and the absolute value of $\beta_2^{(s)} > 0$ then it is more likely that x causes y. (Readers might like to remind themselves of what we mean by cause by looking at Section 1.6.) However, perhaps the most likely outcome is for both the absolute values of $\hat{\alpha}_2^{(s)}$ and $\hat{\beta}_2^{(s)}$ to be significantly greater than zero and in such cases, conclusions about relative causality can only be tentative, especially if $\hat{\alpha}_2^{(s)}$ and $\hat{\beta}_2^{(s)}$ have opposite signs.

Clearly, any statement about the relative strength of the causal relationship should be influenced by the errors attached to the estimated regression coefficients as well as by their actual magnitudes. If x_1 and y_1 are highly correlated—not an unlikely situation—then the standard errors of $\hat{\alpha}_2$ and $\hat{\beta}_2$ will tend to be large, particularly for small samples, and it will then be more difficult to make causal inferences.

4.4 AN ILLUSTRATION OF 2W2V ANALYSIS

Let us now illustrate some of these ideas by going back to the data on worries and mental health presented in Section 4.2. It was argued there that the causal direction is from worries to mental health. Nevertheless, worsening mental health could lead to increased worries because of the influence health might have on behaviour towards children, husband, or job. Let us see whether a change in the level of worries really does lead to a change in mental health, or whether the reverse relationship is more plausible.

Estimating equations (4.9) for the sample of 174 mothers gives the following results, with x referring to worries and y to mental health, and standard errors in brackets:

$$x_2 = 2.3 + 0.49x_1 + 0.02y_1$$
$$\quad\quad (0.08) \quad\quad (0.08) \quad\quad (R^2 = 0.21) \quad\quad (4.12a)$$

$$y_2 = 1.9 + 0.39y_1 + 0.27x_1$$
$$\quad\quad (0.07) \quad\quad (0.07) \quad\quad (R^2 = 0.31) \quad\quad (4.12b)$$

These results appear to support the approach taken in Section 4.2. A comparison of the coefficient of y_1 on x_2 (0.02) with its standard error (0.08) in equation (4.12a) shows that y_1 has no effect on x_2, whereas equation (4.12b) shows that x_1 has some influence on y_2—the coefficient is 0.27 and the standard error only 0.07. In other words, $\alpha_2 = 0$ but $\beta_2 > 0$. (For these data $\hat{\alpha}_2$ and $\hat{\alpha}_2^{(s)}$ are very similar, as are $\hat{\beta}_2$ and $\hat{\beta}_2^{(s)}$.)

As so often happens, the best predictors of the variables at occasion 2 are the corresponding variables at occasion 1. The values of R^2 show that x_1 and y_1 explain 21 % of the variance of x_2 and 31 % of the variance of y_2.

4.5 ELABORATING SIMPLE 2W2V MODELS

Let us now begin to relax some of the assumptions implicit in equations (4.9). There is no particular problem about including terms such as y_1^2 or e^{x_1} to account for any non-linear aspects of the model and, similarly, it would be possible to allow for interactions by including an $x_1 y_1$ term. The inclusion of such terms would, however, mean that a simple comparison of $\hat{\alpha}_2$ and $\hat{\beta}_2$ would no longer be useful in trying to determine causality.

If important variables are omitted from the simple model depicted in Figure 4.1 then $\hat{\alpha}_2$ and $\hat{\beta}_2$ could be biased and false conclusions drawn from their relative values. This kind of mis-specification is a serious problem with 2W2V models just as it is with models like those discussed in Chapter 3; indeed, it is the

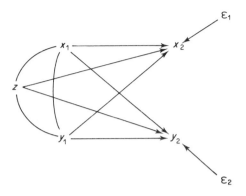

Figure 4.2 As Figure 4.1, but including a
constant exogenous variable

bane of all non-experimental work in the social sciences. Figures 4.2 and 4.3
illustrate some possible ways in which the simple model can be wrongly specified.

In Figure 4.2 the background (or exogenous) variable z is causally related both
to change in x and to change in y and so the corresponding equations are:

$$x_2 = \alpha'_0 + \alpha'_1 x_1 + \alpha'_2 y_1 + \alpha'_3 z + \varepsilon'_1 \qquad (4.13a)$$

$$y_2 = \beta'_0 + \beta'_1 y_1 + \beta'_2 x_1 + \beta'_3 z + \varepsilon'_2 \qquad (4.13b)$$

We see from Figure 4.2 that not only is z a causal determinant of x_2 and y_2, it is
also correlated with x_1 and y_1. This means that estimating the mis-specified
equations (4.9) rather than equations (4.13) would lead to biased estimates of α'_i
and β'_i.

In Figure 4.3, the omitted variable, p, is not constant over time but it is
exogeneous to the system of interest and its omission from a model would have

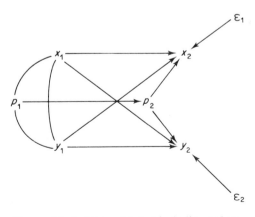

Figure 4.3 As Figure 4.1, but including a changing exogenous variable

the same effect as the omission of z from equations (4.9). That is, it would lead to $\hat{\alpha}_i$ and $\hat{\beta}_i$ being biased estimates of the causal parameters of interest because p_2 is related to x_1 and y_1 via p_1. Although $\hat{\alpha}_2$ and $\hat{\beta}_2$ will both be biased if estimated from models which exclude z or p (or both) when the true model is like Figure 4.2 or Figure 4.3, it is possible that their relative values will be much less affected. Heise (1970) presents the results of simulations which suggest that this is so, and he argues that the simple model might still be useful for determining causal direction. It will not, however, be useful for estimating causal relationships.

Returning to the example in Section 4.4, there are two variables, marital status (z_1) and housing (z_2), which are associated with x and y as in Figure 4.2, and so the estimates given in equations (4.12) may be biased. The re-estimated equations are:

$$x_2 = 2.4 + 0.47x_1 + 0.04y_1 - 1.2z_1 + 0.66z_2 \qquad (4.14a)$$
$$ (0.08) \quad\;\; (0.08) \quad\;\; (0.60) \quad (0.21) \quad\; (R^2 = 0.26)$$

$$y_2 = 2.5 + 0.41y_1 + 0.24x_1 - 1.2z_1 + 0.38z_2 \qquad (4.14b)$$
$$ (0.07) \quad\;\; (0.07) \quad\;\; (0.53) \quad (0.19) \quad\; (R^2 = 0.35)$$

and it can be seen that, for these data, the introduction of z_1 and z_2 into the equations has no important effect on $\hat{\alpha}_2$ and $\hat{\beta}_2$, although the values of R^2 show that they do explain some additional variation in x_2 and y_2.

Although these analyses suggest that the causal influence does go from x to y, the results still depend on untested assumptions and, in particular, they depend on the fact that x_2 and y_2 are not allowed to influence each other. We consider that assumption in more detail in the next section.

In some circumstances, the causal relationship of x and y might be better characterized by a 'feedback' model, as illustrated by Figures 4.4(a) and 4.4(b). In Figure 4.4(a), a change in y leads to a change in x, which in turn leads to a further change in y, whereas in Figure 4.4(b), the sequence is a change in x causing a change in y, followed by another change in x. An example of such a model is an exogeneously determined rise in prices (y_1) leading to a rise in wages (x_2), leading to another rise in prices (y_2). The equations corresponding to Figure 4.4(a) are:

$$x_2 = \alpha_0 + \alpha_1 x_1 + \alpha_2 y_1 + \varepsilon_1 \qquad (4.15a)$$
$$y_2 = \beta_0 + \beta_1 y_1 + \beta_2 x_1 + \beta_3 x_2 + \varepsilon_2 \qquad (4.15b)$$

However, if equation (4.15a) is substituted into equation (4.15b) we see that the two equations have the same form as equations (4.9), and the same is true for the equations corresponding to Figure 4.4(b). And so it is not possible to distinguish feedback models from models like (4.9) if α_2 and β_2 are both different from zero. It is possible to get round this problem with the more complex models discussed in the next section.

The previous three sections have shown that even with longitudinal data, there are still many difficulties in teasing out causal influences with simple 2W2V models.

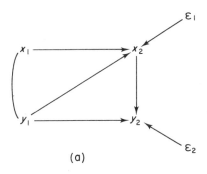

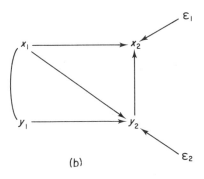

Figure 4.4 (a) Causal diagram for a
feedback model, $y \rightarrow x \rightarrow y$
(b) Causal diagram for a
feedback model, $x \rightarrow y \rightarrow x$

4.6 MORE COMPLEX MODELS FOR 2W2V DATA

So far, we have assumed that a comparison of the partial regression coefficients of x_1 on y_2 and y_1 on x_2 in a properly specified model will enable us to determine causal direction. However, the models in the previous section are not specified in a fully dynamic way. Also, we argued in Section 4.2 for the need for short causal lags and so we should allow x_2 and y_2 to influence one another, as in Figure 4.5.

The equations corresponding to Figure 4.5 are:

$$x_2 = \alpha_0 + \alpha_1 x_1 + \alpha_2 y_1 + \alpha_3 y_2 + \varepsilon_1 \tag{4.16a}$$

$$y_2 = \beta_0 + \beta_1 y_1 + \beta_2 x_1 + \beta_3 x_2 + \varepsilon_2 \tag{4.16b}$$

We saw in Section 4.3 that it will not always be possible to reach a conclusion about causal direction from a comparison of $\hat{\alpha}_2$ and $\hat{\beta}_2$ in equations (4.9) and this is just as true when working with equations (4.16). If $\alpha_3 = 0$ and the absolute value of β_3 is not zero, then, in our terms, x causes y. Reversing α_3 and β_3 in the above statement would lead us to argue that y causes x. If $\alpha_3 = \beta_2 = 0$ then the

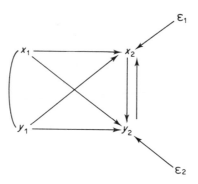

Figure 4.5 Causal diagram for
2W2V data with reciprocal causation
at occasion 2

feedback model of Figure 4.4(a) would be plausible, whereas if $\alpha_2 = \beta_3 = 0$ then Figure 4.4(b) would apply. But, as before, the values of $\hat{\alpha}_3$ and $\hat{\beta}_3$ will sometimes make it difficult to reach definite causal conclusions.

Equations (4.16) may be more realistic than equations (4.9), but they present considerable statistical difficulties. The most formidable of these is that, as they stand, neither of the two equations is 'identified'. This means that however much information is collected on x_1, x_2, y_1, and y_2, it will never be possible to obtain unique estimates of α_i and β_i ($i = 0, 1, 2, 3$). (From this point of view, they are no better than equations (4.10).) Equations (4.16) form a pair of 'non-recursive' simultaneous equations; non-recursive in the sense that the dependent (or endogenous) variables x_2 and y_2 both appear on the right-hand side of the other equation. It is possible to eliminate the simultaneity by substituting from equation (4.16b) for y_2 in equation (4.16a) and vice versa for x_2, to give:

$$x_2 = (1 - \alpha_3\beta_3)^{-1}[(\alpha_0 + \alpha_3\beta_0) + (\alpha_1 + \alpha_3\beta_2)x_1$$
$$+ (\alpha_2 + \alpha_3\beta_1)y_1 + (\varepsilon_1 + \alpha_3\varepsilon_2)] \tag{4.17a}$$
$$= \theta_0 + \theta_1 x_1 + \theta_2 y_1 + v_1$$
$$y_2 = (1 - \alpha_3\beta_3)^{-1}[(\beta_0 + \alpha_0\beta_3) + (\beta_1 + \alpha_2\beta_3)y_1$$
$$+ (\beta_2 + \alpha_1\beta_3)x_1 + (\varepsilon_2 + \beta_3\varepsilon_1)] \tag{4.17b}$$
$$= \theta_3 + \theta_4 y_1 + \theta_5 x_1 + v_2$$

Equations (4.17) are the 'reduced form' of equations (4.16); the reduced form is identified and can be estimated in the usual way. However, this will only give six independent pieces of information (θ_0–θ_5), whereas there are eight 'structural' coefficients (α_0–α_3 and β_0–β_3) in equations (4.16), and so it is not possible to solve for these structural coefficients which are, of course, the coefficients of interest. (The variances and covariance of the errors of the reduced form, v_1 and v_2, can also be estimated, but although this provides three more pieces of information, it also adds three more unknowns, i.e. the variances and covariance of ε_1 and ε_2.)

There are various ways of dealing with a system of under-identified equations such as (4.16), but they all involve using prior knowledge to impose restrictions either on the variables or on the errors. The most common approach to the problem is to suppose that some of the coefficients in the system are zero. The predetermined variables of the system are those variables which are either determined outside the system (exogenous variables), or are 'lagged' values of the endogenous variables such as x_1 and y_1 in equations (4.16), and all the predetermined variables are assumed to be uncorrelated with the errors. An equation within a system of simultaneous equations is identified if the number of predetermined variables omitted from the equation (i.e. the coefficients are zero) is at least equal to the number of endogenous variables in the equation minus one. Suppose there are p endogenous variables and q predetermined variables in the system, and suppose that a particular equation includes p_1 endogenous variables and q_1 predetermined variables; this equation is identified if $(q - q_1)$ $\geqslant (p_1 - 1)$. This is known as the order condition for identifiability and is in general only a necessary condition, although when $p = 2$ (as in this chapter) it is reasonable to regard it as a necessary and sufficient condition. Interested readers should refer to Goldberger (1964) and Fisher (1966) for an extended discussion of the identification issue which has received a good deal of attention from econometricians.

Returning to equations (4.16), we see that in both cases $(q - q_1) = 0$, but $(p_1 - 1) = 1$, and this confirms that they are under-identified. If, however, there were reasons for believing that y_1 did not predict x_2 for fixed values of y_2, and x_1 did not predict y_2 for fixed values of x_2, then α_2 and β_2 could be set to zero; $(q - q_1)$ and $(p_1 - 1)$ would then both be 1 and both equations would be identified. If it were only reasonable to suppose that α_2 was zero, then equation (4.16a) would be identified although equation (4.16b) would not, but if, in addition, it could be assumed that the covariance of the error terms was also zero $(E(\varepsilon_1 \varepsilon_2 = 0))$ then both equations would be identified. The assumption of no covariance between the errors was made for the recursive system (4.9) and is clearly plausible for any correctly specified system. However, it is not a straightforward matter to use both kinds of restrictions when estimating a set of simultaneous equations.

Suppose now that Figure 4.2 or Figure 4.3 is imposed on Figure 4.5; this would mean that equations (4.16) were incorrectly specified and should be replaced by:

$$x_2 = \alpha_0 + \alpha_1 x_1 + \alpha_2 y_1 + \alpha_3 y_2 + \alpha_4 z + \varepsilon_1 \qquad (4.18a)$$

$$y_2 = \beta_0 + \beta_1 y_1 + \beta_2 x_1 + \beta_3 x_2 + \beta_4 z + \varepsilon_2 \qquad (4.18b)$$

Equations (4.18) are like equations (4.13) except that they now include y_2 and x_2 on the right-hand sides and thus are not identified. If, however, z was only related to one of x_2 and y_2 and $E(\varepsilon_1 \varepsilon_2) = 0$, then equations (4.18) would be identified. Alternatively, if there are two other exogenous variables, z_1 and z_2, one of which is related to x_2 and one to y_2, i.e.

$$x_2 = \alpha_0 + \alpha_1 x_1 + \alpha_2 y_1 + \alpha_3 y_2 + \alpha_4 z_1 + \varepsilon_1 \qquad (4.19a)$$

$$y_2 = \beta_0 + \beta_1 y_1 + \beta_2 x_1 + \beta_3 x_2 + \beta_4 z_2 + \varepsilon_2 \qquad (4.19b)$$

then equations (4.19) would be identified. This shows how careful model specification, besides being a good thing in itself, can also eliminate the problem of under-identification. However, identification *cannot* be achieved by adding noise to the system—in other words, by including variables in an equation which have no association with the endogenous variable after allowing for the effects of other variables already in the system.

The second great statistical problem with simultaneous regression equations is that even when they are identified, the application of ordinary least squares (OLS) to each of the equations separately gives biased estimates. An examination of equations (4.17), the reduced form of equations (4.16), shows that x_2 is not independent of ε_2 nor y_2 of ε_1, and so OLS estimation of, say, equations (4.19) would give incorrect results. Various methods have been proposed to deal with this problem and they can be divided into two groups; single equation methods of estimation and system methods of estimation. The second group of methods is only useful if some of the equations in the system are over-identified. Extensive discussion of these methods can be found in econometrics textbooks such as Goldberger (1964) and Johnston (1972), but the most useful of the single equation methods is probably two-stage least squares (2SLS). In terms of equations (4.19), this works in the following way. Replace y_2 in equation (4.19a) and x_2 in equation (4.19b) by predicted values $\hat{y}_2$ and $\hat{x}_2$, these predicted values having been obtained by regressing y_2 and x_2 on all the predetermined variables in the system. Then use OLS to estimate α_i and β_i. So

$$\hat{y}_2 = \hat{\lambda}_0 + \hat{\lambda}_1 x_1 + \hat{\lambda}_2 y_1 + \hat{\lambda}_3 z_1 + \hat{\lambda}_4 z_2 \tag{4.20a}$$

$$\hat{x}_2 = \hat{\gamma}_0 + \hat{\gamma}_1 x_1 + \hat{\gamma}_2 y_1 + \hat{\gamma}_3 z_1 + \hat{\gamma}_4 z_2 \tag{4.20b}$$

where $\hat{\lambda}_i$ and $\hat{\gamma}_i$ are OLS estimates. Then

$$x_2 = \alpha_0 + \alpha_1 x_1 + \alpha_2 y_1 + \alpha_3 \hat{y}_2 + \alpha_4 z_1 + \varepsilon_1 \tag{4.21a}$$

$$y_2 = \beta_0 + \beta_1 y_1 + \beta_2 x_1 + \beta_3 \hat{x}_2 + \beta_4 z_2 + \varepsilon_2 \tag{4.21b}$$

System methods of estimation use all the information in the system of equations to estimate each equation. They are computationally more complex than single equation methods like 2SLS but, for over-identified equations, they are more efficient. However, only small gains in efficiency (reductions in variance) are likely for systems of just two equations. Three-stage least squares (3SLS) and full information maximum likelihood (FIML) are the most used members of this group. If it can be assumed that the joint distribution of the endogenous variables is multivariate normal, then the LISREL program (Jöreskog and Sörbom, 1981) can be used to get FIML estimates. The great advantage of the LISREL approach is that it can handle restrictions on the errors as well as on the variables, and over-identifying restrictions can be tested. These two methods of estimation will not be discussed here, although the general approach advocated by Jöreskog and Sörbom is discussed in more detail in Chapter 5.

4.7 A FURTHER ILLUSTRATION

We now continue with the example started in Section 4.2 and extended in Sections 4.4 and 4.5. If we start with equations (4.19), one might, *a priori*, argue that z_1

(marital status) could be omitted from eqution (4.19a) for worries at occasion 2 and z_2 (housing) from equation (4.19b) for mental health at occasion 2. This means that the right-hand side of equation (4.19a) would contain x_1, y_1, y_2, and z_2, with equation (4.19b) having x_1, y_1, y_2, and z_1 on the right-hand side. The results from estimating these just-identified equations by two-stage least squares are given in Table 4.3 as model 1. The estimates, particularly those when x_2 is the dependent variable, are not really plausible; it is unlikely that the coefficient of y_1 would be negative and it is perhaps the case that z_1 should not have been omitted from equation (4.19a). However, its inclusion would mean that the equation for x_2 was no longer identified.

Suppose instead that z_1 and z_2 appear in both equations, but assume that α_2 and β_2 are both zero in equations (4.18). This rules out the feedback models of Figure 4.4, reasonably so because there is no evidence that either y_1 or y_2 influences x_2. Then 2SLS estimation gives the results in model 2 in Table 4.3 and these estimates are not unreasonable. There is no reason for retaining z_2 in the equation for y_2 in model 2, and omitting it would give one over-identifying restriction so that the equation for x_2 could then be estimated by 3SLS.

Table 4.3 Reciprocal causation of worries and health: parameter estimates and standard errors

Model	Dependent variable	Constant	x_1	x_2	y_1	y_2	z_1	z_2
1	x_2	-0.01	0.24 (0.17)	—	-0.36 (0.24)	0.98 (0.55)	—	0.29 (0.26)
	y_2	1.1	0.03 (0.16)	0.57 (0.29)	0.39 (0.07)	—	-0.52 (0.54)	—
2	x_2	2.2	0.45 (0.11)	—	—	0.10 (0.19)	-1.0 (0.62)	0.63 (0.21)
	y_2	1.3	—	0.50 (0.15)	0.39 (0.07)	—	-0.60 (0.57)	0.05 (0.23)

(Explanatory variables span columns x_1, x_2, y_1, y_2, z_1, z_2.)

The estimates in model 2 are probably the most reasonable ones and they confirm previous conclusions—no influence of y on x but a quite large effect of x on y. In fact, the effect of x on y in model 2 is higher than that given in equation (4.14b)—0.50 against 0.24—and this suggests that a short causal lag is more appropriate for these data. But model 2 does have the disadvantage of not having a fully dynamic specification in the way that was given earlier.

4.8 SUMMARY AND CONCLUSIONS

The first part of this chapter (Section 4.2) shows how longitudinal data can be used to specify different models for known causal direction. Even though there are differences between them, they are all more convincing than models based on cross-sectional data.

The second part sets out to show that great care is needed when analysing longitudinal data to decide between competing causal explanations of an observed association. Many of the published analyses which have used 2W2V data, particularly in psychology, have tended to rely on comparisons of cross-lagged correlations. They have not therefore been satisfactory, and more experience of the models suggested in this chapter is needed. As with non-randomized studies, any conclusions will be open to criticism on the grounds of model specification, but these criticisms should become more muted as analyses are replicated and as knowledge accumulates about the reasonableness of the various assumptions that have to be made. Nevertheless, causal models based on theory, such as those presented in Chapter 3 and Section 4.2, will usually be more convincing than causality determined empirically using methods like the ones in Sections 4.3 to 4.7. On the other hand, there are times when theory is not able to provide any guidance on how important questions should be tackled. There may be a paucity of theory or there may be two equally plausible theories. At these times, the answers obtained by using these models, although inevitably tentative, may be better than no answers at all.

APPENDIX 4.1 BASIC DATA FOR THE WORRIES AND MENTAL HEALTH EXAMPLE

	Means	Variances, covariances, and correlations			
		x_1	x_2	y_1	y_2
Worries index, occasion 1 (x_1)	3.79	9.31	0.48	0.44	0.44
Worries index, occasion 2 (x_2)	4.26	4.86	11.0	0.21	0.47
Mental health index, occasion 1 (y_1)	5.05	4.11	2.16	9.47	0.51
Mental health index, occasion 2 (y_2)	4.95	4.42	4.81	4.86	9.59

The variances are given on the diagonal, covariances below the diagonal, and correlations above the diagonal. The sample size is 174.

CHAPTER 5

The Effects of Measurement Error on Models for Change

5.1 INTRODUCTION

The previous two chapters concentrated on the specification of models for the explanation of change, but they assumed that all the variables of interest had been perfectly measured, so that no distinction was made between observed and true scores on a variable. However, as we saw in Chapter 2, this is often an unrealistic assumption and it can lead to mistaken causal inferences. Goldstein (1979c), for example, illustrates how an analysis of a non-randomized study which corrects for measurement error can reverse the conclusions which would have been reached from an analysis which did not take account of it. In the same paper, Goldstein demonstrates that, for fixed seven-year scores, social class differences in educational attainment for children aged 11 are reduced by about 35% when a correction is introduced for measurement error.

There is a good deal of discussion in the literature about ways of correcting for measurement error, although practical examples of their effects are harder to find. This chapter reviews some of the methods that have been proposed; the simple method of disattenuation in Section 5.2, Fuller's methods in Section 5.3, and Jöreskog's methods in Section 5.4. We return to the analyses of Chapters 3 and 4 to see whether and how their conclusions are affected when different kinds of corrections are made. A new example is introduced in Section 5.5; this section also discusses the issue of the stability of a variable.

5.2 A SIMPLE METHOD OF CORRECTING FOR MEASUREMENT ERROR

Consider the simple regression model

$$y = \alpha + \beta x_1 + \varepsilon \tag{5.1}$$

but suppose that, rather than equation (5.1), the model of interest is

$$y = \alpha^* + \beta^* X_1 + \varepsilon^* \tag{5.2}$$

where x_1 and X_1 are related according to the measurement model given in Chapter 2 (equation (2.5)) so that x_1 refers to the observed score, u to the error of measurement, and X_1 ($= x_1 - u$) to the true score. Then equation (5.2) can be written as

$$y = \alpha^* + \beta^* x_1 + (\varepsilon^* - \beta^* u) \tag{5.3}$$

Equation (5.3) has the same form as equation (5.1) but it shows that x_1 and ε in equation (5.1) are correlated because $x_1 = X_1 + u$ and $\varepsilon = \varepsilon^* - \beta^* u$ and so both x_1 and ε are related to u. This means that the usual least squares estimates of α and β in equation (5.1) (i.e. $\hat{\alpha}$ and $\hat{\beta}$) will be biased estimates of the parameters of interest, α^* and β^*, in equation (5.2). This argument is similar to the one presented in Section 3.3 about model specification, and indeed ignoring measurement error could be regarded as a kind of specification error.

It is easy to show that, providing ε^*, the error term in equation (5.2) (which may include the errors of measurement of y), and u, the measurement error in x, are uncorrelated, then

$$E(\hat{\beta}) = \beta^* \frac{\sigma_{X_1}^2}{\sigma_{X_1}^2 + \sigma_u^2} < \beta^* \tag{5.4}$$

where $E(\hat{\beta})$ is the expected value of $\hat{\beta}$ over repeated samples, $\sigma_{X_1}^2$ is the true score variance, and σ_u^2 is the measurement error variance. However, the expression in brackets in equation (5.4) is just the reliability, ρ, of x_1 and if this is known, it is possible to correct $\hat{\beta}$ (and hence $\hat{\alpha}$) by dividing $\hat{\beta}$ by ρ. This correction is sometimes referred to as *disattenuation* because $\hat{\beta}$ will always underestimate β^* in absolute value. It can also be shown that

$$\hat{\beta}^* = \frac{\hat{\beta}}{\rho} = \frac{\text{cov}(x_1 y)}{\text{var}(x_1) - \sigma_u^2} \tag{5.5}$$

It is straightforward to link this theory with the simple model for relative change, equation (3.4), in Chapter 3. The estimated treatment effect or measure of relative change, $\hat{\beta}_0$, was given there as

$$\hat{\beta}_0 = (\bar{y}_2 - \bar{y}_1) - \hat{\beta}_1 (\bar{x}_{12} - \bar{x}_{11}) \tag{5.6}$$

where the subscripts for x and y refer to the two groups. If $\hat{\beta}_1$, the pooled within-groups regression coefficient of y on x_1, is not corrected then, for $\bar{x}_{12} > \bar{x}_{11}$ and $\beta_1 > 0$, the true relative change or treatment effect is overestimated, and for $\bar{x}_{11} > \bar{x}_{12}$, it is underestimated. Much of the debate about measurement error has derived from the analysis of quasi-experiments in compensatory education when the second of these two conditions—the control group scoring higher than the treatment group before intervention—has often applied, and Campbell and Boruch (1975) discuss the policy implications of this.

It is not necessary to correct $\hat{\beta}_1$ if the allocation to treatment and control groups is made solely on the basis of the observed pre-test (as in the regression discontinuity design described in Section 3.2) or if the allocation is random. There is also no need to correct $\hat{\beta}_1$ if the best predictor of the post-test, given the unreliable pre-test, is required. The emphasis of this chapter, however, is on explanation rather than on prediction.

The correction procedure given above is simple, but it has several limitations. Often, particularly for variables like the indices of health and worries considered in previous chapters, prior information on reliability or error variance is unavailable. Reliabilities and error variances of some standardized educational and psychological tests are given in the manuals for these tests, but they are often based on small, non-probability samples and so may not apply to the population under study. It is often argued that reliabilities are population-specific, but error variances are not, and so the correction given in equation (5.5) is perhaps more useful. Even if reasonable estimates of σ_u^2 are available, they may be subject to considerable sampling error and this sampling error should be incorporated into any correction procedure. Another problem with quoted reliabilities and error variances is that it is often not clear which components of measurement error have been included: it was pointed out in Chapter 2 that what is defined as error will vary according to the purposes of the study, which means that no one estimate will be appropriate for all studies.

A further problem with the simple method is that it does not extend easily to deal with more than one unreliable explanatory variable. All the models put forward in Chapter 4, and most of those in Chapter 3, have more than one explanatory variable and so a method is needed for correcting them. Also, the assumption that the measurement errors of the dependent variable and any explanatory variables are uncorrelated—which is needed for equation (5.4) to be valid—will not always be reasonable. For example, if y and x_1 are both obtained by the same interviewer in a survey or by the same psychological tester, this could introduce correlated measurement error. Moreover, there is always the chance that the measurement errors of explanatory variables will be correlated, particularly as these variables will often have been measured at the same time and so might contain similar 'transitory' errors.

Although several correction methods have been suggested to deal with some of the limitations outlined above, perhaps the two most useful are those proposed by Fuller and his colleagues (Degracie and Fuller, 1972; Warren, White, and Fuller, 1974; Fuller and Hidiroglou, 1978; Fuller, 1980), and those based on the theoretical work of Jöreskog (1970) and further developed by Sörbom (1976, 1978). These two methods are now compared, and their advantages and disadvantages considered.

5.3 CORRECTING FOR MEASUREMENT ERROR (1): APPLYING THE WORK OF FULLER

The methods developed by Fuller and his colleagues extend the simple model in several ways. They can deal with more than one explanatory variable and with a mixture of perfectly and imperfectly measured explanatory variables. They allow for correlated measurement error both between the explanatory variables and between the dependent variable and any of the explanatory variables. Also, if the measurement errors are estimated rather than known, then the variances of the corrected regression coefficients are inflated to take account of this. In this section, the effects of correcting for measurement error are illustrated on some of the examples presented in earlier chapters. More details of the method itself, and the range of situations to which it can be applied, are given in Appendix 5.1.

Let us now return to the National Child Development Study data analysed in

Chapter 3 to see what effects corrections for measurement error have on the results presented there. The most complete analysis of the data was given in equation (3.10), which is repeated here:

$$M16 = 7.11 - 1.57ST + 0.009M11^2 - 1.03SC11 + 1.69PI + 0.09GA11 \quad (5.7)$$
$$(1.32) \quad (0.67) \quad (0.001) \quad (0.62) \quad (0.59) \quad (0.03)$$

Let us assume, perhaps unwisely, that the dichotomous variables school type (ST), social class (SC11), and parental interest (PI) are measured without error. The reliabilities of the eleven-year maths score (M11) and the general ability score (GA11) were estimated to be 0.94 (Steedman, 1980) and 0.84 (Hutchison, personal communication) respectively. These estimates were based on a sample of 300 and so are subject to sampling error, but as this sample is larger than the one analysed here, this sampling error can be ignored. Note that equation (5.7) includes not M11 but $M11^2$, for which the reliability is unknown. However, if M11 is normally distributed, then the reliability of $M11^2$ can be shown to be (Bohrnstedt and Marwell, 1978)

$$\rho_{M11^2} = \frac{\rho_1(\rho_1 + 2k)}{1 + 2k} \quad (5.8)$$

where ρ_1 is the reliability of M11, and

$$k = \left[\frac{\overline{M11}}{\text{s.d.}(M11)} \right]^2$$

Applying equation (5.8) leaves the reliability of $M11^2$ unchanged at 0.94. After correcting for measurement error, equation (5.7) becomes

$$M16 = 5.88 - 1.16\,ST + 0.010\,M11^2 + 0.87\,SC11 + 1.53\,PI + 0.11\,GA11$$
$$(2.15) \quad (0.80) \quad (0.002) \quad (0.63) \quad (0.63) \quad (0.06) \quad (5.9)$$

The corrections raise the coefficients of $M11^2$ and GA11 and reduce the coefficients of ST, SC11, and PI. In particular, the coefficient for school type is reduced from 1.57 to 1.16 which is small and no longer statistically significant ($t = 1.45$, $p > 0.10$). In other words, children in comprehensive and grammar schools make essentially the same amount of progress in mathematics, once measurement error is taken into account.

Consider now the estimates given in Table 4.1 and Table 4.2 for the models of one-way causation. It was suggested that, for perfectly measured variables, model 4 in Table 4.1 and model 6 in Table 4.2 were both reasonable, but serious difficulties arise with models which contain differences, as model 4 does, when the assumption of perfect measurement is dropped. It is often assumed that reliabilities of differences are rather low (not more than 0.5), but these reliabilities are never available. It is straightforward to estimate error variances of differences as the sum of the separate error variances if the error covariance is assumed to be zero, but this will not always be so. Reasonable guesses of error covariances can be made in some situations, but one may not have any prior views about the likely covariance of the errors of two differences, for example. Therefore models which include differences can only be satisfactorily estimated when perfect measurement is not an unreasonable assumption.

No information was available on the error variances of the indices of health and worries used in Section 4.2. Thus, to correct model 6 of Table 4.2, two sets of assumptions have been made which one might suppose are the upper and lower bounds of measurement error for these variables. The first set, referred to as 'high' in Table 5.1, fixes the error variances at values which make the reliability for the study population 0.7 for each of x_1, x_2, and y_1. And, because x_1 and y_1 were measured at the same time, and because y_1 and y_2 were obtained from the same set of 'yes/no' items, small error covariances were assigned to them. The second set ('low') assumes all error covariances are zero and fixes the error variances to make the reliability of x_1, x_2, and y_1 equal to 0.9. The results are presented in Table 5.1, along with the uncorrected estimates ('none') from Table 4.2. There are quite sharp differences between the uncorrected estimates and those corrected by the first set of assumptions, but the differences are unremarkable when the second set is used. In both cases, however, the corrections reduce the coefficient of x_1 and raise those of x_2 and y_1, on y_2 but the standard errors of all the coefficients are higher. A unit change in x_2 for fixed values of x_1 leads to a change of 0.47 units in y_2 for the 'high' row, 0.35 units for the 'low' row, and 0.31 units when there is no correction.

Table 5.1 Estimated regression coefficients and standard errors when model 6 of Table 4.2 is corrected

| Correction | Constant | Explanatory variables | | | R^2 |
		y_1	x_1	x_2	
'High'	0.44	0.47	0.02	0.47	0.46
	(0.50)	(0.13)	(0.18)	(0.13)	
'Low'	0.95	0.43	0.08	0.35	0.43
	(0.39)	(0.09)	(0.10)	(0.07)	
None	1.2	0.39	0.11	0.31	0.40
	(0.39)	(0.07)	(0.07)	(0.06)	

Moving on to the 2W2V analyses of Chapter 4, let us first look at the effects of correcting the recursive system (4.14). The error variances and covariances are fixed at the same high levels as are used in Table 5.1 and both z_1 (marital status) and z_2 (housing index) are assumed to be measured without error. The main effect, as shown in Table 5.2, is to increase the auto-relationships both between x_1 and x_2 and between y_1 and y_2, while the coefficient of y_1 on x_2 is slightly reduced and that of x_1 on y_2 slightly increased. Thus, in one way, the causal inference is made a little sharper, although the fall in precision of the regression coefficients serves also to blur it. The coefficients of the perfectly measured variables, z_1 and z_2, are essentially unaffected by the correction.

Table 5.2. 2W2V data, no reciprocal causation: results from corrected conditional models

(a)

Dependent variable = x_2		Explanatory variables				
		Constant	x_1	y_1	z_1	z_2
Uncorrected						
	Estimate	2.4	0.47	0.04	-1.2	0.66
		(0.71)	(0.08)	(0.08)	(0.60)	(0.21)
Corrected						
	Estimate	2.0	0.62	-0.00	-0.97	0.60
		(0.85)	(0.17)	(0.16)	(0.63)	(0.22)

(b)

Dependent variable = y_2		Explanatory variables				
		Constant	y_1	x_1	z_1	z_2
Uncorrected						
	Estimate	2.5	0.41	0.24	-1.2	0.38
		(0.59)	(0.07)	(0.07)	(0.53)	(0.19)
Corrected						
	Estimate	1.3	0.58	0.26	-1.1	0.42
		(0.69)	(0.16)	(0.16)	(0.57)	(0.21)

Correcting the non-recursive 2W2V system of Section 4.6 does not introduce any extra theoretical problems. Consider, for instance, model 2 of Table 4.3 (but excluding z_2 from the equation for y_2), i.e.

$$x_2 = \alpha_0 + \alpha_1 x_1 + \alpha_2 \hat{y}_2 + \alpha_3 z_1 + \alpha_4 z_2 + \varepsilon_1 \qquad (5.10a)$$
$$y_2 = \beta_0 + \beta_1 y_1 + \beta_2 \hat{x}_2 + \beta_3 z_1 + \varepsilon_2 \qquad (5.10b)$$

where $\hat{y}_2$ and $\hat{x}_2$ are the predicted values of y_2 and x_2 when each is regressed against x_1, y_1, z_1, and z_2. Assuming as before that z_1 and z_2 are perfectly measured, then it is only necessary to eliminate the error variance of x_1 from equation (5.10a) and the error variance of y_1 from equation (5.10b) to ensure that α_i and β_i are estimated in an unbiased way. Clearly $\hat{y}_2$ and $\hat{x}_2$ are not equal to the true values of y_2 and x_2, but their errors of measurement will not be correlated with the error terms, ε_1 and ε_2, in equations (5.10) *after* correcting for the errors in x_1 and y_1. Hence, unbiased estimates of α_i and β_i can be obtained without further correction.

The error variance of y_1 and the error covariance of y_1 and y_2 were fixed at the 'high' levels as before, and a comparison of the uncorrected and corrected versions of equation (5.10b) is given in Table 5.3(b). However, when the 'high' level of the error variance of x_1 was used to correct equation (5.10a), numerical problems arose because observed x_1 and $\hat{y}_2$ are highly correlated ($r = 0.75$) and eliminating the error variance from the variance of x_1 increases this correlation. Multicollinearity of this kind will always be a danger when two-stage least squares (2SLS) is used, as here, to eliminate simultaneous equations bias from equations such as (5.10). Somewhat more precise results are obtained when an error variance corresponding to a reliability of 0.8 rather than 0.7 is used for x_1, and these are given in Table 5.3(a). Even then a substantial, if imprecise, negative coefficient is obtained for $\hat{y}_2$ which is highly unlikely, and note also a sharp rise in the coefficient of x_1; the coefficients of z_1 and z_2 are much less affected. In Table 5.3(b), the coefficient of y_1 is raised and the coefficient of $\hat{x}_2$ is reduced, but the changes are not substantial. (The uncorrected coefficients in Table 5.3(b) differ slightly from those given in Table 4.3 because of the omission of z_2.)

The results given in Table 5.3 are not as clear cut as earlier results and they illustrate the difficulties of analysing non-recursive systems which contain measurement error. On the other hand, taking Tables 5.1, 5.2, and 5.3 together, the bulk of the evidence does suggest that the conclusions in Chapter 4 about the causal relationship of worries and mental health hold up quite well.

Table 5.3 2W2V data, with reciprocal causation: results from corrected conditional models

(a)

Dependent variable = x_2		Explanatory variable				
		Constant	x_1	$\hat{y}_2$	z_1	z_2
Uncorrected	Estimate	2.2	0.45	0.10	−1.0	0.63
		(1.1)	(0.11)	(0.19)	(0.62)	(0.21)
Corrected	Estimate	3.6	0.87	−0.47	−1.4	0.67
		(1.3)	(0.27)	(0.38)	(0.68)	(0.21)

(b)

Dependent variable = y_2		Explanatory variables			
		Constant	y_1	$\hat{x}_2$	z_1
Uncorrected	Estimate	1.2	0.39	0.52	−0.52
		(0.76)	(0.08)	(0.15)	(0.56)
Corrected	Estimate	1.0	0.50	0.44	−0.56
		(0.76)	(0.13)	(0.17)	(0.56)

5.4 CORRECTING FOR MEASUREMENT ERROR (2): APPLYING THE WORK OF JORESKOG

The methods developed by Jöreskog and his colleagues for constructing causal or structural models which are free from the problems of measurement error are linked to the latent variable approach; they tend therefore to be subject to the advantages and disadvantages of that approach which were discussed in Chapter 2. The feature of Jöreskog's (and Sörbom's) method is that it does not require prior knowledge about reliabilities or error variances. Instead it assumes that there are at least two measures or indicators of each of the underlying variables which are then combined, using the more general measurement model of equations (2.9) and (2.10), to provide estimates of error variances for the sample. The method can also handle known error variances, but it cannot incorporate sampling errors of error variances into the estimated variances of the structural coefficients in a way that the methods of the previous section are able to do.

It is assumed that a set of, say, v observed indicators is related to an underlying or latent variable, ξ, as in equation (2.10), i.e.

$$x_j = \mu_j + \lambda_j \xi + \delta_j \qquad (j = 1, 2, \ldots, v) \tag{5.11}$$

The methods of the previous section paid little attention to measurement error in the dependent variables, mainly because they do not usually lead to biased estimates of the regression coefficients, but they will be considered in this section. Thus,

$$y_k = \mu_k + \lambda_k \eta + \varepsilon_k \qquad (k = 1, 2, \ldots, w) \tag{5.12}$$

where y_k are observed variables and η is the latent variable. Equations (5.11) and (5.12), together with the assumptions that the measurement errors, δ_j and ε_k, have zero means and are uncorrelated with ξ and η respectively, define a measurement model. Additionally, the latent variables are related in a linear causal or structural model of the form

$$\eta = \gamma \xi + \zeta \tag{5.13}$$

where ζ is an error term with the usual properties found in regression models. Equations (5.11), (5.12), and (5.13) can be extended to allow for several dependent and explanatory latent variables, and these extensions are presented in Appendix 5.2.

For illustration, consider the analysis of a quasi-experiment with two groups and three pre- and post-test indicators ($v = w = 3$) of a single latent variable. Thus, for each group

$$
\begin{aligned}
x_1 &= \mu_1 + \lambda_1 \xi + \delta_1 \\
x_2 &= \mu_2 + \lambda_2 \xi + \delta_2 \\
x_3 &= \mu_3 + \lambda_3 \xi + \delta_3
\end{aligned}
\tag{5.14}
$$

and

$$
\begin{aligned}
y_1 &= \mu_4 + \lambda_4 \eta + \varepsilon_1 \\
y_2 &= \mu_5 + \lambda_5 \eta + \varepsilon_2 \\
y_3 &= \mu_6 + \lambda_6 \eta + \varepsilon_3
\end{aligned}
\tag{5.15}
$$

It is necessary to constrain λ_1 and λ_4 to be 1 in order to identify λ_i and the variances of ξ and η, and so it is only possible to infer differences among the scales for the indicators. When analysing just one group, it is more convenient to measure x_i and y_i as deviations from their means and to exclude μ_j and μ_k from the models, but this is not possible when wishing to estimate group differences. However, in order to identify μ_i and the means ξ and η, one must fix the means of ξ and η at zero for one of the groups; thus, it is only possible to estimate relative rather than absolute change. The conditional structural model for the first, say the control, group is

$$\eta^c = \beta_2\, \xi^c + \zeta^c \tag{5.16a}$$

with $\bar{\eta}^c = \bar{\xi}^c = 0$, and for the second, say the treatment, group, it is

$$\eta^T = \beta_1 + \beta_2\, \xi^T + \zeta^T \tag{5.16b}$$

so that $\hat{\beta}_1$ is the estimated treatment effect which is equal to $(\bar{\eta}^T - \hat{\beta}_2\, \bar{\xi}^T)$. The unconditional model is just

$$\eta^T - \xi^T = \alpha + \zeta^T \tag{5.17}$$

with α as the unconditional relative change (see Sörbom, 1976).

It would be difficult to talk about relative change if the relationship between the observed variables and the latent variable were not the same for both groups, and so it is assumed that the origins of the scales (μ_i) and the factor loadings (λ_i) are invariant over the groups within occasions. However, the indicator–variable relationship is allowed to vary over time to reflect the fact that, in some situations, an indicator is more appropriate for a particular latent variable at one occasion than it is at another. Also the measurement error variances, $\sigma^2_{\delta_i}$ and $\sigma^2_{\varepsilon_i}$ ($i = 1, 2, 3$), sometimes known as the specific error variances, can vary across groups and across time. If it is assumed that there are no measurement error covariances either within or between the δ_i and ε_i, then the model (equations (5.15), (5.16), (5.17)) generates 29 parameters, 8 from that part of the model concerned with means and 21 concerned with covariances, whereas the observed data produce 54 estimates, 12 means and 42 covariances; see Table 5.4. Thus, the model is over-

Table 5.4 Parameters and estimates for equations (5.15) to (5.17)

Model parameters				Data estimates	
All groups	n	Each group	n	Each group	n
μ_i	6	σ^2_δ	6	$\bar{x}_i$	6
λ_i	4	σ^2_ε	6	$\bar{y}_i$	6
β_2	1	$\bar{\eta}$	1	σ^2_x	6
		$\bar{\xi}$	1	σ^2_y	6
		σ^2_η	2	σ_{xy}	30
		σ^2_ξ	2		
Total	11	Total	18	Total	54

identified with 25 degrees of freedom remaining for testing some of its assumptions such as whether measurement error covariances really are zero or whether the slope parameter, β_2, in equations (5.16), really is constant across groups.

Details of the method of estimating the model parameters and testing for goodness of fit can be found in Appendix 5.2.

5.5 AN EXAMPLE

How does the method described in the previous section work in practice? Let us illustrate it by looking at the stability of language ability over time using data from another part of the Educational Priority Area (EPA) project (see Section 3.9). These data come from the National Pre-School Experiment (NPSE) and were analysed in Payne (1974); here the data from the 14 pre-school groups are amalgamated and treated as if they were a simple random sample. Each child was tested on two occasions with the English Picture Vocabulary Test (EPVT) and with two Reynell Developmental Language Scales (RDLC and RDLE). It is assumed that these three tests measure the same latent variable—language ability—at both occasions, although not everyone would agree that this is a reasonable assumption to make. Complete data were obtained from 222 children. The basic data consist of six variances and 15 covariances and are given in Table 5.5.

Table 5.5 Observed variances and covariances—EPA (NPSE) data

	EPVT1	RDLC1	RDLE1	EPVT2	RDLC2	RDLE2
EPVT1 (y_1)	155					
RDLC1 (y_2)	104	191				
RDLE1 (y_3)	71	110	186			
EPVT2 (y_4)	100	91	66	149		
RDLC2 (y_5)	94	121	70	101	160	
RDLE2 (y_6)	61	75	72	71	84	130

The basic model is shown in Figure 5.1. It is similar to the model described in the previous section, except that there is now only one group and means are of no interest. This model generates 13 parameters: $\lambda_2, \lambda_3, \lambda_5, \lambda_6$ (λ_1 and λ_4 are fixed at 1), β, $\sigma_{\varepsilon_i}^2$ ($i = 1, 2, \ldots, 6$), $\sigma_{\eta_1}^2$, $\sigma_{\eta_2}^2$, and so there are eight ($15 + 6 - 13$) degrees of freedom for testing the model. It is more convenient to express the model just in terms of y and η variables in order to estimate measurement error covariances (see Appendix 5.2).

In fact, the model represented by Figure 5.1 does not fit well ($X^2 = 53.3$, 8 df, $p < 0.001$). An examination of the residuals from the fitted model suggests that there is a case for including measurement error covariance terms, $\sigma_{\varepsilon_i \varepsilon_j}$ ($i = 1, 2, 3; j = i + 3$). These covariances account for the possibility that each test measures

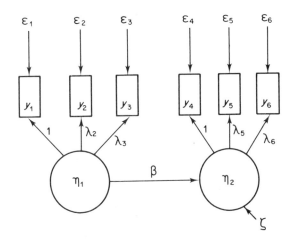

Figure 5.1 Measurement and structural model for
Table 5.5

something other than language ability and that these other abilities are correlated over time. For example, the EPVT could be measuring visual ability as well as language ability. The inclusion of these covariance terms improves the goodness of fit considerably ($X^2 = 15.0$, 5 df, $p < 0.025$) and differencing the two chi-square statistics shows that the set of covariances do indeed differ significantly from zero ($X^2 = 38.3$, 3 df, $p < 0.001$).

As it stands, the model allows the individual tests to have a different relationship to the underlying variable at each occasion, but this is perhaps unnecessary. The imposition of the constraints $\lambda_2 = \lambda_5$ and $\lambda_3 = \lambda_6$ does not significantly worsen the fit ($X^2 = 15.9$, 7 df, $p < 0.05$) and a difference of 0.9 in the two values of X^2 is clearly unimportant. Overall, the model fits pretty well, especially when we remember that the data are an amalgam of rather disparate studies. The results are given in Table 5.6.

These results give a number of insights into the structure of the data. They

Table 5.6 EPA (NPSE) data: final LISREL model

Parameter	Estimate	s.e.	Parameter	Estimate	s.e.	Parameter	Estimate	s.e.
λ_1	1	Fixed	$\sigma^2_{\varepsilon_1}$	74.6	9.57	$\sigma_{\varepsilon_1 \varepsilon_4}$	26.8	6.90
λ_2	1.30	0.11	$\sigma^2_{\varepsilon_2}$	49.6	11.7	$\sigma_{\varepsilon_2 \varepsilon_5}$	8.13	8.19
λ_3	0.91	0.08	$\sigma^2_{\varepsilon_3}$	114	12.3	$\sigma_{\varepsilon_3 \varepsilon_6}$	20.6	7.39
λ_4	1	Fixed	$\sigma^2_{\varepsilon_4}$	67.9	8.44			
$\lambda_5 \, (= \lambda_2)$	1.30	0.11	$\sigma^2_{\varepsilon_5}$	36.5	9.56			
$\lambda_6 \, (= \lambda_3)$	0.91	0.08	$\sigma^2_{\varepsilon_6}$	71.8	8.24			
β	0.81	0.06						
$\sigma^2_{\eta_1}$	83.5	13.5						
σ^2_{ζ}	19.7	4.62						

show that the stability of language ability (as given by β) is 0.81 and this corresponds to a correlation of 0.86. The values of λ_i show that the second test (RDLC, the comprehension sub-test of the RDLS) has a stronger influence on the latent variable than the other two tests. The values of the measurement error variances, particularly for the third test, show some variation over time; they can be combined with the observed variances in Table 5.5 to get reliability estimates. Thus, for EPVT1, the reliability is $1 - \sigma^2_{\varepsilon_1}/\sigma^2_{y_1} = 0.52$ and for the other tests they are 0.74, 0.39, 0.54, 0.77, and 0.45 respectively, and so the reliabilities show essentially no variation over the two occasions. From the error covariances, $\sigma_{\varepsilon_i \varepsilon_j}$, we see that the first and third tests appear to be measuring other abilities, but not the second.

It is possible to compare the 'LISREL' approach with the method given in Section 5.3. A pilot study of 61 children was carried out to examine the reliability of the EPVT for an EPA-type population (Stevenson and Payne, 1972) and estimated the test–retest error variance and reliability as 37 and 0.76 respectively. When these figures are used to correct the simple conditional model (EPVT2 regressed against EPVT1), we get the results given in Table 5.7.

Table 5.7 EPA (NPSE) data: uncorrected and corrected conditional model

	Stability (β)	s.e.
Uncorrected model	0.64	0.07
Corrected, known measurement error variance	0.84	0.07
Corrected, known reliability	0.84	0.09
Corrected, estimated measurement error variance	0.84	0.13

Table 5.7 shows a marked difference between the uncorrected and corrected estimates of stability but no differences within the set of corrected estimates. It also shows that the corrected estimates are all close to the estimate of stability in Table 5.6. However, the standard error of the estimate is substantially higher in the final row of the table where it is recognized that the error variance is only estimated from a sample about a quarter of the size of the study sample rather than known exactly (or estimated from a much larger sample).

Let us spend a little longer on this idea of stability, which we first raised in the opening chapter. We have used a regression (or structural) coefficient to measure it as did Wheaton, Muthen, Alwin, and Summers (1977) in their analysis of the stability of alienation. But stability is more often measured by correlating what is assumed to be the same variable on different occasions; for example, Hindley and Owen (1978) used Pearson's product moment coefficient to describe the stability of children's IQ scores over time and Cox (1978) used Kendall's tau b rank correlation coefficient to describe the stability of children's behaviour in school.

However, it is just as important to correct correlation coefficients for measurement error as it is to correct regression coefficients, and this is usually done by disattenuating the observed correlation by the square root of the product of the reliabilities, i.e.

$$r_T = r_0 / \sqrt{\rho_{x_1} \rho_{x_2}} \qquad (5.18)$$

where r_T is the correlation between the true variables, r_0 the observed correlation, and ρ_{x_t} ($t = 1, 2$) are the reliabilities of the variable at the two occasions. This correction comes directly from the simple model for measurement error given in Section 5.2 and so it shares that model's drawbacks. The observed correlation between the two EPVT tests is 0.66 (from Table 5.5), but when corrected using equation (5.18), and assuming the reliability is the same at both occasions, the true correlation is 0.87. This is very close to the value obtained from Jöreskog's model.

The arguments for using correlation or regression coefficients as measures of stability are essentially the same as the arguments in Section 4.3 for unstandardized or standardized regression coefficients in causal models. However, sampling errors are much easier to calculate for corrected regression coefficients than they are for corrected correlations.

5.6 COMPARING THE TWO METHODS

What are the relative advantages of these two methods of correcting for measurement error? They have rather different origins, with the Jöreskog/LISREL approach linked more to the psychometric tradition, whereas Fuller's work is more closely related to econometrics, although these two disciplines have plenty in common. The LISREL method comes into its own when there are multiple indicators of each variable, as in the previous example. However, multiple indicators are often not available. It is useful to be able to introduce sampling variability of measurement error variances and reliabilities into analyses. This advantage of the Fuller approach is, however, confined to models estimated on samples which are much larger than those used to estimate measurement error statistics, and to models where both samples are small. Another advantage of the LISREL approach is that it does allow error variances and covariances to vary between groups when analysing a non-randomized study, and this could be important for some analyses.

It would be wrong to argue that one approach is uniformly superior to the other, and potential users should consider the relevance of the above points and whether a latent variable model is appropriate before deciding which to use. Also, the two methods described in detail in this chapter are not the only ways of coming to grips with measurement error. One alternative is to use 'instrumental' variables as described by Ecob and Goldstein (1983) and another is to use grouping estimates as Steedman (1980) did in the study of children's progress in secondary school referred to earlier. However, these methods are generally less satisfactory, although instrumental variable methods are useful for estimating reliabilities.

5.7 SUMMARY AND CONCLUSIONS

In this chapter, a number of techniques for eliminating measurement error from models for change are presented. The application of these techniques is not restricted to models requiring longitudinal data; they can be applied regardless of whether models are estimated with longitudinal or cross-sectional data. But, as we have seen, longitudinal data are often essential if there is to be any chance of determining causality and so correction for measurement error is especially important when analysing change. Longitudinal data also lead to particular error structures; for example, we have seen that the measurement of the same variable on two occasions can produce an error covariance if a latent variable approach is adopted and, with multiple measures, this covariance can be estimated. On the other hand, cross-sectional data can result in important error covariances between dependent and explanatory variables because they can share the same transitory variation and, for survey data, the same interviewer variation, but these covariances will usually be difficult to estimate.

It is still uncommon to find analyses of change which take account of measurement error. Indeed, the concept of measurement error is not as widely appreciated by social scientists as it should be. But it is also true that those who wish to correct for measurement error have to grapple with somewhat difficult statistical techniques. We might therefore consider just how large measurement error has to be before it has an important effect on results, as there may be times when it can safely be ignored.

For the simple conditional model (equation (3.4)), it is easy to show that the difference between the uncorrected and corrected estimates of relative change is

$$D = \hat{\beta}_1 (\bar{x}_2 - \bar{x}_1) \left(\frac{1-\rho}{\rho} \right) \tag{5.19}$$

where $\hat{\beta}_1$ is the uncorrected estimate of the slope coefficient, $\bar{x}_i$ ($i = 1, 2$) are the pre-test means for the two groups, and ρ is the reliability. Clearly, D increases as $\hat{\beta}_1$ increases, the difference between the group pre-test means increases, and ρ decreases. If ρ is unknown, then a range of likely values can be tried to see whether any correction will change the conclusions about relative change.

Unfortunately, no simple expression for D exists when there is more than one explanatory variable. If, in Section 5.3, the reliabilities of GA11 and M11^2 had both been set at 0.9, the estimate for school type would have been the same as the one given in equation (6.9), when the reliabilities were 0.84 and 0.94 respectively. And so, even when quite high values are assumed for ρ, conclusions can be modified, although, as the other example in Section 5.3 shows, they need not be.

APPENDIX 5.1 FULLER'S METHODS OF CORRECTING FOR MEASUREMENT ERROR

This appendix gives a little more detail about the methods described in Section 5.3. It does not, however, give formulae for estimates and their standard errors as these tend to be rather complicated; interested readers can find them in the articles referred to below. A computer program, SUPER CARP (Hidiroglou, Fuller, and

Hickman, 1980) is available and it will produce estimates for most of the cases listed below.

Consider a multiple regression model

$$y = \beta_0 + \sum_{i=1}^{k} \beta_i x_i + e \qquad (A5.1)$$

where e is the error term with the usual properties—a mean of zero, constant variance σ_e^2, uncorrelated both across observations and with the explanatory variables, x_i.

Suppose that y and some or all of x_i are measured with error so that

$$y = Y + w \qquad (A5.2)$$

$$x_i = X_i + u_i \qquad (i = 1, 2, \ldots, k) \qquad (A5.3)$$

where Y and X_i are true values and w and u_i are measurement error terms with zero means and variances σ_w^2 and σ_i^2 $(i = 1, 2, \ldots, k)$.

Allow the measurement error terms to be correlated and denote the measurement error covariances by σ_{wi} for the dependent variable and any one of the explanatory variables and σ_{ij} within the set of k explanatory variables.

If σ_q^2 is the true error variance then

$$\sigma_e^2 = \sigma_w^2 + \sigma_q^2 \qquad (A5.4)$$

Consistent estimates of the regression coefficients (estimates which may be biased for small samples but not for large ones) and their standard errors have been obtained for the following situations:

(i)   All the σ_i^2, σ_{ij}, σ_{wi}, and σ_w^2 are known exactly or are known to be zero. σ_q^2 is positive but unknown (Fuller, 1980).

(ii) As (i) but some or all of the measurement error statistics are estimates from samples whose sizes are known (Fuller, 1980). The standard errors of the regression coefficients are proportional to the reciprocal of these sample sizes.

(iii) As (i) except σ_w^2 is unknown and so σ_e^2 is positive but unknown (Hidiroglou, Fuller, and Hickman, 1980).

(iv) As (ii) but no estimate of σ_w^2 available (Hidiroglou, Fuller, and Hickman, 1980).

(v), (vi)   As (iii), (iv) but all $\sigma_{wi} = 0$ (Fuller, 1980).

(vii), (viii) As (v), (vi) but all $\sigma_{ij} = 0$ (Warren, White, and Fuller, 1974).

(xix), (x)   As (iii), (iv) but with only one explanatory variable as in analysis of covariance (Degracie and Fuller, 1972).

(xi), (xii)   As (i), (ii) but $\sigma_q^2 = 0$, i.e. there is a functional relationship between the true dependent variable and the set of true explanatory variables. For one explanatory variable, this is the classical errors-in-variables model (Fuller, 1980). However, most social scientists shy away from supposing that a particular dependent variable is determined exactly by one or more explanatory variables so this case will rarely apply.

(xiii) The *reliabilities* of each explanatory variable are either known or estimated. The reliability of the dependent variable may or may not be available (Fuller and Hidiroglou, 1978).

APPENDIX 5.2 JÖRESKOG'S METHODS OF CORRECTING FOR MEASUREMENT ERROR

This appendix gives a little more detail about the methods described in Section 5.4. It is very much easier to do this by using matrix algebra of an elementary kind. It is also easier to describe the models in terms of data for just one group so that the observed variables have zero means; Jöreskog and Sörbom (1981) show how the models can be extended to allow for non-zero means, which is needed when comparing groups. But, in this appendix, the μ_j of equation (5.11) and μ_k of equation (5.12) are zero, just as they were in the example in Section 5.5.

Suppose there are q observed variables for the n underlying explanatory or predetermined variables and p observed variables for the m underlying dependent or endogeneous variables. The measurement model is then

$$x = \Lambda_x \xi + \delta \qquad (A5.5)$$

$$y = \Lambda_y \eta + \varepsilon \qquad (A5.6)$$

where x and δ are $(q \times 1)$ vectors, y and ε are $(p \times 1)$ vectors, ξ is an $(n \times 1)$ vector, η is an $(m \times 1)$ vector, and Λ_x and Λ_y are $(q \times n)$ and $(p \times m)$ matrices respectively. The Λ matrices show the relationship between the observed variables (x and y) and the latent variables (ξ and η) and, in the language of factor analysis, can be regarded as matrices of factor loadings.

The structural model is

$$\eta = B\eta + \Gamma\xi + \zeta \qquad (A5.7)$$

where B $(m \times m)$ and Γ $(n \times n)$ are parameter matrices and ζ $(m \times 1)$ is a vector of errors with the usual properties found in regression models. It is also assumed that the measurement error vectors (δ and ε) are uncorrelated with their latent variables and with ζ and, further, that δ and ε are themselves uncorrelated. This final assumption explains why the example in Section 5.5 was framed solely in terms of y and η variables; the assumption is not needed for models which use means to compare groups.

The matrix B always has zeros on its diagonal. For a non-recursive system of simultaneous equations, B will be a full matrix, for a recursive system it will be triangular with zeros above the diagonal, and for single equation models with known causal direction, it will be zero throughout.

Equations (A5.5), (A5.6), and (A5.7) define a general model and estimation of that model proceeds by equating the $(p + q) \times (p + q)$ matrix of observed variances and covariances to a matrix expressed in terms of the parameters of the model and their variances and covariances. However, many models of interest are less general; for example, in Section 5.5, Λ_x, δ, and Γ are all zero and B is triangular.

It is, of course, possible to put forward a model which has too many parameters given the data available. In other words, the model is not identified, where identification has the same meaning given in Chapter 4. A necessary condition for the model to be identified is that the total number of parameters to be estimated from equations (A5.5), (A5.6), and (A5.7) should be less than $\frac{1}{2}(p+q)(p+q+1)$, which is the number of observed variances and covariances.

If version V of LISREL is used to estimate the model, then two estimation methods are available. The parameters can be estimated either with unweighted least squares or with the method of maximum likelihood, and both use iterative computing algorithms. The latter is more commonly used and is the more efficient of the two, but it does require the observed variables, x and y, to have a multivariate normal distribution. This is a reasonable assumption for the data in Section 5.5, but it will not always be reasonable, and the least squares approach, which does not require distributional assumptions, is perhaps more robust. The two estimation methods produce very similar results for the data in Section 5.5.

Having estimated a model, one then needs to assess how well this model fits the observed data and how it might be improved, either by making it more general or by imposing further reasonable constraints in the interests of parsimony. There are various ways of assessing fit, ranging from intelligent consideration of the reasonableness of parameter estimates and their standard errors through to examination of test statistics when maximum likelihood is used. The likelihood ratio test statistic (X^2) from a maximum likelihood estimation has a χ^2 distribution with degrees of freedom equal to $\frac{1}{2}(p+q)(p+q+1)-r$, where r is the number of parameters estimated. However, for large samples, this statistic will nearly always be significant at conventional levels even if the fit is reasonable. A more useful role for these statistics is to examine differences between them in order to assess the importance of particular constraints; differences in X^2 statistics are also distributed as χ^2 with $(r_2 - r_1)$ degrees of freedom, where r_2 is the number of parameters estimated in the more complex model and r_1 the number in the relatively less complex model. An indication of how a model might be improved can be obtained from an examination of the residuals from a model, and Jöreskog and Sörbom (1981) suggest ways of looking at residuals from a LISREL run.

This appendix has aimed to give no more than an outline of this particular approach to the problem of measurement error when analysing change. However, readers can consult the references cited earlier for more details. The computer program LISREL, which is almost synonymous with the method, is powerful and widely used.

As well as estimating causal models, the method can be used for other kinds of longitudinal analyses. One of these is longitudinal factor analysis and, in fact, the analysis of the EPA data given in Section 5.5 is a simple example of this kind of analysis which is restricted to considering whether there are changes in loadings (i.e. λ_i) of the three observed variables on the single factor or latent variable assumed to exist at each occasion. More sophisticated analyses using the LISREL approach can be found in Jöreskog and Sörbom (1977) and Olsson and Bergman (1977). An alternative approach to what is more generally the analysis of covariance structures is given by McDonald (1978, 1980).

CHAPTER 6

Models for Change when the Data are Categorical (1)

6.1 INTRODUCTION

The previous three chapters were all concerned with models for the analysis of change when the data are essentially continuous and measured on at least an interval scale. However, many variables in the social sciences are measured either on an ordered or on an unordered categorical scale, and techniques are needed to deal with these variables. For a long time, the analysis of categorical data tended to be restricted to the calculation of various measures of association but, during the last 10 to 15 years, the development of statistical models for categorical data has proceeded apace In this chapter and the next we will consider ways in which these models can be applied to categorical data on change. Again, extensions to three or more occasions are discussed in Chapter 8 and, in a rather different way, in Chapter 9.

Simple methods for making inferences about change are given in Section 6.2, but the bulk of this chapter is concerned with models for relative change. Hence, the ideas presented in Sections 6.3 and 6.4 are analogous to those presented in Chapter 3 for continuous variables. Logistic and log-linear models underpin these sections and readers unfamiliar with these models should first look at a specialist book in the area, such as Everitt (1977) and Fienberg (1980). Appendix 6.1 does present the basic ideas, but it should be seen as a refresher course for those who have previously been exposed to the underlying theory.

6.2 SOME SIMPLE METHODS

Suppose data on net change are obtained from two cross-sectional studies and suppose also that the variable of interest is binary and so has just two categories. Then, as we saw in Chapter 2, an obvious measure of net change is $p_2 - p_1$ where $p_t (t = 1, 2)$ is the sample proportion of 'successes' at each occasion. Elementary theory from the binomial distribution can then be used to test whether P_2 equals P_1 in the population and to construct confidence intervals for the net change (see, for example, Blalock, 1981, Ch. 13).

Suppose instead the variable of interest is polytomous with, say, three unordered categories. The data can be put into a table like Table 6.1, where n_{tj} is the number of sample observations at occasion $t (t = 1, 2)$ the category $j (j = 1, 2, 3)$, and $n_1.$ and $n_2.$ (the total number of observations for each occasion) are in general different. There is now no simple measure of net change. It is, however, straightforward to test for the statistical significance of net change with the usual chi-square test (with two degrees of freedom in Table 6.1). If the categories are ordered, then the significance of net change can be assessed more efficiently with a chi-square test for trend as described by, for example, Maxwell (1961, Ch. 4).

Table 6.1 Representing data on a three-category variable from two cross-sectional samples

Occasion (t) \ Category (j)	1	2	3	Total
1	n_{11}	n_{12}	n_{13}	$n_{1.}$
2	n_{21}	n_{22}	n_{23}	$n_{2.}$
Total	$n_{.1}$	$n_{.2}$	$n_{.3}$	$n_{..}$

Data such as those just described cannot of course provide any information on individual change. Suppose instead we have longitudinal data on a binary variable. Table 6.2 gives the number of mothers whose mental health was rated on two occasions, 12 months apart, taken from the study by Moss, Plewis, and Bax (1979). The row and column totals give the data which would have been obtained from two cross-sectional studies with the same sized sample at each occasion. The individual cells provide the longitudinal information and show that little net change can hide a lot of change at the individual level; 24 % (47/195) of the sample changed health levels between the two occasions, but the net change is only -0.08 ((58 − 73)/195). (It is possible that some of the apparent individual change arises because of measurement, or classification, error; we return to this issue in Section 6.7.)

Table 6.2 Longitudinal data for two occasions on mental health

Occasion 1 \ Occasion 2	Good	Poor	Total
Good	106	16	122
Poor	31	42	73
Total	137	58	195

The simplest way of testing whether $P_2 − P_1$ is zero in this case is to test whether the 2 × 2 table is symmetrical, i.e. whether the off-diagonal cells, $N_{12}(n_{12} = 16)$ and $N_{21}(n_{21} = 31)$ are equal. This is easily done by calculating the statistic given first by Bowker (1948):

$$X^2 = \frac{(n_{12} - n_{21})^2}{n_{12} + n_{21}} \tag{6.1}$$

which is distributed as χ^2 with one degree of freedom. For Table 6.2, $X^2 = 4.79$, which is statistically significant at the 5% level. Hence, one would conclude that there has been some net change with a fall in the proportion of mothers in poor mental health over time, or, equivalently, more individual change from poor to good health than from good to poor.

If only the cross-sectional information, the information in the margins in Table 6.2, had been available then the net change would not have been significant. The standard error of $(p_2 - p_1)$ is 0.067 when independence is assumed and the Z-statistic is 1.15, a good deal lower than the critical value of 1.96.

The association between the variable at occasion 1 and occasion 2 is a measure of its stability. Perhaps the best way to measure stability for dichotomous variables is to use Yule's Q:

$$Q = \frac{n_{11}n_{22} - n_{12}n_{21}}{n_{11}n_{22} + n_{12}n_{21}} \tag{6.2}$$

which equals 0.8 from Table 6.2.

Things become a little more complicated when we move from 2×2 to $r \times r$ tables such as we get when collecting longitudinal data on a polytomous variable. Suppose we have a 3×3 table, like Table 6.3.

Table 6.3 Representing longitudinal data on a three-category variable

Occasion 2	Occasion 1 1	2	3	Total
1	n_{11}	n_{12}	n_{13}	$n_{1.}$
2	n_{21}	n_{22}	n_{23}	$n_{2.}$
3	n_{31}	n_{32}	n_{33}	$n_{3.}$
Total	$n_{.1}$	$n_{.2}$	$n_{.3}$	$n_{..}$

Testing for the statistical significance of net change means asking whether $N_{i.} = N_{.i}(i = 1, 2, 3)$, and this is known as a test of marginal homogeneity. However, although symmetry implies marginal homogeneity, marginal homogeneity does not imply symmetry for $r > 2$, so separate tests of these two hypotheses are needed. The test for symmetry is a straightforward extension of equation (6.1):

$$X^2 = \frac{(n_{12} - n_{21})^2}{n_{12} + n_{21}} + \frac{(n_{13} - n_{31})^2}{n_{13} + n_{31}} + \frac{(n_{23} - n_{32})^2}{n_{23} + n_{32}} \tag{6.3}$$

and this is distributed as χ^2 with three degrees of freedom. Extensions to larger square tables follow automatically with $r(r-1)/2$ df.

A number of tests of marginal homogeneity have been proposed (see Plackett, 1981), but they are all complicated and require matrix manipulation. They therefore are not presented here, but one version is presented in the next section. The notion of quasi-symmetry links marginal homogeneity and symmetry, in that quasi-symmetry and marginal homogeneity together imply symmetry. For a 3×3 table, quasi-symmetry implies the equality of the cross-product ratios $N_{12}N_{33}/N_{13}N_{32}$ and $N_{21}N_{33}/N_{23}N_{31}$, but again the actual test is computationally difficult and the results are not easy to interpret in terms of change.

The methods given in this section can only deal with rather simple and not especially interesting questions about change and they do not easily generalize to questions about the explanation rather than just the description of change. However, square tables have received a lot of attention in the analysis of social mobility and, to a lesser extent, in the analysis of voting behaviour. Social mobility is usually defined as the inter-generational movement, from fathers to sons, between occupational classes, and these data are normally obtained by retrospective questioning within a cross-sectional study (e.g. Goldthorpe, 1980). Social mobility represents a type of change which can be treated as movement between unordered or ordered categories where the categories, in a table like Table 6.3, are occupational classes. Hauser (1980) presents a detailed description of one way of analysing social mobility tables which does not assume ordering and uses the idea of quasi-symmetry mentioned earlier in this section. Goodman (1979) does allow the categories to be ordered, and Bartholomew (1982) shows how Markov models can be used to analyse social mobility tables.

6.3 UNCONDITIONAL MODELS FOR GROUP COMPARISONS (A): BINARY DEPENDENT VARIABLE

This section presents unconditional models for the analysis of non-randomized studies, when the dependent variable is binary. The logic behind the use of unconditional and conditional models is not of course changed by the type of data available. It is still the case that only conditional models are suitable for the analysis of quasi-experiments, but the arguments against unconditional models for observational studies are perhaps less strong when the data are categorical. It is often reasonable to suppose that the meaning of a categorical variable does not change over time. For example, if different reading tests are used on two occasions to define two groups of readers, adequate and poor, then there could be sound practical reasons for supposing that this binary or dichotomous variable has the same meaning on both occasions, although this might not be justified in a study with a strong theoretical basis. Also, the question of whether to standardize for variances which change over time does not arise with categorical data unless scores are allocated to the categories. (But if the proportion of poor readers is forced to be the same at each occasion then this is a form of standardization.)

Suppose, for simplicity, that we are dealing with a study which involves longitudinal data on just two groups. If there are no other 'pre-treatment' variables, then these data can be represented as a three-way, $2 \times 2 \times 2$ contingency table such as Table 6.4 with cells n_{rst} where r $(r = 1, 2)$ defines the groups, s $(s = 1, 2)$ defines the first occasion measure, and t $(t = 1, 2)$ defines the second occasion measure.

As always, we want to know whether one group changes more than the other

Table 6.4 Notation for the group by pre-test by post-test contingency table

Occasion 1	Occasion 2						Total
	Group 1			Group 2			
	1	2	Total	1	2	Total	
1	n_{111}	n_{112}	$n_{11.}$	n_{211}	n_{212}	$n_{21.}$	$n_{.1.}$
2	n_{121}	n_{122}	$n_{12.}$	n_{221}	n_{222}	$n_{22.}$	$n_{.2.}$
Total	$n_{1.1}$	$n_{1.2}$	$n_{1..}$	$n_{2.1}$	$n_{2.2}$	$n_{2..}$	$n_{...}$

and, as before, we know that there are at least two ways of approaching this question. Consider first unconditional models; Koch *et al.* (1977) propose building models for the *marginal* probabilities ϕ_{ijk} from Table 6.4 where i ($i = 1, 2$) defines the groups, j ($j = 1, 2$) defines the occasions, and k ($k = 1, 2$) defines the binary dependent variable, so that

$$\phi_{i1k} = \frac{n_{rs.}}{n_{r..}} \qquad (6.4a)$$

are the four pre-test or pre-treatment marginal probabilities with $i = 1, 2; i = r$, and $k = 1, 2; k = s$, and

$$\phi_{i2k} = \frac{n_{r.t}}{n_{r..}} \qquad (6.4b)$$

are the four post-treatment marginal probabilities with $i = 1, 2; i = r$, and $k = 1, 2; k = t$. Because the response is binary, $\phi_{i11} + \phi_{i12} = \phi_{i21} + \phi_{i22} = 1$. A general model for the ϕ_{ijk}, which is rather like a model for a repeated measures analysis of variance (see Chapter 8) can then be written as

$$F(\phi_{ijk}) = \mu_k + \alpha_{i.k} + \gamma_{.jk} + \delta_{ijk} \qquad (6.5)$$

where μ_k is just the mean, for category k, of the chosen function, F, of the marginal probabilities, $\alpha_{i.k}$ is the overall group effect, $\gamma_{.jk}$ is the overall time or occasion effect, and δ_{ijk} is the group–time interaction. Constraints are put on the parameters to ensure that $\sum_k \phi_{ijk} = 1$. It is δ_{ijk} which is the term of major interest as it gives the relative unconditional change. But a test of $\gamma_{.jk} = 0$ can be interpreted as a test of marginal homogeneity mentioned in the previous section, that is, a test of whether there was any overall change in the distribution of the variable over time.

Equation (6.5) does not model just the probabilities, ϕ_{ijk}, but a function, F, of them, and the choice of F will depend both on the substantive nature of the problem at hand and also on statistical theory. With a binary variable, then $F(\phi) = \phi$ is possible, and equation (6.5) would then be modelling the probability of 'success'. However, there are statistical reasons for preferring

$$F(\phi) = \log \frac{\phi}{1 - \phi}$$

known as logit ϕ; one of the reasons is that it avoids estimated probabilities falling outside the permitted range of 0 to 1. Also, it is often more convenient to work with a scale which varies between $-\infty$ and ∞ as the logit scale does, rather than just between 0 and 1. If a logit function is used then the logarithm of the odds of a success is modelled; there are some, although not many, situations for which the ease of interpretation of $F(\phi) = \phi$ is more important.

Whatever the choice of F, estimates of the parameters in equation (6.5) can be obtained by the method of weighted least squares (WLS) as originally described for categorical data by Grizzle, Starmer, and Koch (1969) and modified by Koch et al. (1977), and readers are referred to these articles for details. The test of whether $\delta_{ijk} = 0$ leads to a statistic distributed as χ^2 with, for Table 6.4, one degree of freedom. A computer program, GENCAT (Landis, Stanish, Freeman, and Koch, 1976) is available for parameter estimation and hypothesis testing. (Further details about this approach can be found in Chapter 8 and Appendix 8.1.)

Let us illustrate these ideas with an example which is just a little more complicated in that there are five groups, so subscript i in equations (6.4) and (6.5) runs from 1 to 5. The data were originally presented by Marascuilo and Serlin (1979) and re-analysed by Plewis (1981b); they are measures of a dichotomous variable at two occasions for five ethnic groups and are given in Table 6.5. The responses are replies by a sample of high school students to the item 'the most important qualities of a husband are determination and ambition' (!).

Table 6.5 Marascuilo and Serlin data. (Reproduced from Plewis (1981b) by permission of The British Psychological Society)

Response at occasion		Ethnic group					
1	2	Asian	Black	Chicano	Indian	White	Total
True	True	60	72	62	86	243	523
True	False	50	30	29	28	208	345
False	True	22	30	19	47	112	230
False	False	68	41	25	39	381	554
Total		200	173	135	200	944	1652

Marascuilo and Serlin constructed a non-parametric test for (unconditional) relative change. The re-analysis focused on the alternative statistical models described in this section and the next. Two versions of equation (6.5)—the unconditional model—were applied to the data; the first put $F(\phi) = \phi$ and so modelled the probability of a 'true' response, and the second put $F(\phi) = \text{logit } \phi$ and thus modelled the log of the odds on a true response (Table 6.6). The values of the test statistics for these two models are given in Table 6.7, which shows that very similar χ^2 values were obtained for the two models, and that each of the effects was highly significant. It is not surprising to find similar results for linear and logit models for these data because there are no low (say less than 0.2) or high

Table 6.6 Linear and logit marginal probabilities from Table 6.5

Occasion		Ethnic group				
		Asian	Black	Chicano	Indian	White
1	Prob. (true)	0.55	0.59	0.67	0.57	0.48
	Log-odds (true)	0.20	0.36	0.73	0.28	−0.09
2	Prob. (true)	0.41	0.59	0.60	0.67	0.38
	Log-odds (true)	−0.36	0.36	0.41	0.69	−0.51

Table 6.7 Unconditional model: test statistic values (χ^2). (Reproduced from Plewis (1981b) by permission of The British Psychological Society)

Effect	Parameter	df	Function	
			Linear	Logit
T	$\gamma_{.jk}$	1	26.3	24.2
G/T	$\alpha_{i.k}$	4	80.3	70.9
G.T/G,T	δ_{ijk}	4	23.1	22.2

Notes: T—main effect of time
G/T—main effect of group after fitting T
G.T/G,T—interaction after fitting main effects

(greater than 0.8) marginal probabilities. Differences are more likely to emerge when some of the probabilities are close to their bounds of 0 and 1.

It is also possible to analyse Table 6.5 using the transformation suggested in Chapter 2 (Section 2.10) and thus creating Table 6.8.

Table 6.8 An alternative presentation of Table 6.5

Change Category	Ethnic group					Total
	Asian	Black	Chicano	Indian	White	
True → False	50	30	29	28	208	345
False → True	22	30	19	47	112	230
No Change	128	113	87	125	624	1077
Total	200	173	135	200	944	1652

It is straightforward to test for an association between the change categories and ethnic group and the resulting χ^2 value is 26.9 which, for eight degrees of freedom, is highly significant. However, this association is not measuring only relative change; it is not necessary for there to be relative change or indeed net change for an association to exist. There will be an association if the proportion of people changing response categories varies across the groups. However, in Table 6.8, this proportion is almost constant at around 35 %.

6.4 CONDITIONAL MODELS FOR GROUP COMPARISONS (A): BINARY RESPONSE

Moving on to conditional models for situations illustrated by Table 6.4, let us now draw a distinction between the variable measured at the first occasion and the variable measured at the second occasion. In the unconditional model, the measures at both occasions are treated as 'responses', so both can vary, but in the conditional model the variable at the first occasion becomes a 'factor', which means that it is regarded as fixed. (It is not now necessary for the pre-test and post-test to be measured in the same way with the same number of categories.) This distinction is essentially the same as the one made for continuous variables, and the question to be answered is the same: what is the relationship between the group and the response for fixed values of the variable at the first occasion? However, the most appropriate model is somewhat different.

When the response is binary then the easiest way of expressing the conditional model is

$$\text{logit } P_{rs} = \kappa + \theta_r + \psi_s + \zeta_{rs} \tag{6.6}$$

where P_{rs} is the expected probability of 'success' at the second occasion and so logit P_{rs} equals $\log N_{rs1}/N_{rs2}$, where N_{rst} are the expected cell numbers in Table 6.4. For two groups ($R = 2$) and a binary pre-test ($S = 2$) there are four values of logit P_{rs} and these are completely determined by an overall mean, κ, the within-group association between pre-test and post-test (ψ_s), the association between group and post-test for fixed values of the pre-test (θ_r), and the interaction of group and pre-test on post-test (ζ_{rs}). As each of these terms has just one degree of freedom, constraints have to be imposed and the easiest way to do this is to put redundant terms equal to zero so that $\theta_2 = \psi_2 = \zeta_{12} = \zeta_{21} = \zeta_{22} = 0$.

When analysing a non-randomized study, we first want to know whether the omission of the ζ_{rs} term from equation (6.6) results in a statistically significant reduction in the goodness of fit of the model to the data. If it does, then this is analogous to the existence of a group-covariate interaction or nonparallel regression lines as described for continuous variables in Chapter 3. Whereas there are ways of estimating an average treatment effect in the presence of such an interaction with continuous variables, it is not possible to do this with unscaled categorical data. It is therefore difficult to make any statements about a treatment effect (i.e. θ_r) when $\zeta_{rs} \neq 0$. The interaction itself may, however, be interesting. If $\zeta_{rs} = 0$ then e^{θ_1} can be interpreted as the conditional effect of the treatment on the relative odds of success at occasion 2. Further details about estimating and testing model (6.6) can be found in Appendix 6.1.

A drawback of the conditional approach as described here is that it only allows for one explanatory variable or factor besides the group factor, and it was emphasized in Chapter 3 that models which adjust only for the pre-test will often be mis-specified. There is no difficulty in principle in putting more factors into the logit model but if they are categorical, their inclusion can soon lead to very sparse multi-way contingency tables with consequent problems of estimation and testing. The extra factors could of course be continuous variables and the method of logistic regression (see Fienberg, 1980) could be applied to the mixture of categorical and continuous variables. Often, however, it will be more difficult than usual to conduct a satisfactory conditional analysis with categorical pre- and post-tests. This suggests that resources which are directed towards the construction of a satisfactory continuous measure or sensible scale values, at the pilot stage of a project, will often be well spent.

The application of the conditional logit model (6.6) with $R = 5$ to the data in Table 6.5 gave a test statistic of 2.23 for the 'group-covariate interaction' term ζ_{rs} which is distributed as χ^2 with four degrees of freedom and so is clearly unimportant. It is therefore possible to go on to look at the term of interest, θ_r, and this produces a test statistic of 70.7, which is also distributed as χ_4^2 and is highly significant. It is also a good deal larger than the χ^2 value for δ_{ijk} in Table 6.7 and this suggests that there are differences between the results for the unconditional and conditional models.

These differences can be seen more clearly when we look at the pairwise contrasts, C_m ($m = 1, 2, \ldots 10$), or estimated differences, between the groups in Table 6.9. The contrasts for the unconditional and conditional logit models can be compared and there are some rather sharp differences—for example, the unconditional 'Chicano–White' contrast is 0.1, but the conditional contrast is 0.7—and these differences are reinforced when the squared relative contrasts, $C_m^2/\text{var}(C_m)$, are compared.

These results show how conclusions can be affected by the choice of model and thus how important it is to choose an appropriate model for the particular data to hand. An unconditional model is perhaps better suited to the data of Table 6.5,

Table 6.9 Comparing unconditional and conditional contrasts. (Reproduced from Plewis (1981b) by permission of the British Psychological Society)

Contrasts (C_m)	Unconditional logit		Conditional logit	
	C	$C^2/\text{var}(C)$	C	$C^2/\text{var}(C)$
Asian–Black	−0.565	5.09	−0.746	11.36
Asian–Chicano	−0.243	0.76	−0.677	8.12
Asian–Indian	−0.968	15.14	−1.128	26.83
Asian–White	−0.148	0.64	0.060	0.13
Black–Chicano	0.321	1.24	0.069	0.08
Black–Indian	−0.404	2.41	−0.382	2.86
Black–White	0.417	4.33	0.805	20.79
Chicano–Indian	−0.725	6.36	−0.451	3.46
Chicano–White	0.096	0.17	0.736	13.99
Indian–White	0.821	17.06	1.187	47.61

although we would need to know more about the purpose of the study before making a definite decision.

It could be argued that because it is possible to estimate an unconditional model with categorical data from two cross-sections then there is no great advantage in collecting longitudinal data when analysing relative change. This argument is not convincing. Although it is true that a model like equation (6.5) can be estimated with cross-sectional data, the estimates will not be as precise as those estimated from longitudinal data (just as the estimate of net change in Table 6.2 was less precise when only the marginal information was used). Also, it would not be entirely satisfactory to conclude that relative change is zero when the data are as follows:

	p_1	p_2
Group 1	0.5	0.7
Group 2	0.3	0.5

where p_t $(t = 1, 2)$ is the proportion of 'successes' at the two occasions, without knowing that the underlying situation is:

Occasion 1 \ Occasion 2	\multicolumn{3}{c}{Group 1}	\multicolumn{3}{c}{Group 2}
	S	F	Total	S	F	Total
S	50	0	50	0	30	30
F	20	30	50	50	20	70
Total	70	30	100	50	50	100

Clearly the pattern of individual change in the two groups is very different, a point which is brought out by a conditional analysis of the longitudinal data. The argument is rather like the one in Chapter 3 (Section 3.8) where it is pointed out that estimates of unconditional relative change can mask differences in pre-test, post-test associations within groups.

6.5 UNCONDITIONAL MODELS FOR GROUP COMPARISONS (B): POLYTOMOUS DEPENDENT VARIABLE

Suppose that, instead of being binary, the variable measured at the two occasions has K categories. Thus, the data are now represented as a $2 \times K \times K$ table, although the structure is the same as that of Table 6.4. The method of calculating marginal probabilities is the same as that given in equation (6.4) but with $k, s,$ and t all running from 1 to K. The basic model is still given by equation (6.5) but there are now $(K - 1)$ degrees of freedom attached to the interaction term, δ_{ijk}.

With $K > 2$, further questions arise about which function, F, of the marginal probabilities, ϕ_{ijk}, should be modelled. It will not usually be satisfactory to use the linear function, $F(\phi) = \phi$, because one category would have to be omitted and the results will be influenced by the omitted category. However, it is easy to extend the logit formulation by considering

$$F(\phi_{ijk}) = \log\frac{\phi_{ijk}}{\phi_{ijK}} \tag{6.7}$$

where k runs from 1 to $K-1$, and this is sometimes referred to as a multivariate logit. Equation (6.7) does not introduce any arbitrary omissions.

Let us illustrate the use of the multivariate logit with some data from the British Election Study (see Särlvik and Crewe, 1983). Table 6.10 gives the numbers voting for the three major parties in the February 1974 and May 1979 General Elections broken down by whether they owned their own homes or lived in rented accommodation in 1974.

Table 6.10 Voting behaviour by housing tenure, February 1974 and May 1979

| Vote, February 1974 | Owner-occupiers | | | | Renters | | | |
| | Vote, May 1979 | | | | Vote, May 1979 | | | |
	Con	Lab	Lib	Total	Con	Lab	Lib	Total
Conservative	137	4	7	148	40	1	1	42
Labour	13	80	8	101	12	118	11	141
Liberal	25	14	36	75	16	11	15	42
Total	175	98	51	324	68	130	27	225

A Labour government was elected in 1974 and a Conservative government in 1979 so it is not interesting to test for the net change, i.e. marginal homogeneity. But it would be interesting to know whether there was any relative change in voting behaviour between these two social groups. A test of $\delta_{ijk} = 0$ in equation (6.5) using the functional form given in equation (6.7) produces a test statistic of 5.98 which is very close to the critical value of 5.99 for χ^2 with two degrees of freedom. So there is some evidence for relative change and we can gain more insight into this by examining Table 6.11. This gives the multivariate logits for the two occasions and two groups and shows that any relative change is due

Table 6.11 Multivariate logits from Table 6.10

| | Owner-occupiers | | | Renters | | |
	1974	1979	1979–1974	1974	1979	1979–1974
$\log\dfrac{Con}{Lib}$	0.68	1.23	0.55	0	0.92	0.92
$\log\dfrac{Lab}{Lib}$	0.30	0.65	0.35	1.21	1.57	0.36

to the greater change in the odds of voting Conservative rather than Liberal in the renting group. There is no relative change in the odds of voting Labour rather than Liberal.

A more complete analysis would take account of changes in housing tenure between 1974 and 1979. It is plausible to suppose that those voters who move out of the rented sector into owner-occupation are particularly likely to change their vote. The effects of changes in housing tenure on changing behaviour can, in principle, be analysed with the methods of the first part of the next chapter, but in fact only a small proportion (3 %) of this sample reported changes in housing tenure.

It is likely that the categories of a polytomous variable will be ordered. One might therefore want to construct a function of the marginal probabilities which uses this information. There are a number of ways of doing this. McCullagh (1980) suggests using proportional odds with

$$F(\phi_{ijk}) = \log \frac{\sum_{k=1}^{m} \phi_{ijk}}{1 - \sum_{k=1}^{m} \phi_{ijk}} \tag{6.8}$$

or proportional hazards with

$$F(\phi_{ijk}) = \log \left[-\log \sum_{k=1}^{m} (1 - \phi_{ijk}) \right] \tag{6.9}$$

whereas Fienberg (1980) proposes continuation odds or continuation ratios with

$$F(\phi_{ijk}) = \log \frac{\sum_{m \geq k} \phi_{ijm}}{\phi_{ijk}} \tag{6.10}$$

where m goes from 1 to $K-1$ in each case. Alternatively, some kind of scoring system might be preferred.

The way in which continuation odds are defined implies that movement can take place only in one direction as, for example, in levels of educational attainment, and so this restricts their use.

It could be argued that the categories in Table 6.10 (Conservative, Labour, Liberal) can be ordered on a crude 'Right–Left' dimension as (Conservative, Liberal, Labour). And so these data were analysed to take account of this ordering by using the functions given in equations (6.8) and (6.9). (Continuation odds are not appropriate as movement can clearly take place in both directions.) One would hope to get a more parsimonious model by using the ordering. In particular, one would hope to find that the effects of housing tenure would be the same for the two ratios generated by the ordering. In the case of proportional odds, these two ratios are

$$\log \frac{\text{Conservative}}{\text{Liberal} + \text{Labour}} \quad \text{and} \quad \log \frac{\text{Conservative} + \text{Liberal}}{\text{Labour}}.$$

Similarly, one would hope to get equal effects of time on the two ratios.

In fact, neither of the functions produce the desired level of parsimony. The effects of time are not the same for the two ratios and this suggests that the assumed ordering is not actually appropriate, at least for changes over time. We can see from Table 6.10 that there is more movement from Labour to Conservative than from Labour to Liberal (10 % of Labour voters in 1974 voted Conservative in 1979 but only 8 % voted Liberal), whereas one might expect more movement from Labour to Liberal if the ordering did reflect the true position of the three parties. However, the effects of housing tenure on the two ratios are essentially the same whether proportional odds or proportional hazards models are fitted and so the ordering would seem to be valid for differences between these two groups. Overall, though, there would seem to be no great advantage in ordering voting behaviour in this way and the somewhat equivocal results about relative change given earlier are probably the best that can be obtained from these data. There was, however, an election between February 1974 and 1979, in October 1974, and so we return to the data for three occasions in Chapter 8.

6.6 CONDITIONAL MODELS FOR GROUP COMPARISONS (B): POLYTOMOUS RESPONSE

Consider now an example of a quasi-experiment. The data come from the same project on pre-school families mentioned in Chapter 1, part of which was concerned with the 'desire' of mothers for pre-school services for their children (Plewis, 1978). The data in Table 6.12 give levels of desire measured on an ordered four-point scale on two occasions, 12 months apart, for three non-randomly formed groups. Two of these groups were subject to an intervention, the third was a control group. Did the intervention—in fact, the introduction of new, free, comprehensive services—have the effect of raising the levels of desire above the levels for the control group? This is clearly a situation for which only a conditional model is appropriate.

Equation (6.6) can be extended to allow for responses with more than two categories in essentially the same way as the unconditional model is extended. In other words, multivariate logits for the response probabilities within each factor combination are modelled. However, it is more convenient to use a log-linear model as described in Appendix 6.1. It is possible to set up a log-linear model for $2 \times K \times K$ contingency tables as follows:

$$\log N_{rst} = \lambda + \lambda_r^A + \lambda_s^B + \lambda_t^C + \lambda_{rs}^{AB} + \lambda_{st}^{BC} + \lambda_{rt}^{AC} + \lambda_{rst}^{ABC} \qquad (6.11)$$

where N_{rst} are the expected cell numbers, A and r $(r = 1, 2)$ refer to the group variable, B and s $(s = 1, 2, \ldots, K)$ refer to the measure at occasion 1, and C and t $(t = 1, 2, \ldots, K)$ to the measure at occasion 2, and A and B are factors and C is the response.

Given equation (6.11) for the $2 \times K \times K$ table, we want to know first whether it is reasonable to omit λ_{rst}^{ABC} from the model—this term corresponds to ζ_{rs} in equation (6.6) and in turn corresponds to a group-covariate interaction as

Table 6.12 Pre-school data: group by desire at occasion 1 by desire at occasion 2 (percentage in brackets)

Desire/ Occasion 1	Desire/Occasion 2														
	Treatment 1					Treatment 2					Control				
	None	Part-time	School day	All day	Total	None	Part-time	School day	All day	Total	None	Part-time	School day	All day	Total
None	15	17	16	3	51 (50)	4	4	4	1	13 (38)	8	4	4	3	19 (32)
Part-time	0	4	11	6	21 (21)	0	1	3	1	5 (15)	1	3	5	0	9 (15)
School day	0	1	10	8	19 (19)	0	1	2	1	4 (12)	1	1	6	5	13 (22)
All day	0	1	0	9	10 (10)	1	0	2	9	12 (35)	0	0	3	15	18 (31)
Total	15 (15)	22 (22)	38 (38)	26 (26)	101 (100)	5 (15)	6 (18)	11 (32)	12 (35)	34 (100)	10 (17)	8 (14)	18 (31)	23 (39)	59 (100)

described in Chapter 3 (Section 3.8). If the λ_{rst}^{ABC} are unimportant, then attention turns to λ_{rt}^{AC} and we want to know whether the following model

$$\log N_{rst} = \lambda + \lambda_r^A + \lambda_s^B + \lambda_t^C + \lambda_{rs}^{AB} + \lambda_{st}^{BC} \tag{6.12}$$

gives a satisfactory fit to the data. If it does, then there is no evidence for a treatment effect, but if it does not then λ_{rt}^{AC} is included in the model and gives the estimates of the treatment effect. A test of the hypothesis that $\lambda_{rst}^{ABC} = 0$ in equation (6.11) gives a test statistic (the deviance) of 19.7 for the data in Table 6.12. This is distributed as χ_{18}^2 and so there is no evidence for a group-covariate interaction. A test of $\lambda_{rt}^{AC} = 0$ further increases the deviance by only 2.94 which, for six degrees of freedom, is very small, so there is also no evidence for any kind of treatment effect.

However, this approach is not sensitive to the particular characteristics of these data because it ignores the ordering in the measure taken on the two occasions. Also, it does not take account of the fact that half the cells below the diagonals are zero and the other half are all small. In fact, the second point flows directly from the first, as 'desire' can reasonably be treated as a variable for which change is only possible in one direction. This is because it is very unusual for mothers to want less pre-school provision for their children as the children get older. All the cells below the diagonals (i.e. desire at time 2 less than desire at time 1) can therefore be treated as 'structural' zeros. This means that they do not arise from sampling fluctuations but from the nature of the data and so are zero *a priori*. Hence Table 6.12 can be analysed as an *incomplete* multi-way table. If we accept this argument, then those cells below the diagonals which are not zero can only have arisen because of measurement error of some kind and should therefore be re-allocated to other cells, and the most sensible relocation would appear to be the diagonal cells. Bishop, Fienberg, and Holland (1975, Ch. 5) discuss the analysis of incomplete tables in some depth, but the essential details of the theory for complete tables go over to incomplete tables, with the null hypotheses expressed in terms of independence for the non-zero cells. This means that the structural zeros are omitted from the fitting process, and this kind of independence is known as *quasi-independence*. The only problem is the calculation of the correct degrees of freedom, particularly for multi-way tables. In fact, when the tables form a set of 'block triangular' tables as will happen with longitudinal data of this kind, then the degrees of freedom are unchanged for the term of interest, that is, λ_{rt}^{AC}, but they are different for λ_{rst}^{ABC}. For the incomplete version of Table 6.12, the degrees of freedom for λ_{rst}^{ABC} are calculated as the number of degrees of freedom usually associated with the model for the complete table (18 in our case) minus the number of structural zeros (18) plus the number of zero entries in the three 2-way tables obtained by collapsing over the third variables, which is six in our case, all from the table relating desire at the two occasions for all groups combined. Treating Table 6.12 as an incomplete table gives a deviance of 8.22 for λ_{rst}^{ABC} which is small when compared with χ_6^2 ($p > 0.20$) and a deviance of 1.54 for λ_{rt}^{AC} which is also small when compared with χ_6^2.

Thus, in this example, the conclusions are unchanged from those obtained for the complete table. But remember that the conclusions might be different if it were possible to re-specify the model to include other background variables as factors.

Of course, change will take place in both directions for many ordered categorical variables, and models for incomplete tables will not then be appropriate. The ordering in these variables can be taken into account within the framework of a conditional analysis by modelling the proportional odds or the proportional hazards within each factor combination.

It is also possible to take account of ordering by allocating scores to the categories, and the simplest, and most usual, way of doing this is to give scores 1, 2, . . . , K to categories 1, 2, . . . , K respectively. If this scoring system is adopted then the log-linear model is written rather differently (equation (A6.7) in Appendix 6.1) but the principles of model fitting are unchanged. Instead of fitting the term λ_{st}^{BC}, which represents the interaction between pre-test and post-test, the 'linear by linear' component of this interaction is fitted which has just one degree of freedom. And, instead of fitting λ_{rt}^{AC}, the 'linear' interaction having $(r-1)$ degrees of freedom is fitted and it is this linear interaction which now represents the treatment effect.

If it is reasonable to leave out the non-linear components of λ_{st}^{BC} and λ_{rt}^{AC} and all of λ_{rst}^{ABC} then, again, we want to know whether the linear part of λ_{rt}^{AC} can be omitted from the model.

This simple scoring method was applied to the data in Table 6.12 so that the category 'none' was given a score of 1 and the category 'all day' was given a score of 4. The model without the 3-way interaction and the non-linear components of λ_{st}^{BC} and λ_{rt}^{AC} fits well ($X^2 = 28.6$, 30 df) and the linear part of the treatment effect is essentially zero ($X^2 = 1.61$, 2 df).

All the conditional methods used to analyse these data lead to the same conclusion: the interventions had no effect on levels of desire for pre-school provision. But rather different results are obtained from an unconditional analysis, an analysis based on the marginal probabilities rather than on the cell probabilities. Continuation odds (equation (6.10)) are well suited to these data because change essentially takes place in one direction. The test of the hypothesis that $\delta_{ijk} = 0$ in equation (6.5) gives a test statistic of 11.3, distributed as χ_6^2 ($p < 0.08$). So an unconditional approach gives at least some evidence of a treatment effect which was not apparent with the conditional approach. This reinforces the point made earlier that it is very important to choose the right model for the data and this will depend on the nature of the study. The unconditional model is not appropriate for these data and gives a misleading result.

6.7 MEASUREMENT ERROR IN CATEGORICAL DATA

The whole of Chapter 5 was devoted to the problems caused by measurement error for continuous variables. Unfortunately, very much less is known about the effects of measurement error, usually referred to as classification error, when the data are categorical. It is difficult to know just how important an issue it is, as there is little evidence about the extent of misclassification, either in terms of variables particularly susceptible to misclassification or of situations particularly likely to cause it. On the other hand, the temptation to ignore the problem in the hope that it will not lead to distorted inferences is perhaps unwise. One of the difficulties of using the framework of Chapter 5 with categorical data is that the link between misclassification rates and conventional notions of error variance and reliability is not entirely clear. Sometimes classification error is estimated by re-measuring a sub-sample in the same way as the main sample and this is analogous to measuring reliability as a test–retest coefficient. But when misclassification is estimated by using a more accurate method of classification on a sub-sample, then the ensuing rates would seem to be measuring a mixture of reliability (or error variance) and validity (or bias). Bross (1954), Assakul and Proctor (1967), and others have looked at the effects of misclassification on hypothesis testing for 2-way tables. But only Korn (1981) has considered the problem within the context of fitting models to multi-way tables and he is concerned only with the effects of misclassification on the form of model selected from the observed data and not with its effects on estimates from the model.

Another approach to measurement error in categorical data is taken by Colemar (1964a) who distinguishes 'states' from 'responses'. Responses are variables for which the underlying distribution is continuous, even though they are measured categorically, whereas states such as martial status are genuinely categorical. Clearly, most variables measured as ordered categories are, in this sense, responses and one form of measurement error—response uncertainty—is postulated to arise because, for any point on the underlying continuum, there is a probability (less than one) of responding as a particular category. Thus there is a chance that all members of a sample could have the same value on the underlying continuum at two occasions but the observed table of individual change could have non-zero off-diagonal cells. But it is also possible for the diagonal, 'no change' cells to contain individuals whose score on the underlying continuum did change. Further research into the problem of measurement error in categorical data is needed and should consider the effects of both misclassification and response uncertainty.

6.8 SUMMARY

This chapter starts by describing some simple methods for analysing relative change when the data are categorical. However, these methods are limited in their scope and much greater understanding can be obtained from analyses based on explicit statistical models. A clear distinction can then be made between the conditional and unconditional approaches, the importance of which was stressed in earlier chapters. Again we see that we get different results depending on which approach is used for a particular data set. It is also possible to frame the models so that they can deal both with unordered and with ordered categorical data, and various ways of analysing ordered data are presented.

APPENDIX 6.1 LOG-LINEAR MODELS

A brief introduction to log-linear models and associated issues is given in this appendix. Consider first the 2×2 table shown in Table A6.1.

Table A6.1 Simple 2×2 table

		Variable B		
		1	2	Total
Variable	1	n_{11}	n_{12}	$n_{1.}$
A	2	n_{21}	n_{22}	$n_{2.}$
	Total	$n_{.1}$	$n_{.2}$	$n_{..}$

In the table, n_{ij} are the observed values in category i of variable A and category j of variable B. If there is no association between the two variables in the population, then the expected value of n_{ij} is

$$\hat{n}_{ij} = \frac{n_{i.}n_{.j}}{n_{..}} \tag{A6.1}$$

Equation (A6.1) can be transformed from a multiplicative structure to a simpler additive one by taking logs, so that

$$\log \hat{n}_{ij} = \log n_{i.} + \log n_{.j} - \log n_{..} \tag{A6.2}$$

If the two variables in Table A6.1 are associated then this association can be measured by the cross-product ratio, α, where

$$\alpha = \frac{n_{11}n_{22}}{n_{21}n_{12}} \tag{A6.3}$$

The full model for Table A6.1 should allow for association and can be written as

$$\log \hat{n}_{ij} = \lambda + \lambda_i^A + \lambda_j^B + \lambda_{ij}^{AB} \tag{A6.4}$$

with either:

(A) $\quad \lambda_2^A = \lambda_2^B = \lambda_{12}^{AB} = \lambda_{21}^{AB} = \lambda_{22}^{AB} = 0$

or

(B) $\quad \lambda_2^A = -\lambda_1^A; \ \lambda_2^B = -\lambda_1^B; \ \lambda_{11}^{AB} = \lambda_{22}^{AB}; \ \lambda_{12}^{AB} = -\lambda_{11}^{AB}; \ \lambda_{21}^{AB} = -\lambda_{11}^{AB}$

If the first set of constraints is adopted, then $\lambda_{11}^{AB} = \log \hat{\alpha}$, and if the second set is adopted then $\lambda_{11}^{AB} = \frac{1}{4} \log \hat{\alpha}$. The other terms in equation (A6.4) can be regarded as an overall mean (λ), the main effect of variable A or the difference between $n_{1.}$ and $n_{2.}$ (λ_i^A), and the main effect of variable B or the difference between $n_{.1}$ and $n_{.2}$ (λ_j^B). Equation (A6.4) is very like the equation which lies behind a two-way analysis of variance for continuous data.

Clearly the basic log-linear model (A6.4) can be generalized to two-way tables for variables with more than two categories and, more importantly, to multi-way tables. If variable A or variable B or both have more than two categories then equation (A6.4) is unchanged but the constraints become:

(A) $\lambda_i^A = \lambda_j^B = \lambda_{ij}^{AB} = \lambda_{ij}^{AB} = 0$

or

(B) $\sum_i \lambda_i^A = \sum_j \lambda_j^B = \sum_i \lambda_{ij}^{AB} = \sum_j \lambda_{ij}^{AB} = 0$

Now consider the three-way table with variables A, B, and C having I, J, and K categories respectively. Then equation (A6.4) becomes

$$\log \hat{n}_{ijk} = \lambda + \lambda_i^A + \lambda_j^B + \lambda_k^C + \lambda_{ij}^{AB} + \lambda_{ik}^{AC} + \lambda_{jk}^{BC} + \lambda_{ijk}^{ABC} \tag{A6.5}$$

which is the same as equation (6.11). In this equation, the terms λ_{ij}^{AB}, λ_{ik}^{AC}, λ_{jk}^{BC} are the first-order interactions or associations. So λ_{ij}^{AB} represents the association between A and B within any level of C and λ_{ijk}^{ABC} is the second-order interaction which measures the extent to which the association between any two variables is influenced by the third.

It was pointed out in Section 6.4 that categorical variables can either be responses or factors so, for the three-way table, we must distinguish between:

(a) each of A, B, and C a response;
(b) one factor and two responses;
(c) one response and two factors.

(A model in which all of A, B, and C are factors is not sensible.)

The final model will be influenced by whether situations (a), (b), or (c) apply. If situations (a) or (b) hold, then it will be usual for a model to include λ, λ_i^A, λ_j^B, λ_k^C so that the margins of the three variables are fixed. If (c) holds, and if A and B are factors, then any model must also include λ_{ij}^{AB} because this association is fixed by design and is not of any interest.

As it stands, the model (A6.5) will fit any three-way table exactly and is therefore known as a saturated model. Clearly the aim of any analysis is to try to produce a simplified version of (A6.5). However, the form of any unsaturated model will be determined by the design of the study (i.e. (a), (b), or (c) above) and by the hierarchy principle. The hierarchy principle states that if an interaction containing particular variables is included in the model then all lower-order interactions and main effects containing those variables must also be included. In other words, if λ_{ijk}^{ABC} is included in equation (A6.5) then all other terms must also be included.

Suppose, in situation (c), that the response has just two categories. Then equation (A6.5) can be transformed from a log-linear model to a logit model:

$$\log \frac{\hat{n}_{ij1}}{\hat{n}_{ij2}} = \lambda + \lambda_i^A + \lambda_j^B + \lambda_1^C + \lambda_{ij}^{AB} + \lambda_{i1}^{AC} + \lambda_{j1}^{BC} + \lambda_{ij1}^{ABC}$$

$$- \lambda - \lambda_i^A - \lambda_j^B - \lambda_2^C - \lambda_{ij}^{AB} - \lambda_{i2}^{AC} - \lambda_{j2}^{BC} - \lambda_{ij2}^{ABC}$$

$$= \lambda_1^C + \lambda_{i1}^{AC} + \lambda_{j1}^{BC} + \lambda_{ij1}^{ABC} \tag{A6.6a}$$

or

$$= 2\lambda_1^C + 2\lambda_{i1}^{AC} + 2\lambda_{j1}^{BC} + 2\lambda_{ij1}^{ABC} \tag{A6.6b}$$

Equation (A6.6a) applies for the set of constraints labelled 'A' and equation (A6.6b) for constraints 'B'. These two equations are each equivalent to equation (6.6).

Let us now consider the situation described in Section 6.6. We have a polytomous response C $(K > 2)$ which is ordered and one ordered factor, B $(J > 2)$, and one unordered factor, A $(I > 2)$. Suppose scores α_j and β_k are allocated to the categories of B and C such that $\sum_j \alpha_j = \sum_k \beta_k = 0$. Then equation (A6.5) can be expressed as

$$\log \hat{n}_{ijk} = \lambda + \lambda_i^A + \lambda_j^B + \lambda_k^C + \lambda_{ij}^{AB} + \beta_k \lambda_i^{AC} + \alpha_j \beta_k \lambda^{BC} + \lambda_{ijk}^{ABC} \tag{A6.7}$$

Equation (A6.7) is not in fact a hierarchical model, but if λ_{ijk}^{ABC} is unimportant (see below) then λ_i^{AC} represents the linear component of the AC interaction and λ^{BC} represents the 'linear by linear' component of the BC interaction. It is possible to break down the AB interaction into linear and non-linear components, but this is not sensible when A and B are both factors. Further details of these kinds of models are given by Fienberg (1980).

The most usual ways of writing log-linear models have been given here, but other, essentially equivalent, formulations are possible—see, for example, Grizzle, Starmer, and Koch (1969).

Having written down an appropriate model, a method is needed to estimate the parameters and to test hypotheses about these parameters. It is usually assumed that each cell in a multi-way table has an independent Poisson distribution with the expected cell counts as the parameters of these distributions; or that, within each factor combination, the response (or responses) follow a multinomial distribution. In fact, these two assumptions are essentially the same. (Remember, however, that they are assumptions and they may be invalid, particularly if the data are collected using a complex sample design with stratification and clustering.)

Probably the most popular way of estimating the parameters in equations (A6.5), (A6.6), and (A6.7) is to use iterative maximum likelihood (ML) and numerical methods for doing this are built into the computer programs GLIM (Baker and Nelder, 1978), ECTA (Goodman and Fay, 1973) and BMDP3F (Dixon and Brown, 1979). Note that GLIM uses the first set of constraints given earlier (i.e. 'A'), whereas the other two programs use the second set ('B'). An alternative approach to estimation is to use non-iterative weighted least squares (WLS) as built into GENCAT. (Kershner and Chao, 1976, compare GENCAT with some ML programs.) The two approaches are equivalent for very large samples, but ML is generally to be preferred (although WLS has to be used for unconditional analyses as ML methods have yet to be developed for them, or for complex sampling schemes).

The fit of the model of interest can be assessed with the likelihood ratio test statistic if ML is used which, for large samples, has a χ^2 distribution. It is often known as the 'deviance' (Nelder and Wedderburn, 1972). The deviance has a convenient additive property so that it is possible to assess not only the adequacy of the fitted model but also the contribution to the fit of the last term or group of terms fitted. This method of assessing fit is, of course, the same as the one described in Appendix 5.2 for LISREL-type models. Goodness of fit statistics from the WLS approach are based on Pearson's chi-square statistic and there is some evidence (Larntz, 1978) that this is better than the likelihood ratio test statistic for small expected values. On the other hand, the Pearson statistic does not have the convenient additive property possessed by the deviance.

This appendix has provided a necessarily brief and deliberately non-rigorous guide to log-linear models. Readers wishing to put flesh on to these bare bones should consult one of the specialist books in the area—for example, Bishop, Fienberg, and Holland (1975), Everitt (1977), and Fienberg (1980).

CHAPTER 7

Models for Change when the Data are Categorical (2)

7.1 INTRODUCTION

In this chapter we return to the issues that were first raised in Chapter 4. There ways were presented of estimating causal models both for situations where the causal direction is known and where it has to be determined, if possible, from the data. All the models in that chapter deal with variables measured on interval scales. Here we are concerned with the same kinds of questions and models, but this time applied to categorical data. And so, in Sections 7.2 and 7.3, a number of ways of estimating the strength of a known causal relationship are presented. This is followed, in Section 7.4, by a short discussion of the kinds of models that might be considered when the causal direction is unknown, with one approach given in detail. (Another approach can be found in Chapter 9.) The ideas are presented very much in terms of examples and I have striven for detailed explanations of the meaning of the results because the notion of cause presents a few new problems when the data are categorical. Again, however, readers will find this chapter easier after acquiring a basic understanding of log-linear and logistic models.

7.2 PROPORTIONAL AND RELATIVE ODDS MODELS FOR KNOWN CAUSAL DIRECTION

In Chapter 4 we looked at the strength of a presumed causal relationship between worries and mental health in mothers with pre-school children. We do the same here, but with the variables representing worries and mental health dichotomized so that mothers either are or are not worried and have either good or poor mental health. Table 7.1 shows that the two variables are indeed associated, both at

Table 7.1 Worries and mental health: cross-sectional relationships

(a) Occasion 1				(b) Occasion 2			
MH Worries	Good	Poor	Total	MH Worries	Good	Poor	Total
No	77	17	94	No	83	8	91
Yes	45	56	101	Yes	54	50	104
Total	122	73	195	Total	137	58	195

occasion 1 (Table 7.1a) when the cross-product ratio is 5.64, and at occasion 2 (Table 7.1b) when it is 9.61.

These cross-product ratios are equivalent to the relative odds of having poor mental health when the mother is worried compared with when she is not (i.e. (56/45)/(17/77) at occasion 1 and (50/54)/(8/83) at occasion 2). Also the logs of the cross-product ratios ($= \lambda$) are equivalent to the difference in the logits for the two categories of worry:

$$\lambda = \text{logit } p_2 - \text{logit } p_1 \tag{7.1}$$

where p_i is the proportion of mothers in poor mental health in worry category i ($i = 1, 2$) and

$$\text{logit } p_i = \log \frac{p_i}{1 - p_i}$$

But these associations cannot of course be given a causal interpretation; it is likely that there are other variables associated both with worries and with mental health which, if they were included in a model, would have the effect of reducing or even eliminating the cross-sectional association. One way of dealing with this problem for interval scale data is to eliminate the effects of constant background variables by taking differences between occasion 2 and occasion 1 scores for the dependent and explanatory variables and estimating a regression model on the difference scores (i.e. equations (4.4) and (4.5)). It is not possible to reproduce these models with dichotomous data, but it is possible to construct models which share some of the characteristics of equations (4.4) and (4.5).

One such model can be created from the composite variables suggested in Chapter 2 (Section 2.10) and in Chapter 6 (Section 6.3). These variables have three categories: 'no change', a category representing 'improvement', and a category representing 'deterioration'. This produces Table 7.2 for these data.

Table 7.2 Change in mental health by change in worries

Worries \ MH	Improvement (1)	No change (2)	Deterioration (3)	Total
Improvement	11	17	1	29
No change	14	108	12	134
Deterioration	6	23	3	32
Total	31	148	16	195

The mental health composite is the response, which can reasonably be regarded as ordered, and the worries composite is the factor, or explanatory variable. Suppose the ordering is best exploited by a proportional odds model (see Section 6.5); then the basic data are given in Table 7.3.

Table 7.3 Proportional odds from Table 7.2

Worries	$\log\dfrac{p_1}{p_2 + p_3}$	$\log\dfrac{p_1 + p_2}{p_3}$
Improvement	-0.49	3.33
No change	-2.12	2.32
Deterioration	-1.47	2.27

The model underlying Table 7.3 is

$$\log\frac{p_{1k}}{p_{2k} + p_{3k}} = \alpha_1 + \beta_{1k} \tag{7.2a}$$

$$\log\frac{p_{1k} + p_{2k}}{p_{3k}} = \alpha_2 + \beta_{2k} \tag{7.2b}$$

where P_{jk} are expected probabilities in category j of mental health and category k of worries ($\sum_j P_{jk} = 1$), α_1 and α_2 are means, and β_{1k} and β_{2k} ($k = 1, 2$) represent the effects of improvement and no change in worries compared with a deterioration ($\beta_{13} = \beta_{23} = 0$). The dependent variable in equation (7.2a) is the log of the expected odds of mental health getting better, while the dependent variable in equation (7.2b) is minus the log of the expected odds of mental health getting worse. As in Chapter 6, we would hope that the use of proportional odds would produce parsimony in the sense that $\beta_{1k} = \beta_{2k}$. This is in fact the case with these data where the test statistic for the equality of β_{11} and β_{21}, and β_{12} and β_{22} jointly is 1.02 with 2 df ($p > 0.6$). The estimated means of the two proportional odds are -1.40 (s.e. $= 1.22$) and 2.84 (s.e. $= 0.30$) which confirms something than can be seen from the last row of Table 7.2—overall improvement in mental health is more likely than deterioration. The estimates of β_k show that the odds of mental health getting worse are three times as high if the mother becomes worried compared with becoming unworried (and so the odds of an improvement in mental health in this situation are one-third as high). They also show that the odds of worsening health are about two-thirds as high if the mother becomes worried compared with no change (and so the corresponding odds of getting better are 1.5).

It is not possible to use $p_2 - p_1$ as a dependent variable for data of this kind in the way that $y_2 - y_1$ was used before. (But $p_2 - p_1$ could be used when the dependent variable is binary and the explanatory variable is continuous.) However, an analogous measure is the relative odds of being in poor (or good) mental health at the two occasions:

$$\frac{p_2/(1 - p_2)}{p_1/(1 - p_1)}$$

where p_t ($t = 1, 2$) is the probability of being in poor mental health at occasion t. Again it is not possible sensibly to relate the relative odds of being in poor mental health to the relative odds of being worried, but it is possible to relate the relative odds (preferably the log of the relative odds) to worries at occasion 1 and occasion 2 separately. The model is

$$\log\left[\frac{P_{2ij}/(1 - P_{2ij})}{P_{1ij}/(1 - P_{1ij})}\right] = \kappa + \delta_1 + \theta_1 \qquad (7.3)$$

where the dependent variable is now the log of the expected relative odds of being in poor mental health at occasion 2 compared with occasion 1, in category i of worries at occasion 1 and category j of worries at occasion 2. The overall mean of these four relative odds is κ, δ_1 is the effect of being worried at occasion 1 ($\delta_2 = 0$), and θ_1 is the effect of being worried at occasion 2 for fixed values of the worry variable at time 1 ($\theta_2 = 0$). It is θ_1 which is the term of interest as it represents the effect of a change in the explanatory dichotomous variable on the dependent dichotomous variable. However, θ_1 can only be interpreted in this way if equation (7.3) gives a satisfactory fit to the data; in other words, there should be no important effect on the log of the relative odds, of the interaction between the explanatory variable at occasions 1 and 2. If there were an interaction then we would have a similar situation to the one in equation (4.6) when the effect of a change in x varies according to the initial value of x.

The complete data for the two occasions are given in Table 7.4. From them, it is possible to calculate the four values of the dependent variable in equation (7.3), and these are given in Table 7.5. The relative odds in Table 7.5 are calculated from the marginal distributions of the four tables linking mental health at the two occasions.

It is possible to estimate equation (7.3) using weighted least squares with the program GENCAT. The model without the interaction fits well ($X^2 = 1.68$, 1 df,

Table 7.4 Mental health and worries: raw data

Mental health, Occasion 1		Good				Poor			
Worries, Occasion 1		No		Yes		No		Yes	
Worries, Occasion 2		No	Yes	No	Yes	No	Yes	No	Yes	Total
Mental	Good	53	20	13	20	6	6	11	8	137
health,	Poor	1	3	1	11	2	3	4	33	58
Occasion 2	Total	54	23	14	31	8	9	15	41	195

Table 7.5 Log relative odds from Table 7.4

	No worries, both occasions	Worries, occasion 1. No worries, occasion 2	No worries, occasion 1. Worries, occasion 2	Worries, both occasions
Log relative odds	− 1.07	− 1.64	− 0.53	0.17

$p < 0.20$). The estimate of κ is -0.71 (s.e. $= 0.24$), again indicating an overall decline over time in poor mental health. The estimate of δ_1 is 0.25 (s.e. $= 0.33$) and θ_1 is estimated to be 1.35 (s.e. $= 0.33$). So the relative odds of being in poor mental health at occasion 2 compared with occasion 1 are 3.86 times as high ($= e^{1.35}$) if the mother is worried at occasion 2 than if she is not worried and regardless of whether she was worried or not at occasion 1. This is a statistically significant finding ($X^2 = 8.22$, 1 df, $p < 0.01$). We see that the effect of *becoming* worried compared with staying unworried on a *change* in mental health is the same as the effect of *staying* worried compared with becoming unworried, and is less than the estimated effects of *being* worried on the *odds* of poor mental health at any one time. Alternatively, the effects of becoming worried (compared with staying unworried) and becoming unworried (compared with staying worried) are equal in magnitude and opposite in sign. But this would not be true if the interaction term were needed in equation (7.3).

There is a third model which is a hybrid of the first two. Equation (7.3) can be rewritten as

$$\log\left[\frac{P_{2k}/(1 - P_{2k})}{P_{1k}/(1 - P_{1k})} \right] = \alpha + \beta_k \tag{7.4}$$

This time the dependent variable is the log of the expected relative odds of being in poor mental health at occasion 2 compared with occasion 1 in category k of the composite worries variable in Table 7.2. Hence β_k ($k = 1, 2; \beta_3 = 0$) are the effects on the log of the relative odds, of an improvement compared with a deterioration in worries (β_1) and no change compared with deterioration (β_2).

The second and third columns of Table 7.5 are unchanged when estimating equation (7.4) but the first and fourth are combined to give a value for the log of the relative odds of -0.06. A test of the significance of the β_k terms gives a statistic, distributed as χ^2 with 2 df, of 8.26 ($p < 0.02$). The individual estimates show that the relative odds are three times as high if the mother becomes worried rather than unworried, but are only 0.63 times as high if the mother becomes worried compared with no change in worry status.

The results from the third analysis are very similar to those obtained from the first analysis. They are not entirely convincing: it is curious that the odds of a deterioration in mental health are higher when there is no change in worries status compared with a worsening. They suggest that it is not sensible to create a 'no change' category, because this category compresses two rather different situations—a period free from worry and a period of chronic worry. The second analysis, however, maintains the separation of the two no-change categories and the results are both clear cut and *a priori* reasonable.

7.3 LOGISTIC MODELS FOR KNOWN CAUSAL DIRECTION

Each of the models discussed in the previous section (i.e. equations (7.2), (7.3), and (7.4)) has the advantage of being specified dynamically. However, none of them share the strength of the differencing approach incorporated into equation (4.4) of eliminating the effects of constant background variables. The effects of these can only be eliminated with certainty here if they are included in the models, although it is reassuring to note that the longitudinal relationships are lower than the cross-sectional ones, suggesting that the dynamic models are freer from specification error. A disadvantage of these three models is that they do not extend easily to polytomous variables. There is not an easily interpretable extension of the relative odds and a single 'no change' category becomes even less plausible as the number of categories increases. It also becomes more difficult to order change categories as they were ordered in Table 7.2. An alternative approach is given by Goodman (1973) which is rather like equation (4.8) for continuous data, and which uses all the information in the 2^4 table linking the two variables on the two occasions (see Table 7.4).

Call the four variables W1, W2, H1, and H2. Then Figure 7.1 is a reasonable representation of the causal system—W1 and H1 are regarded as exogenous, W2 is determined only by W1, and H2 is determined by each of W1, H1, and W2. The effect of W2 on H2 for fixed values of W1 and H1 is the causal parameter of interest. Goodman shows that the parameters of the causal system can be estimated separately from two equations, one for the expected log odds (or logit)

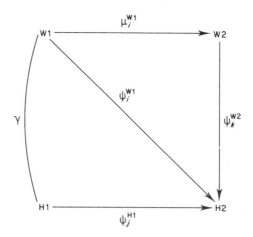

Figure 7.1 Causal diagram for a 2^4 table when the causal direction is known

of W2 related to W1 and one for the expected log odds of H2 related to W1, H1, and W2 as follows:

$$\log \frac{P_{ij1}}{P_{ij2}} = \mu + \mu_i^{W1} \tag{7.5a}$$

and

$$\log \frac{P_{ijk1}}{P_{ijk2}} = \psi + \psi_i^{W1} + \psi_j^{H1} + \psi_k^{W2} \tag{7.5b}$$

where i (the subscript for W1), j (the subscript for H1), and k (the subscript for W2) each take 2 values, and where μ_2^{W1}, ψ_2^{W1}, μ_2^{H1}, and ψ_2^{W2} are all zero. The parameters from these logistic models are shown in Figure 7.1. Note that γ in Figure 7.1 may be estimated from the 2×2 table after collapsing over W2 and H2 (i.e. Table 7.1(a)) but it has no causal significance.

The goodness of fit of equations (7.5) can be calculated in the usual way (see Appendix 6.1). If equation (7.5a) does not fit the data in the 2^3 table formed by W1, H1, and W2, then the assumption of the worries variable unambiguously causing the mental health variable becomes questionable because μ_j^{H1} and, perhaps, μ_{ij}^{W1H1} need to be included in the model. Also, if equation (7.5b) does not fit the 2^4 table, then some higher-order interactions such as ψ_{ij}^{W1H1} and ψ_{ijk}^{W1H1W2} need to be included. Goodman shows that the overall goodness of fit of the data to the system shown in Figure 7.1 is just the sum of the two separate goodness of fit statistics, and he also shows how to calculate the expected frequencies for the overall table. If some or all of W1, H1, W2, and H2 are polytomous then the method can easily be extended to deal with this, and more details of this generalization can be found in the next section.

When Table 7.4 is collapsed over H2, equation (7.5a) fits well ($X^2 = 3.38$, 2 df, $p > 0.18$) and equation (7.5b) fits the 4-way table ($X^2 = 2.37$, 4 df, $p > 0.5$) and so the overall goodness of fit is also satisfactory ($X^2 = 5.75$, 6 df, $p > 0.4$). The estimated parameters (from the program GLIM) are shown in Figure 7.2. The

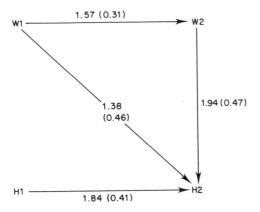

Figure 7.2 Coefficients for the relationship between worries and mental health (S.E. in brackets)

odds of a mother being in poor mental health at occasion 2 are seven times as high (i.e. $e^{1.94}$) if she is worried at occasion 2 regardless of her health and worries status at occasion 1. Although the *odds* of being in poor mental health when the mother is worried compared with when she is not do not vary with earlier positions on the health and worries variables, the *prevalences* of poor mental health are of course different. Only 5 % of mothers with good mental health and no worries at occasion 1 have poor mental health at occasion 2, whereas 66 % of mothers having poor mental health and worries at occasion 1 have poor mental health at occasion 2.

The results from this analysis have a slightly different interpretation from those given in the previous section. Here we have shown that the odds of poor mental health at occasion 2 are 7 times higher if the mother becomes worried rather than staying unworried, or if she stays worried rather than becoming unworried, regardless of her mental health at occasion 1. When we apply equation (7.3) to the same data, we show that the *relative* odds of poor mental health at occasion 2 compared with occasion 1 are 3.9 times as high for the same kinds of change in worries. (Both these estimates assume that the model has been adequately specified.) Models couched in terms of relative odds are perhaps more obviously related to change than is Goodman's model. However, Goodman's model does link better with established theory for log-linear models, it does use all the data, and it can be extended both to polytomous variables and, as we shall see, to situations where the causal direction is unknown.

7.4 MODELS FOR UNKNOWN CAUSAL DIRECTION

Let us now move on to the question of determining causal direction for dichotomous and polytomous variables measured on two occasions, that is categorical 2W2V data. As in the previous sections, the data can be represented as a 2^4, or sixteen-fold, table. The analysis of sixteen-fold tables has quite a history which goes back to work by Lazarsfeld in the early 1940s. Much of Lazarsfeld's early work was not published until 1972 (Lazarsfeld, 1972a, b) and two main strands can be distinguished in the developments which have followed his pioneering ideas. The first is the work of Coleman (1964b) and, more recently, of Singer and Spilerman (1976a, b), who have been interested in modelling dynamic processes using Markov-type models. They have looked not at a 2^4 table, but at a 4×4 table which gives all the transitions between the two occasions of measurement. This approach is described in more detail in Chapter 9. The other strand is best exemplified by Goodman's (1973) paper which considers not only recursive systems but also the equivalent of a non-recursive system when data are categorical rather than continuous. This strand can be seen as a more satisfactory alternative, from the statistical point of view, to the earlier work of Campbell (1963) because Goodman formulates the problem in terms of a statistical model, whereas Campbell focused on the comparison of the cross-lagged associations. We have already pointed out in Chapter 4 (Section 4.3), that cross-lagged associations can be misleading for continuous data, and this is equally true for categorical data.

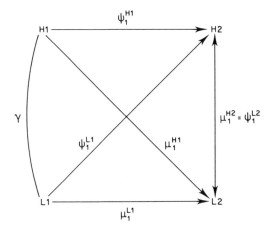

Figure 7.3 Causal diagram for a 2^4 table when the
causal direction is unknown

Let us illustrate how Goodman's non-recursive model works with a set of data
which is different from the one used in the previous two sections, but related to it.
Table 7.6 is a sixteen-fold table relating mental health (good/poor) and loneliness
(absent/present) on two occasions. We want to know whether mothers' mental
health is influenced by loneliness or whether it is the loneliness variable which
influences mental health. (The cross-product ratios at occasions 1 and 2 are 3.5
and 2.9.) The causal diagram corresponding to this admittedly simplistic question
is given in Figure 7.3. Goodman shows that relating the expected log odds (or
logit) of being lonely at occasion 2 to H1, L1, and H2, together with a model for
the expected log odds of being in poor mental health at occasion 2 related to H1,
L1, and L2, is in fact equivalent to a log-linear model for the table as a whole. In
other words, if the equations

$$\log \frac{P_{ijk1}}{P_{ijk2}} = \mu + \mu_i^{H1} + \mu_j^{L1} + \mu_k^{H2} \tag{7.6a}$$

which is the same as equation (7.5b), and

$$\log \frac{P_{ij1l}}{P_{ij2l}} = \psi + \psi_i^{H1} + \psi_j^{L1} + \psi_l^{L2} \tag{7.6b}$$

where i, j, k and l each take two values, and where $\mu_2^{H1}, \psi_2^{H1}, \mu_2^{L1}$, etc., are all zero, are
simultaneously true, then they are equivalent to

$$\log P_{ijkl} = \lambda + \lambda_i^{H1} + \lambda_j^{L1} + \lambda_k^{H2} + \lambda_1^{L2} + \lambda_{ij}^{H1L1} + \lambda_{ik}^{H1H2}$$
$$+ \lambda_{il}^{H1L2} + \lambda_{jk}^{L1H2} + \lambda_{jl}^{L1L2} + \lambda_{kl}^{H2L2} \tag{7.7}$$

which is essentially the same kind of log-linear model as equation (A6.4) and it is
assumed that the first set of those constraints apply. (Note that μ_1^{H1} and ψ_1^{L1} can be
obtained directly from equation (7.7) but the formulation in equations (7.6)

Table 7.6 Mental health and loneliness: raw data (a)

Mental health, Occasion 1		Good				Poor				
Loneliness, Occasion 1		Absent		Present		Absent		Present		
Loneliness, Occasion 2		Absent	Present	Absent	Present	Absent	Present	Absent	Present	Total
Mental health, Occasion 2	Good	72	11	15	7	13	2	4	11	135
	Poor	8	2	2	4	11	7	8	12	54
	Total	80	13	17	11	24	9	12	23	189

emphasizes the asymmetries involved with L2 as the dependent variable in one model and H2 as the dependent variable in the other.

Thus, if it can be shown that a model like equation (7.7), which excludes all the second- and higher-order interactions, fits the data adequately, then the estimated parameters from equations (7.6) can be fitted on to Figure 7.3 as shown. (Note that γ in Figure 7.3 is again estimated from the 2×2 table after collapsing over L2 and H2.) If ψ_1^{L1}, say, is close to zero and μ_1^{H1} is importantly different from zero then one might reasonably conclude that the causal direction is from mental health to loneliness, and μ_1^{H1} tells us how the log odds of L2 change when health is poor at occasion 1 compared with when health is good. Alternatively, e^{μ_1} tells us how the actual odds of L2 are changed. However, if ψ_1^{L1} and μ_1^{H1} both differ from zero then causal conclusions will be more tentative, and if equation (7.7) is too simple a model for the data, so that higher-order interactions need to be included, then a causal interpretation of the data will usually be very difficult. (Rather than looking at ψ_1 and μ_1 separately, it is possible to test whether they are equal—see Duncan (1980). However, it is possible for both estimates to be small but to have opposite signs, and to reject the hypothesis that they are equal rather than accept the hypothesis that they are not different from zero could lead to a result which is difficult to interpret in causal terms.)

The fit of the model (7.7) to the data in Table 7.6 is good ($X^2 = 5.60$, 5 df, $p > 0.3$). The application of equations (7.6) to the data produces the estimates given on the causal diagram in Figure 7.4 with the usual test of $\mu_1^{H1} = 0$ giving $X^2 = 3.59$ (1 df, $p < 0.06$) and a test of $\psi_1^{L1} = 0$ giving $X^2 = 0.32$ (1 df, $p > 0.5$). Thus the evidence from this analysis seems just to favour the hypothesis that the causal direction is indeed from mental health to loneliness. The odds of a mother being lonely given that she was in poor mental health 12 months earlier are 2.1 times higher than if her mental health was good. On the other hand, the odds of being in poor mental health given that she was lonely 12 months earlier are only 1.3 times higher than if she were not lonely.

However, there is one problem with this approach. One cannot distinguish

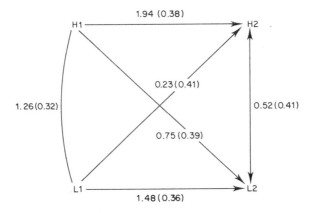

Figure 7.4 Coefficients for the relationship between
mental health and loneliness (s.e. in brackets)

between the 'simultaneous' effects H2 → L2 and L2 → H2 because they are both
measured by the same parameter in the log-linear model, i.e. λ_{kl}^{H2L2} in equation
(7.7). Thus, it is only by comparing the cross-lagged effects, μ_1^{H1} and ψ_1^{L1}, that one
might determine causal direction, and this is restrictive if the time between
measurements is not reasonably close to the causal lag. This restriction did not, of
course, apply when an identified non-recursive system was estimated with
continuous data. There is no reason for the H2 → L2 and L2 → H2 effects to be
the same, but it is difficult to see how to specify a sensible model for the cell
probabilities that would separate them. One way of identifying the simultaneous
effects with continuous data is to introduce two (or more) exogeneous variables,
one related only to L2 and the other only to H2, but this does not resolve the issue
when the data are categorical.

The analysis presented so far is deficient in that we know that there are
background variables related both to mental health and to loneliness which ought
to be included for the model to be properly specified. Unfortunately, the sample is
too small to allow the inclusion of more than one of these background variables.
However, it was possible to include marital status (MS) and so to work with a 2^5
table, although even this table has many small cells and so the analysis is not very
powerful. The inclusion of marital status means that the dependent variable in
equation (7.6a) is now log P_{hijk1}/P_{hijk2} and the right-hand side includes an extra
term, μ_h^{MS}. Similarly, the dependent variable in equation (7.6b) is log P_{hij11}/P_{hij2l}
and the right-hand side includes ψ_h^{MS}. The corresponding log-linear model is:

$$
\begin{aligned}
\log P_{hijkl} = {} & \lambda + \lambda_h^{MS} + \lambda_i^H + \lambda_j^{L1} + \lambda_k^{H2} + \lambda_l^{L2} \\
& + \lambda_{hi}^{MSH1} + \lambda_{hj}^{MSL1} + \lambda_{hk}^{MSH2} + \lambda_{hl}^{MSL2} \\
& + \lambda_{ij}^{H1L1} + \lambda_{ik}^{H1H2} + \lambda_{il}^{H1L2} + \lambda_{jk}^{L1H2} \\
& + \lambda_{jl}^{L1L2} + \lambda_{kl}^{H2L2} + \lambda_{hij}^{MSH1L1}
\end{aligned}
\tag{7.8}
$$

which just extends equation (7.7) in an obvious way but does include λ_{hij}^{MSH1L1}

which is the second-order interaction between the exogeneous variables. Equation (7.8) fits the enlarged table well and Figure 7.5 gives the amended causal diagram. Figure 7.5 shows that the effect of H1 on L2 is reduced with the odds down from 2.1 to 1.9 and a test of $\mu_1^{H1} = 0$ giving $X^2 = 2.63$ (1 df, $p > 0.1$), but the effect of L1 on H2 is unchanged. Thus, the conclusions from the analysis of the 2^4 table are made more tentative by the inclusion of marital status. (The coefficients for the paths linking MS and H1 and MS and L1 are obtained from the 2×2 tables having collapsed over all other variables, but the coefficient for the path linking H1 and L1 is obtained after controlling for MS.)

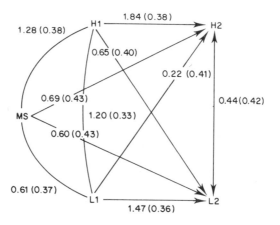

Figure 7.5 As Figure 7.4 but including marital status

Originally, both mental health and loneliness were measured on 4-point scales, but the data are too sparse to fit models to the 256 cells of a 4^4 or even to the 81 cells of a 3^4 table. However, there were just enough data to look at a $3 \times 3 \times 2 \times 2$ table with mental health measured with three categories, and loneliness staying as a dichotomy. These data are given in Table 7.7. With H2 having three categories, equation (7.6b) has to be extended to allow for this, and can be thought of as two models, one which takes $\log P_{ij1l}/P_{ij3l}$ as dependent and the other taking $\log P_{ij2l}/P_{ij3l}$ as dependent (i.e. the multivariate logit first introduced in equation (6.7)). The three models taken together are equivalent to equation (7.7). Some of the 'paths' in Figure 7.3 must now be represented by more than one parameter; the H2 → L2, H1 → L2, and L1 → H2 paths have two, while the H1 → H2 path has four, with just the L1 → L2 path remaining with one. Thus, one has to contrast two sets of coefficients in order to make any causal inferences from data represented by a table with more than 16 cells. This is clearly more difficult unless both (or all) members of one set are smaller than the two or more members of the other set.

The simple model, equation (7.7), still fits Table 7.7 well ($X^2 = 20.1$, 16 df,

Table 7.7 Mental health and loneliness: raw data (b)

Mental health, Occasion 1		Good				Moderate				Poor				
Loneliness, Occasion 1		Absent		Present		Absent		Present		Absent		Present		
														Total
Loneliness, Occasion 2		Abs	Pres	Abs	Pres	Abs	Pres	Abs	Pres	Abs	Pres	Abs	Pres	
Mental Health, Occasion 2	Good	34	3	7	1	13	3	4	3	7	2	1	2	80
	Moderate	13	1	2	1	12	4	2	2	6	0	3	9	55
	Poor	2	0	1	3	6	2	1	1	11	7	8	12	54
	Total	49	4	10	5	31	9	7	6	24	9	12	23	189

$p > 0.2$). A test of whether the effect of H1 on L2 is zero gives a test statistic of 6.06 (2 df, $p < 0.05$) and the test of whether L1 → H2 effect is zero gives $X^2 = 0.90$ (2 df, $p > 0.5$) so the evidence again favours a causal link which goes from mental health to loneliness. The coefficients are given in Figure 7.6 and we see that both H1 → L2 coefficients are higher than the L1 → H2 values.

The coefficients in Figure 7.6 do not have a straightforward interpretation. However, the three categories of the mental health variable are ordered and an analysis which takes account of this might lead to more easily interpretable

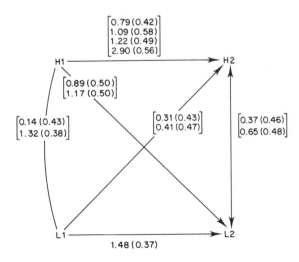

Figure 7.6 As Figure 7.4 but with mental health measured in three categories

results. One way of doing this is to allocate scores to the categories of the polytomous variables (as in Section 6.6) and to see whether the data can be represented by 'linear by linear' components of the various interaction terms.

Suppose in general that scores $\alpha_i, \beta_j, \gamma_k$, and δ_l are allocated to variables A, B, C, and D with $\sum \alpha_i = \sum \beta_j = \sum \gamma_k = \sum \delta_l = 0$ as in equation (A6.7). Then the general version of equation (7.7) is

$$\log P_{ijkl} = \lambda + \lambda_i^A + \lambda_j^B + \lambda_k^C + \lambda_l^D + \lambda_{ij}^{AB} + \alpha_i \gamma_k \lambda_L^{AC} + \alpha_i \delta_l \lambda_L^{AD}$$
$$+ \beta_j \gamma_k \lambda_L^{BC} + \beta_j \delta_l \lambda_L^{BD} + \gamma_k \delta_l \lambda_L^{CD} \qquad (7.9)$$

where L signifies the linear by linear component of the interaction (the main effects and λ_{ij}^{AB} could be partitioned but are not interesting). Then it can be shown that, for the $3 \times 3 \times 2 \times 2$ case, with α_i and γ_k taking the values $-1, 0, 1$, and β_j and δ_1 taking the values -0.5 and 0.5,

$$\log \frac{P_{ijk1}}{P_{ijk2}} = \lambda_1^{L2} - \alpha_i \lambda_L^{H1L2} - \beta_j \lambda_L^{L1L2} - \gamma_k \lambda_L^{H2L2} \qquad (7.10a)$$

$$\log \frac{P_{ij1l}}{P_{ij3l}} = \lambda_1^{H2} - 2\alpha_i \lambda_L^{H1H2} - 2\beta_j \lambda_L^{L1H2} - 2\delta_l \lambda_L^{H2L2} \qquad (7.10b)$$

$$\log \frac{P_{ij2l}}{P_{ij3l}} = \lambda_2^{H2} - \alpha_i \lambda_L^{H1H2} - \beta_j \lambda_L^{L1H2} - \delta_l \lambda_L^{H2L2} \qquad (7.10c)$$

Thus, it is still not possible to separate the H2 → L2 and L2 → H2 effects. Model (7.9) fits Table 7.7 well ($X^2 = 22.4$, 22 df, $p > 0.4$) and so a test of all the non-linear parts of the interactions (obtained from the comparison of the fits of equations (7.7) and (7.9)) gives a test statistic of 2.3 $(22.4 - 20.1)$ (6 df, $p > 0.5$). A test of $\lambda_L^{H1L2} = 0$ gives $X^2 = 5.51$ (1 df, $p < 0.02$) and a test of $\lambda_L^{L1H2} = 0$ gives $X^2 = 1.02$ (1 df, $p > 0.3$) and the 'linear' coefficients are shown in Figure 7.7. The odds of

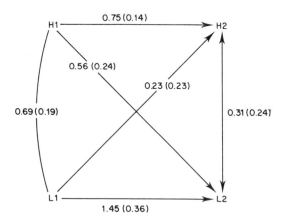

Figure 7.7 As Figure 7.6 but estimating only 'linear' effects

being lonely at occasion 2 are 1.75 (i.e. $e^{0.56}$) times as high for adjacent categories of H1 but are 3.1 (i.e. $e^{1.12}$) times as high when health at occasion 1 is poor than when it is good. The scoring system adopted here is the simplest and others are possible, although any scoring system is arbitrary. One might prefer to take account of ordering by using proportional odds or continuation odds as described in the previous chapter. Unfortunately, these models cannot be related to the underlying log-linear model in the same way and it is therefore difficult to see how to take account of the simultaneity in the system.

There are other ways of analysing these data. For example, it could be argued that the mental health and loneliness variables are just indicators of an underlying variable which one might ingenuously call 'satisfaction'. One would then look for ways of combining them into a single scale, perhaps to measure the stability of this scale rather as the three tests were combined to form a scale of language ability in Chapter 5.

Let us end this section by looking at Table 7.8 which relates mental health to physical health (PH) at two occasions. For these data, equation (7.7) does not fit well ($X^2 = 11.2$, 5 df, $p < 0.05$); a comparison of the cross-lagged effects suggests that only the relationship between physical health at occasion 1 and mental health at occasion 2 is important ($\psi_1^{PH1} = 0.91$, $\mu_1^{H1} = 0.05$) but this is misleading as that effect is changed both by mental health at occasion 1 and by physical health at occasion 2. It is only by testing whether equation (7.7) fits all the data that misleading inferences can be avoided; a simple comparison of the cross-lagged correlations would have indicated, mistakenly, that poor physical health leads unambiguously to poor mental health.

Table 7.8 Mental health and physical health: raw data

Mental health, Occasion 1		Good			Poor				
Physical health, Occasion 1		Good	Poor		Good		Poor		Total
Physical health, Occasion 2		Good	Poor	Good	Poor	Good	Poor	Good	Poor
Mental	Good	80	9	10	7	16	2	10	3	137
health,	Poor	2	5	6	3	10	7	9	14	56
Occasion 2	Total	82	14	16	10	26	9	19	17	193

In Sections 7.2 and 7.3, we have seen how the odds, and the relative odds, of poor mental health are affected by changes in worries. In this section we have shown that the evidence favours a causal link from mental health to loneliness rather than the other way round. However, because the H2 → L2 and L2 → H2 parameters cannot be estimated separately, we should talk less about *change* in mental health affecting the odds of being lonely and more about the *presence* of poor mental health at occasion 1 increasing the odds of being lonely at occasion 2, and the presence of good mental health at occasion 1 lowering the odds of being lonely at occasion 2.

There is a symmetry when using log-linear models in the causal analysis of categorical data just as there is in the corresponding regression models for interval data. The models described in Chapter 4 assume that if the causal link is from x to y then, providing there are no interactions, a unit increase in x and a unit decrease in x produce equal and opposite effects on y. Here, again providing there are no interactions, the acquisition of a condition compared with its continued absence has an equal and opposite effect on the response to the loss of a condition compared with its continued presence. However, it is possible to get a more disaggregated picture of the causal mechanisms involved when the data are dichotomous, as we shall see in Chapter 9.

7.5 SUMMARY

This chapter deals with a similar range of issues as in Chapter 4, but for categorical rather than for continuous data. The problems which stand in the way of making sound causal inferences from non-experimental categorical data are also familiar: model specification, or the problem of omitted variables, and causal lag, or the problem of how causal inferences manifest themselves over time, are the most marked. But categorical data do present additional difficulties. There are a number of ways of formulating the model, particularly the response variable, when the causal direction is known and these are described in Sections 7.2 and 7.3. And when the causal direction is unknown (Section 7.4), it is not possible to solve the identification problem if the variables at occasion 2 are allowed to influence each other, at least not in the same way as it was for continuous data. The interpretation of results from causal models tends to be more long-winded when the data are categorical.

CHAPTER 8

Models for Data Collected on Three or More Occasions

8.1 INTRODUCTION

All the models up to now have been presented in terms of measurements collected about just two occasions. But, for many people, the essence of an analysis of change comes with the collection of data about several occasions. It was argued earlier that if a satisfactory description of change and a satisfactory model for the analysis of change can be found for two occasions, then extensions to three or more occasions will not produce serious extra problems. The purpose of this chapter is to show just how the models of Chapters 3 to 7 can be extended. Chapter 9 presents different kinds of models for data collected on several occasions.

First, however, let us see how the definition of individual change given in Chapter 2 (equation (2.2)) extends to more than two occasions. The advantage of data on several occasions is that, rather than just using differences, individual change can be modelled as follows:

$$x_t = \alpha + \beta t + \gamma t^2 + \delta t^3 + \ldots \tag{8.1}$$

where x_t is the value for an individual on variable x at time t and $\alpha, \beta, \gamma, \delta, \ldots$ are parameters to be estimated. The complexity of equation (8.1) will depend on the number of measurement occasions; a quadratic relationship (i.e. terms up to t^2) will fit exactly for three occasions, a cubic relationship (terms up to t^3) will fit exactly for four occasions, etc. Ideally, one would hope that even with several measurement occasions, individual change could be represented adequately by a linear equation (as in Figure 1.1), so that only α and β had to be estimated. This general approach is most valuable for developmental change and, in a linear equation, β represents the growth rate. Also, values of β (and γ, δ, etc.) can be related to other characteristics of individuals such as social class.

Models like equation (8.1) have been explored in great detail for physical measures, particularly height, and Goldstein (1979a) gives a comprehensive review. However, the problems of the unconditional model for individual change for two occasions, which were discussed in Chapter 2, are exacerbated by extensions to three or more occasions. In particular, the interpretation of equation (8.1) would seem crucially to depend on the assumption that the same underlying variable is being measured at each occasion, which was discussed in terms of operationalization in Chapter 2 (Section 2.3). There would seem to be few situations in the social sciences for which such models are appropriate, apart perhaps from certain experimental situations in psychology when the interval between measurements is very small, as in Anderson and Plewis (1977).

It is true that Hindley and Owen (1979) estimate polynomial models for each member of a study whose IQs were measured on up to eight occasions, but the results are not easy to interpret. Bock (1963) uses a time-related or unconditional model to analyse relative change in tests of educational attainment, but he does not consider how his strategy of standardizing to constant within-group-occasion variance affects his results.

It is, of course, possible to estimate a polynomial model like equation (8.1) for each individual only with longitudinal data. However, if different cross-sections are measured at each occasion, polynomial curves can be fitted to the occasion means (i.e. $\bar{x}_t$) rather than to the individual values (x_t) to give a description of aggregate change. But we know from Figure 1.4 that this description can hide more than it reveals.

8.2 UNCONDITIONAL MODELS FOR RELATIVE CHANGE

It was pointed out in Chapter 3 that an unconditional model for relative change was equivalent to a two-way analysis of variance with repeated measures, although such an analysis was not strictly necessary for data for just two occasions. Now consider a study consisting of K groups, each with independent samples of n individuals. Suppose that each of the Kn individuals are measured on $T\,(> 2)$ equally spaced occasions and that the dependent variable is measured on an interval scale. Suppose also that the researcher wants to know whether one group changes more than another or, putting this another way, whether there is an interaction between group and occasion or time. Studies of this type are commonly analysed using the method given by, for example, Winer (1971, Ch. 7). The variance is partitioned into 'between subjects' and 'within subjects' components and there are therefore two error terms. The first of these, the 'between subjects' term, is used to test for differences between the groups and the other, the 'within subjects' term, is used to test the effect of time and the interaction between group and time. The resulting analysis of variance (ANOVA) table looks like Table 8.1.

However, the F-tests for the two within-subjects effects are only valid if, in addition to the usual assumptions needed for ANOVA, the within-group variances of the dependent variable are constant across occasions and if the correlations between measures are constant for all pairs of occasions. The second of these two conditions is rarely satisfied; much more likely is a pattern of decreasing correlations as the time between measurements increases. One solution to this problem, given by Winer, is to adjust the degrees of freedom for the F-tests, so instead of the F-test for the interaction having $(K-1)\,(T-1)$ and $K(n-1)\,(T-1)$ df, it has $(K-1)$ and $K(n-1)$ df. However, this adjustment will often result in tests which are too 'conservative' in the sense that the true significance level will be lower than the nominal level.

A more satisfactory solution is to change from a univariate to a multivariate

Table 8.1 ANOVA table for repeated measures experiments

Source of variation	df	Mean square	F
Between subjects			
Group	$K-1$	a	a/b
Error 1	$K(n-1)$	b	
Within subjects			
Time	$T-1$	c	c/e
Group. Time	$(K-1)(T-1)$	d	d/e
Error 2	$K(n-1)(T-1)$	e	

mode of analysis and so to treat the T measures for each individual on the dependent variable as a multivariate set (Bock, 1975). This approach to testing the within-subjects effects assumes that the samples from the groups come from K multivariate normal distributions each having the same variances and covariances. But it does not impose any conditions on the pattern of within-group correlations between occasions.

Both the univariate and the multivariate tests of the group–time interaction test only whether the time curves for the groups are parallel, but they do not give any information about the form of the curves. For example, do straight lines with different slopes account for the variation in the dependent variable over the T occasions or is the relationship curvilinear for one group but not for another? This extra information can be obtained by partitioning a statistically significant interaction into components, using either orthogonal or ordinary polynomials to describe the relationship with time. (Cohen and Cohen, 1975, describe how to apply polynomial regression with and without orthogonal polynomials. Orthogonal polynomials are convenient for assessing the shape of the relationship (whether it is linear, quadratic, cubic, etc.) and have computational advantages, but the coefficients from ordinary polynomials are easier to interpret.)

Often, the variation over time can be adequately modelled with just a straight line. In this case, the interaction can be characterized by the following equation:

$$x = \gamma + \delta_i t \qquad (8.2)$$

where x is the dependent variable, t is time, and δ_i ($i = 1, 2, \ldots, K$) gives the slope of the straight line relating x to t for group i. If there were no group–time interaction, then δ_i would not vary from group to group and if there were no time effect then $\delta_i = 0$. The constant term, γ, would vary from group to group if there is a group effect.

8.3 AN EXAMPLE

Let us turn now to the EPA study data first introduced in Chapter 3 (Section 3.9). The children in the study were tested with the English Picture Vocabulary Test

(EPVT) on each of five occasions. The pre-school version of the test was used for the first two occasions, and version 1 was used for occasions 3, 4, and 5, and both raw and standardized test scores were available for analysis. It would not be sensible to apply an ANOVA-type model to all the raw scores because the scale changes after the second occasion, and this change of scale would also make an analysis of the standard scores rather difficult to interpret. However, because 19 children were given both versions of the test at occasion 2, the relationship between the raw scores on the two versions can be characterized well by:

$$EPVT_1 = -3.73 + 0.50 \, EPVT_{ps} \tag{8.3}$$

Assuming that equation (8.3) applies to all the sample both at occasion 2 and at occasion 1, it is possible to estimate a raw score on version 1 of the test whenever the pre-school version was used. Some of the estimated values are negative but as the scale is arbitrary, this does not matter. Table 8.2 gives the occasion means and standard deviations for the three groups. A seemingly obvious question to ask of these data is whether the experimental groups changed more, or 'grew' faster, than the control group over time. This question does, of course, assume that there is no dispute about what is growing.

Table 8.2 Raw scores on EPVT 1: means and standard deviations

Group	Occasion 1	2	3	4	5
C	4.3	6.9	12.3	17.2	19.9
(n = 15)	(4.2)	(5.2)	(6.2)	(6.6)	(7.3)
E1	1.2	6.4	10.4	16.3	21.5
(n = 15)	(1.1)	(3.8)	(4.0)	(5.2)	(4.3)
E2	0.3	4.5	11.8	15.9	21.4
(n = 15)	(2.5)	(3.6)	(3.6)	(5.9)	(4.1)

There are no significant differences between the groups when averaged over the five occasions ($F_{2,42} = 0.47$, $p > 0.6$). The within-subjects effects were analysed by transforming the dependent variables to orthogonal polynomials and then using multivariate analysis of variance. The main effect of time is highly significant ($F_{4,39} = 187.0$, $p < 0.001$) but there is also a significant group–time interaction with an F-statistic of 2.69 with 8 and 80 df ($p < 0.02$). It is clear from the univariate test statistics that nearly all the group–time interaction is accounted for by the linear orthogonal polynomial and so the analysis was carried out again using an ordinary linear transformation (see Goldstein, 1979a, Appendix 4.1, for details). The resulting coefficients—δ_i in equation (8.2)—were 0.36 for the control group and 0.45 and 0.47 for the two experimental groups (see Figure 8.1). One would therefore conclude from this analysis that the experimental groups show a similar growth pattern in the abilities measured by the EPVT

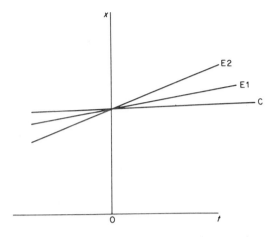

Figure 8.1 EPA study: growth rates for the three
groups

over the four years of the study and one which is indeed different from the control group.

It has not been possible to go into some of the statistically more complex aspects of this method of analysis here, and interested readers are referred to Goldstein (1979a), Guire and Kowalski (1979), and Bock (1979) for these. However, those who have read Chapter 3 might realize that this method is not well suited to these data, and a more appropriate analysis is presented in the next section.

8.4 CONDITIONAL MODELS FOR RELATIVE CHANGE

The conditional model for relative change can be written as a set of recursive equations (see Section 4.3) which, for three occasions and two groups, would be:

$$x_2 = \alpha_1 + \beta_1 x_0 + \gamma_1 x_1 + \varepsilon_1 \qquad (8.4a)$$

$$x_3 = \alpha_2 + \beta_2 x_0 + \gamma_2 x_2 + \gamma_3 x_1 + \varepsilon_2 \qquad (8.4b)$$

where x_0 is a '0–1' variable defining the two groups, and extensions to more than three occasions are obvious. If there are more than two groups then extra dummy variables have to be included, but the number of dummy variables must always be one less than the number of groups. Note that, for both equations, the within-group regressions are assumed to be the same for the two groups, although this is not necessary. If the two error terms, ε_1 and ε_2, are uncorrelated, and if the usual assumptions for ordinary least squares hold, then fully efficient estimates can be obtained by estimating each equation separately. For quasi-experiments, a causal interpretation can be given to β_1 and β_2 providing the models are properly specified. And β_1 is, of course, the parameter which would be estimated if there were just two occasions of measurement. Expectations about the sign and size of

β_2 will depend very much on the study design. For quasi-experiments with just a treatment and a control group, with the treatment withdrawn at the second occasion and with a positive initial treatment effect, β_1, then β_2 might be zero. This would show that the effect of the treatment had been maintained. A positive value of β_2 would show that the treatment had a further effect after its withdrawal which could be thought of as a kind of 'sleeper' effect. If β_2 is negative then one would conclude that at least some of the effect washes out as soon as the treatment is withdrawn; if x_3 is regressed against x_1 only and β_2 is zero, then all the effect washes out. For observational studies, one would usually expect β_1 and β_2 to have the same sign; Goldstein (1979c), for example, found this when he examined social class differences in educational attainment at age 11 for fixed 7-year scores and at age 16 for fixed 7- and 11-year scores.

Even with true experiments, a conditional model is needed to estimate additional treatment effects which occur after the second measurement occasion either from a continuing treatment or from one which had been withdrawn. On the other hand, providing attrition or loss is the same for both groups, one could be sure that conditioning on x_{t-1} would eliminate all the differences between the groups and so the estimate of the effect due to the treatment between occasions $t-1$ and t would be unbiased. This point is the same as the one made in Section 3.2 about the regression discontinuity design which assigns elements to treatment and control groups on the basis of a pre-treatment measure.

When conditional models are estimated from the EPA data, conclusions emerge which are rather different from those presented in the previous section. Four equations were estimated using the standard scores (Table 8.3), the first relating x_2 to x_1, x_{01}, and x_{02} (i.e. equation (8.4a)) but with two dummy variables because there are three groups, and the other three relating x_t to x_{t-1}, x_{t-2}, x_{01}, and x_{02} ($t = 3, 4, 5$). Even though the treatments were in operation only between occasions 1 and 2, there was no evidence of any difference between the groups at occasion 2 after controlling for x_1 ($F_{2,41} = 0.66$, $p > 0.5$). However, in the year after the treatment was withdrawn, there is some evidence of an effect ($F_{2,40} = 3.70$, $p < 0.04$) with all this effect concentrated in the second experimental group which gained 7.2 points more than the control group. There is again no

Table 8.3 EPVT standard scores: means and standard deviations

Group	Occasion 1	2	3	4	5
C	97.8 (11.4)	95.0 (12.3)	98.6 (14.8)	97.6 (13.0)	91.1 (12.8)
E1	92.8 (8.8)	95.8 (10.5)	98.9 (10.8)	98.9 (9.3)	96.1 (9.0)
E2	88.4 (10.2)	90.6 (11.0)	100.9 (9.8)	97.0 (11.4)	95.5 (7.0)

evidence for a group effect from the other two equations ($F_{2,40} = 0.17, p > 0.8$ and $F_{2,40} = 2.11, p > 0.13$ respectively). Both x_{t-1} and x_{t-2} make statistically significant contributions to the explanation of x_t when $t = 5$ but not when $t = 3$ and 4. Curiously, x_2 is a better predictor of x_4 than x_3 is. Other terms in x_{t-k} could, in theory, have been included, but were not necessary.

An alternative approach is to relate x_t to x_1, x_{01}, and x_{02} for $t = 2, 3, 4, 5$. Again, no convincing pattern emerges with a group effect only when $t = 5$, which is not easy to explain.

The results from the conditional analyses are given in Table 8.4. For each dependent variable, two sets are presented—the first set is uncorrected for measurement error and the second set is corrected for measurement error assuming that the error variance is 37 for these data just as it was for the other EPA study in Chapter 5.

A prudent person would conclude that there is little evidence for treatment effects from these analyses and certainly no evidence for an effect of the treatment applied to the first experimental group. This is in sharp contrast to the results from the unconditional analyses which provide apparently unequivocal evidence for faster growth in the two experimental groups. Of course, the conditional

Table 8.4 Conditional analysis: parameter estimates and standard errors

Dependent variable	Analysis	Treatment effects		Explanatory variables				R^2
		E1–C	E2–C	x_1	x_2	x_3	x_4	
x_2	Uncorrected	3.95 (3.40)	1.53 (3.62)	0.63 (0.13)	—	—	—	0.35
	Corrected	5.58 (3.67)	4.59 (3.81)	0.96 (0.22)	—	—	—	0.51
x_3	Uncorrected	−0.39 (2.89)	5.85 (2.87)	—	0.82 (0.10)	—	—	0.59
	Corrected	−0.64 (3.01)	7.23 (3.27)	—	1.13 (0.16)	—	—	0.82
x_4	Uncorrected	0.77 (2.69)	2.42 (3.61)	—	0.70 (0.12)	—	—	0.48
	Corrected	0.56 (2.84)	3.65 (3.94)	—	0.97 (0.18)	—	—	0.67
x_5	Uncorrected	4.43 (2.61)	3.65 (2.19)	—	—	0.40 (0.08)	0.35 (0.09)	0.63
	Corrected	4.32 (2.66)	3.50 (2.35)	—	—	0.48 (0.19)	0.41 (0.21)	0.75

analyses are limited by the fact that they take no account of other variables; nevertheless, the differences between the two analyses are striking and arise because, as Tables 8.2 and 8.3 show, there are substantial differences between the group means on the pre-test.

8.5 OTHER CAUSAL MODELS

(*This section is a little more difficult than the others*)

We saw in Chapter 4 how longitudinal data on just two occasions could be used to estimate a causal model when the causal direction is known. The extension to more than two occasions of these models (Section 4.2) is straightforward. If the true model for y_t is

$$y_t = \alpha_t + \beta x_t + \sum_k \gamma_k z_k + \varepsilon_t \tag{8.5}$$

then the dynamic model corresponding to equation (4.4) is expressed in terms of deviations from the individual's mean:

$$y_t - \bar{y} = (\alpha_t - \bar{\alpha}) + \beta (x_t - \bar{x}) + (\varepsilon_t - \bar{\varepsilon}) \tag{8.6}$$

where $\bar{y}$ and $\bar{x}$ are the means for each individual taken over all T occasions of measurement and $\bar{\varepsilon}$ is the mean error term for an individual. If β is not constant over time then the model corresponding to equation (4.6) is

$$y_t - \bar{y} = (\alpha_t - \bar{\alpha}) + \beta_t (x_t - \bar{x}) + (\beta_t - \bar{\beta})\bar{x} + (\varepsilon_t - \bar{\varepsilon}) \tag{8.7}$$

where $\bar{\beta}$ is the mean 'slope' coefficient over all occasions. Given a sample of n individuals measured on a total of T occasions ($t = 1, 2, \ldots, T$), then there are $n(T-1)$ independent observations in equations (8.6) and (8.7), and ordinary least squares estimation of these equations will give unbiased estimates. However, these estimates will not be fully efficient if the error terms, ε_t, are correlated over time. One way of taking account of these correlations, known as autocorrelations, or serial correlation, is given by Nickell (1982).

Equation (8.5) implies that neither y_{t-k} nor $x_{t-k}(k \geqslant 1)$ are causally related to y_t and so, in equation (8.6), we see that all the causal effect of x on y is concentrated in one time period. This may not be realistic—another manifestation of the problems of not knowing the correct causal lag—but the inclusion of lagged variables in equation (8.5) would lead to problems when estimating equation (8.6).

If $y_t - \bar{y}$ is not acceptable as a measure of change, then the alternative approach must be used and equations (4.8) can be written as

$$y_t = \alpha_t + \beta_{1t} y_{t-1} + \beta_{2t} x_{t-1} + \beta_{3t} x_t + \varepsilon_t \tag{8.8}$$

Equation (8.8) assumes that neither y_{t-k} nor x_{t-k} ($k \geqslant 2$) directly affect y_t. These assumptions will not always hold, as the example in the previous section shows, but they can be tested by a stepwise procedure with samples of reasonable size. It may also be reasonable to assume that α_t and β_{jt} ($j = 1, 2, 3$) are constant over time and they could then be estimated more precisely from all the data.

It is likely that the error term, ε, in equation (8.8) will be autocorrelated because it will contain omitted variables which themselves will be correlated over time. Clearly the best way to reduce, if not to eliminate, the problem of autocorrelation is to ensure that equations like equation (8.8) include all the important explanatory variables. This is, of course, difficult to achieve, although we know that the omission of important variables from equation (8.8) will result in biased estimates of β_j. Nevertheless, the cumulative effect of omitted variables, none of which are important on their own, or the effect of measurement errors which are correlated over time, may be sufficient to produce significant autocorrelation. Suppose that any autocorrelation can be represented in the following way:

$$\varepsilon_t = \rho \varepsilon_{t-1} + v_t \qquad (8.9)$$

where ρ can vary between $+1$ and -1 but will usually be positive, and where v_t has a mean of zero, constant variance over time, and is not itself autocorrelated.

Equation (8.9), together with the assumptions about v_t, is known as a first-order autoregressive process and it assumes that error terms two or more time points apart are uncorrelated, which may not be unreasonable for a well specified model. It can be seen from equations (8.8) and (8.9) that y_{t-1} is related to ε_t (because both y_{t-1} and ε_t are related to ε_{t-1}). Thus, if equation (8.9) holds, the lagged dependent variables in equation (8.8) are not independent of the error term and so ordinary least squares (OLS) estimation of equation (8.8) will give biased estimates of β_j.

Just as the models for known causal direction can be extended, so can the models for unknown causal influence given in Chapter 4 (Section 4.3). Thus, equations (4.9) can be written as

$$x_t = \alpha_0 + \alpha_1 x_{t-1} + \alpha_2 y_{t-1} + \varepsilon_{1t} \qquad (8.10a)$$
$$y_t = \beta_0 + \beta_1 y_{t-1} + \beta_2 x_{t-1} + \varepsilon_{2t} \qquad (8.10b)$$

One would need to assume that α_i and β_i are constant over time in order to make statements about causal direction. The underlying causal system is often referred to as being in 'equilibrium' when this assumption is made, just as it is when equation (8.6) rather than equation (8.7) is estimated. But, least squares estimates of equations (8.10) also may be biased by autocorrelation so there is an additional hazard when trying to determine causal direction for variables which change over time.

Taking simple differences when $T = 2$ or taking within-individual deviations from their means when $T > 2$ is likely to reduce autocorrelation (if $\rho = 1$ in equation (8.9), then it will eliminate it) and the autocorrelation which remains will, if uncorrected, lead to inefficient and not to biased estimates of the parameters. This is an advantage of the simple difference approach; but remember that this approach is not available when the causal direction is unknown. It is reassuring to note that in Chapter 4, the estimates of the parameters of interest for the simple difference model (i.e. model 3 in Table 4.1) and for the models with the lagged dependent variables, x_1 and y_1, (i.e. Table 4.2) are very close, and this suggests that autocorrelation was of little importance for these data.

For quasi-experiments, and for most observational studies, it will be reasonable to suppose that lagged dependent variables are truly exogeneous and so the error terms will not then be autocorrelated. This is because group comparisons of various kinds usually are concerned only with what goes on between the occasions of measurement and therefore pre-tests can be regarded as fixed. Hence the strictures of this section do not apply to the previous section or to Chapter 3. However, in all of Chapter 4 we are looking for causal statements which apply more generally than just to the time interval observed. The lagged variables (i.e. x_1, y_1) are not then exogeneous to the system, and so the results obtained from data collected at just two occasions can be distorted by hidden autocorrelation.

What can be done about autocorrelation in the presence of lagged dependent variables? One solution would be to replace x_{t-1} in equations (8.8) and (8.10a) by an 'instrumental' variable (IV) (see Johnston, 1972) which is highly correlated with x_{t-1} but uncorrelated with ε_{1t}. Similarly, y_{t-1} in equations (8.8) and (8.10b) could be replaced by another instrumental variable. Unfortunately, satisfactory IVs are often hard to find, particularly when data are only collected at two time points. However, the situation is eased if three or more waves of data are collected because if the causal direction is known then all of x_{t-k} and y_{t-k} ($k \geq 2$) can be used to predict y_{t-1}; that is,

$$\hat{y}_{t-1} = \hat{\delta}_0 + \sum_k (\hat{\delta}_k y_{t-k} + \hat{\psi}_k x_{t-k}) \tag{8.11}$$

The parameters δ_i and ψ_i can be estimated by ordinary least squares and $\hat{y}_{t-1}$, the predicted value of y_{t-1}, which is also its instrumental variable, can be substituted in equation (8.8). It will not be correlated with the error term ε_t providing equation (8.9) is a correct representation of the autocorrelation, and so least squares can then be used to estimate the modified version of equation (8.8) which is:

$$y_t = \phi_t + \theta_{1t}\hat{y}_{t-1} + \theta_{2t}x_{t-1} + \theta_{3t}x_t + u_t \tag{8.12}$$

The new error term, u_t, may still be autocorrelated, but this autocorrelation will not lead to biased estimates of the parameters although it will bias downwards the estimates of their standard errors. This procedure is very similar to the two-stage least squares method described earlier in Chapter 4. The same approach can be used to correct equations (8.10).

A further advantage of having more than two waves of data is that it provides another way of identifying causal models. Suppose there are three waves of data but still two variables (3W2V data)—one possible causal diagram is illustrated by Figure 8.2.

The equations for this rather complicated diagram are:

$$x_3 = \alpha_0 + \alpha_1 x_1 + \alpha_2 x_2 + \alpha_3 y_1 + \alpha_4 y_2 + \alpha_5 y_3 + \varepsilon_1 \tag{8.13a}$$
$$y_3 = \beta_0 + \beta_1 y_1 + \beta_2 y_2 + \beta_3 x_1 + \beta_4 x_2 + \beta_5 x_3 + \varepsilon_2 \tag{8.13b}$$

but neither of equations (8.13) is identified. However, it is most unlikely that all α_i

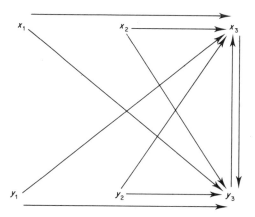

Figure 8.2 Causal diagram for a 3W2V model

and β_i differ from zero. Thus, one might suppose that α_3 and β_3 would be zero, and providing α_1 and β_1 were not zero, then equations (8.13) would be identified. Further, one might argue that either (α_4, β_4) or (α_5, β_5) would be zero and the system would then be over-identified and the restrictions could be tested with, for example, a LISREL approach (see Chapter 5). Data from three waves provide additional flexibility when looking for causal inferences because they make identification easier, and because they make it possible to consider a wider range of causal lags. But they are not a substitute for a properly specified model.

This rather difficult section has introduced yet another obstacle—autocorrelation—barring the way to a successful causal analysis. It was there, although hidden, in earlier chapters but it becomes apparent when there are three or more occasions of measurement. However, the example from Chapter 4 shows that the effects of autocorrelation need not be severe and it is certainly the case that they will be less severe, the better the specification of the causal models. It is also possible that attempts to correct for autocorrelation by using instrumental variables will lead to less satisfactory estimates—a small bias may be eliminated at the cost of a substantial fall in precision. As before, we need to be aware of all the threats to the validity of any causal analysis of non-experimental data, but we also need more experience of these models in order to begin to gauge the likely magnitudes of the different kinds of biases.

8.6 MODELS FOR CATEGORICAL DATA

The models for categorical data presented in Chapter 6 can be extended to multiple-occasion data and this will be illustrated by using an extended version of the data set on voting behaviour analysed in Section 6.5.

Table 8.5 gives the marginal distributions for the three elections held between 1974 and 1979. (These marginal distributions are obtained from longitudinal data. All the analyses take account of this by using information on all 27 (i.e. 3^3)

Table 8.5 Voting behaviour: marginal distributions

Election \ Party	Conservative	Labour	Liberal
Feb 1974	0.35	0.44	0.22
Oct 1974	0.38	0.46	0.18
May 1979	0.44	0.41	0.14

response profiles to estimate models more precisely. Further details on how to transform these response profiles in order to construct dependent variables are given in Appendix 8.1. See also Landis and Koch, 1979.) As before, it is not interesting to find out whether there was any overall change in voting behaviour over the three elections, but it would be interesting to know whether the change could be represented by, say, a linear relationship with time. In view of the results given in Chapter 6 (Section 6.5), it seems reasonable to restrict ourselves to a multivariate logit formulation. These logits are given in Table 8.6 and both show a trend over time.

Table 8.6. Multivariate logits from Table 8.5

	$\log \dfrac{\text{Con}}{\text{Lib}}$	$\log \dfrac{\text{Lab}}{\text{Lib}}$
Feb 1974	0.48	0.71
Oct 1974	0.66	0.73
May 1979	1.13	1.06

The underlying model (essentially equation (6.5)) is

$$\log \frac{\phi_{i1}}{\phi_{i3}} = \mu_1 + \delta_1 t \tag{8.14a}$$

$$\log \frac{\phi_{i2}}{\phi_{i3}} = \mu_2 + \delta_2 t \tag{8.14b}$$

where i ($i = 1, 2, 3$) represents the elections, ϕ_i are the marginal distributions, $\mu_j (j = 1, 2)$ are the means of the multivariate logits, t is time, and δ_j are the coefficients for time. This model has 4 parameters (μ_j and δ_j) and as there are 6 observations in Table 8.6, this leaves 2 degrees of freedom for testing. It is possible to represent t in at least two ways; as 1, 2, 3 which is the 'election' time or as 0, 8, 63 which is the chronological time in months. If election time is used, the model (8.14) does not fit well ($X^2 = 15.5$, 2 df, $p < 0.001$), but the fit for chronological time is quite good ($X^2 = 4.87$, 2 df, $p < 0.09$). This suggests that changes in political allegiance for the period in question took place steadily over time. The two time parameters, δ_1 and δ_2, are 0.01 and 0.004 with standard errors of 0.0018 in both cases.

It is also possible to extend the unconditional analysis of relative change in Section 6.5 to three occasions and so to look at relative change for owner-occupiers and renters. The raw data consist of 54 response profiles, 27 for each group, and are given in Appendix 8.1; the corresponding marginal distributions are given in Table 8.7 and the multivariate logits in Table 8.8. It can be seen from Table 8.8 that there is a trend for both groups. We want to know whether this trend is more marked for the renters compared with the owner-occupiers or vice versa.

Table 8.7 Voting behaviour: marginal distributions for the two groups

	Owner-occupiers			Renters		
	Conservative	Labour	Liberal	Conservative	Labour	Liberal
Feb 1974	0.46	0.31	0.23	0.19	0.63	0.19
Oct 1974	0.47	0.33	0.22	0.19	0.66	0.15
May 1979	0.54	0.30	0.16	0.30	0.58	0.12

Table 8.8 Multivariate logits from Table 8.7

	Owner occupiers		Renters	
	$\log \dfrac{\text{Con}}{\text{Lib}}$	$\log \dfrac{\text{Lab}}{\text{Lib}}$	$\log \dfrac{\text{Con}}{\text{Lib}}$	$\log \dfrac{\text{Lab}}{\text{Lib}}$
Feb 1974	0.68	0.30	0	1.21
Oct 1974	0.85	0.50	0.23	1.47
May 1979	1.23	0.65	0.92	1.57

The model is now

$$\log \frac{\phi_{il1}}{\phi_{il3}} = \mu_1 + \alpha_{.1} + \delta_{1l}^t \tag{8.15a}$$

$$\log \frac{\phi_{il2}}{\phi_{il3}} = \mu_2 + \alpha_{.2} + \delta_{2l}^t \tag{8.15b}$$

which is like equations (8.14) but with the extra subscript, l ($l = 1, 2$) representing the two groups and $\alpha_{.j}$ representing the group effects. Note that the δ, the coefficients for time, also contain a subscript l, showing that they can be different for the two groups. We want to know whether, together, $\delta_{11} = \delta_{12}$ and $\delta_{21} = \delta_{22}$ which would be the case if there were no linear group–time interaction. As it stands, model (8.15) has 8 parameters, so there are 4 degrees of freedom for testing its fit, which essentially means testing whether a linear relationship with time is reasonable.

Defining t as chronological time, then the fit is good ($X^2 = 5.04$, 4 df, $p < 0.28$). A test of the equality of the δ coefficients as given above provides some evidence for an interaction ($X^2 = 5.77$, 2 df, $p < 0.06$). If the interaction is considered sufficiently important then its parameters show a more marked change in $\log \text{Con}/\text{Lib}$ for the renting group (i.e. $\delta_{12} > \delta_{11}$) but essentially no difference for $\log \text{Lab}/\text{Lib}$ (i.e. $\delta_{21} = \delta_{22}$). These results are basically the same as those given earlier (Section 6.5) for just two occasions.

The unconditional analysis just presented does not fully take into account individual change. It uses the information in the individual response profiles to get efficient estimates of the parameters in equations (8.15) but it does not consider how people voted at election i in terms of how they voted at election $i-1$. A conditional analysis of the $3 \times 3 \times 3 \times 2$ contingency table—the table obtained by simultaneously cross-tabulating voting at the three elections (VF, VO, and VM) and housing tenure (HT)—can, in principle, do this. In practice, 71% of the sample of 549 voters who provided complete information voted in the same way at each of the three elections. Thus, the cells containing information on individual change are sparse, with two-thirds having less than five observations. Hence, the test statistics from the conditional analyses reported below (obtained from GLIM) should be treated with some caution.

There are three plausible conditional models which can be fitted to the four-way table:

$$\log N_{jklm} = \lambda + \lambda_j^A + \lambda_k^B + \lambda_l^C + \lambda_m^D + \lambda_{jk}^{AB}$$

$$+ \lambda_{jm}^{AD} + \lambda_{km}^{BD} + \lambda_{jkm}^{ABD} + \lambda_{kl}^{BC} + \lambda_{lm}^{CD} \tag{8.16a}$$

$$\log N_{jklm} = \text{as (8.16a) but} + \lambda_{jl}^{AC} \tag{8.16b}$$

$$\log N_{jklm} = \text{as (8.16b) but} - \lambda_{kl}^{BC} \tag{8.16c}$$

where N_{jklm} is the expected size of cell $jklm$, j, k, and l all run from 1 to 3, m runs from 1 to 2, A (and j) represents VF, B (and k) represents VO, C (and l) represents VM, D (and m) represents HT.

For all three models, VF, VO, and HT are treated as factors and so all terms involving them are fixed, and VM is the response. The term of interest is always the association between VM and HT, i.e. VM . HT or λ_{lm}^{CD}, and so, for each model, we want to know whether λ_{lm}^{CD} can be omitted without a significant reduction in the goodness of fit. In (8.16a), we want to know if there is a relationship between VM and HT having taken account of the association between VM and VO (λ_{kl}^{BC}); in (8.16b) we want to know if there is a relationship between VM and HT having taken account of the association between VM and VO and VM and VF (λ_{jl}^{AC}); whereas in (8.16c) only the association between VM and VF is accounted for. In other words, in (8.16a) the relationship between voting behaviour at elections i and $i-1$ is fixed, in (8.16c) the relationship between voting behaviour at elections i and $i-2$ is fixed, but in (8.16b) the relationships between i and $i-1$ and between i and $i-2$ are both fixed. However, in all three cases, there is no evidence of a relationship between VM and HT for these data (which do, of course, exclude those not voting at each election and those voting for a minor party as well as those lost from the sample). The corresponding test statistics are 0.85, 1.30, and 1.90, all with 2 degrees of freedom and all very much less than the critical value of 5.99 for $\chi^2_{2,0.05}$. (Both the unconditional and conditional analyses ignore changes in housing tenure – see Chapter 6 (Section 6.5).)

Interestingly, there is a relationship between VM and VF after allowing for the relationship between VM and VO ($X^2 = 52.1$, 4 df, $p < 0.001$). This suggests that voters are influenced not only by their choice at the immediately preceding election but additionally by their choice (or choices) in elections prior to that. There are, however, other explanations for such a pattern to which we will return in the next chapter.

So once more we see differences in the results obtained from conditional and unconditional analyses of categorical data. It is clear from the conditional analyses that there is no relative change in voting behaviour between renters and owner-occupiers so that once we know how individuals voted in the past, it does not help us to know their housing tenure in order to predict how they voted in May 1979. However, there is at least some evidence that when we ignore initial differences in voting patterns between the groups as we do in an unconditional analysis, then the odds of voting Conservative rather than Liberal rose more sharply in the renting group than in the owner-occupiers.

8.7 SUMMARY

This chapter generalizes to more than two occasions those models presented in earlier chapters. Growth curve models are introduced as extensions of individual change measured as a difference score, but again it is argued that these models are rarely suitable for social science data. A simple growth curve model is estimated in what is an unconditional analysis of relative change and when the results are compared with the more appropriate conditional analysis, important differences are found. The problem of autocorrelated error terms is introduced as a further difficulty when trying to estimate satisfactory causal models for change. Earlier models for categorical data are extended although these extensions are confined to analyses of relative change. The causal models for categorical data presented in Chapter 7 can be generalized quite easily; these generalizations are not considered in this chapter, although they are touched on in the next.

APPENDIX 8.1 SETTING UP AN UNCONDITIONAL ANALYSIS OF CATEGORICAL DATA

This appendix presents the raw data for the example in Section 8.6 and then shows how to transform these data into a form which can be analysed using equations (8.15). These transformations are presented in terms of matrices for convenience.

The raw data linking voting at the three elections to housing tenure are shown in Table A8.1.

Table A8.1

VF	VO	VM	Owner-occupiers		Renters	
			Count	Prob.	Count	Prob.
C	C	C	124	0.38	37	0.16
C	La	C	1	0.003	0	0
C	Li	C	12	0.04	3	0.01
La	C	C	1	0.003	2	0.009
La	La	C	9	0.03	9	0.04
La	Li	C	3	0.009	1	0.004
Li	C	C	12	0.04	3	0.01
Li	La	C	0	0	5	0.02
Li	Li	C	13	0.04	8	0.04
C	C	La	2	0.006	0	0
C	La	La	2	0.006	0	0
C	Li	La	0	0	1	0.004
La	C	La	2	0.006	1	0.004
La	La	La	77	0.24	114	0.51
La	Li	La	1	0.003	3	0.01
Li	C	La	1	0.003	0	0
Li	La	La	9	0.03	9	0.04
Li	Li	La	4	0.01	2	0.009
C	C	Li	4	0.01	0	0
C	La	Li	0	0	0	0
C	Li	Li	3	0.009	1	0.004
La	C	Li	0	0	0	0
La	La	Li	5	0.02	10	0.04
La	Li	Li	3	0.009	1	0.004
Li	C	Li	6	0.02	0	0
Li	La	Li	4	0.01	1	0.004
Li	Li	Li	26	0.08	14	0.06

Within each of the two groups, or populations, the probabilities add up to 1. That is, $\Sigma_j p_{ij} = 1$ where i ($i = 1, 2$) defines the groups and j ($j = 1, 2, \ldots, 27$) defines the combinations of voting behaviour. For each group, the cell probabilities can be arranged as a (27×1) column vector, p, and can then be transformed to marginal probabilities with the (9×27) matrix A_1.

$$A_1 = \begin{bmatrix}
1 & . & . & . & . & . & . & . & . & 1 & 0 & . & . & . & . & . & . & . & . & . & . & . & . & . & . & . & 0 \\
0 & . & . & . & . & . & . & . & . & 0 & 1 & . & . & . & . & . & 1 & 0 & . & . & . & . & . & . & . & . & 0 \\
0 & . & . & . & . & . & . & . & . & . & . & . & . & . & . & . & 0 & 1 & . & . & . & . & . & . & . & . & 1 \\
1 & 1 & 1 & 0 & 0 & 0 & 0 & 0 & 0 & 1 & 1 & 1 & 0 & 0 & 0 & 0 & 0 & 0 & 1 & 1 & 1 & 0 & 0 & 0 & 0 & 0 & 0 \\
0 & 0 & 0 & 1 & 1 & 1 & 0 & 0 & 0 & 0 & 0 & 0 & 1 & 1 & 1 & 0 & 0 & 0 & 0 & 0 & 0 & 1 & 1 & 1 & 0 & 0 & 0 \\
0 & 0 & 0 & 0 & 0 & 0 & 1 & 1 & 1 & 0 & 0 & 0 & 0 & 0 & 0 & 1 & 1 & 1 & 0 & 0 & 0 & 0 & 0 & 0 & 1 & 1 & 1 \\
1 & 0 & 0 & 1 & 0 & 0 & 1 & 0 & 0 & 1 & 0 & 0 & 1 & 0 & 0 & 1 & 0 & 0 & 1 & 0 & 0 & 1 & 0 & 0 & 1 & 0 & 0 \\
0 & 1 & 0 & 0 & 1 & 0 & 0 & 1 & 0 & 0 & 1 & 0 & 0 & 1 & 0 & 0 & 1 & 0 & 0 & 1 & 0 & 0 & 1 & 0 & 0 & 1 & 0 \\
0 & 0 & 1 & 0 & 0 & 1 & 0 & 0 & 1 & 0 & 0 & 1 & 0 & 0 & 1 & 0 & 0 & 1 & 0 & 0 & 1 & 0 & 0 & 1 & 0 & 0 & 1
\end{bmatrix}$$

The (9×1) vector of marginal probabilities, ϕ_{ij} ($= A_1 p$) is then transformed to log ϕ_{ij} with i ($i = 1, 2, 3$) representing the elections and j ($j = 1, 2, 3$) representing the voting categories. This vector is then transformed to a (6×1) vector of logits, log ϕ_{ij}/ϕ_{i3} ($j = 1, 2$), with the (6×9) matrix A_2:

$$A_2 = \begin{bmatrix} 1 & 0 & -1 & 0 & . & & . & . & . & 0 \\ 0 & 1 & -1 & 0 & . & & & . & . & 0 \\ 0 & 0 & 0 & 1 & 0 & -1 & 0 & 0 & & 0 \\ 0 & 0 & 0 & 0 & 1 & -1 & 0 & 0 & & 0 \\ 0 & . & & . & . & . & 0 & 1 & 0 & -1 \\ 0 & . & & . & . & . & 0 & 0 & 1 & -1 \end{bmatrix}$$

The logits from the two groups can then be put together to form the dependent variable which we can call y, where y is a (12×1) vector. Then we can set up a model

$$y = X\beta \tag{A8.1}$$

with the (8×1) vector of parameters to be estimated, β:

$$\beta = \begin{bmatrix} \mu_1 \\ \mu_2 \\ \alpha_1 \\ \alpha_2 \\ \delta_1 \\ \delta_2 \\ \alpha_1\delta_1 \\ \alpha_2\delta_2 \end{bmatrix}$$

and the (12×8) 'design' matrix, X:

$$X = \begin{bmatrix} 1 & 0 & 1 & 0 & 0 & 0 & 0 & 0 \\ 0 & 1 & 0 & 1 & 0 & 0 & 0 & 0 \\ 1 & 0 & 1 & 0 & 8 & 0 & 8 & 0 \\ 0 & 1 & 0 & 1 & 0 & 8 & 0 & 8 \\ 1 & 0 & 1 & 0 & 63 & 0 & 63 & 0 \\ 0 & 1 & 0 & 1 & 0 & 63 & 0 & 63 \\ 1 & 0 & -1 & 0 & 0 & 0 & 0 & 0 \\ 0 & 1 & 0 & -1 & 0 & 0 & 0 & 0 \\ 1 & 0 & -1 & 0 & 8 & 0 & -8 & 0 \\ 0 & 1 & 0 & -1 & 0 & 8 & 0 & -8 \\ 1 & 0 & -1 & 0 & 63 & 0 & -63 & 0 \\ 0 & 1 & 0 & -1 & 0 & 63 & 0 & -63 \end{bmatrix}$$

Model (A8.1) is essentially the same as equations (8.15) even though the time effect and group–time interaction are parameterized in a slightly different way.

It is then possible to estimate β and to test hypotheses about elements of β using non-iterative weighted least squares as described by Koch *et al.* (1977) and implemented in the computer program GENCAT. The estimates of β and their standard errors are:

$$\hat{\beta}^{\mathrm{T}} = [0.41 \quad 0.85 \quad 0.32 \quad -0.47 \quad 0.01 \quad 0.004 \quad -0.003 \quad 0.0002]$$

$$\mathrm{s.e.}(\hat{\beta}^{\mathrm{T}}) = [0.12 \quad 0.11 \quad 0.12 \quad 0.11 \quad 0.002 \quad 0.002 \quad 0.002 \quad 0.002]$$

CHAPTER 9

Models for Transition and Duration

9.1 INTRODUCTION

Like Chapters 6 and 7 and some of Chapter 8, this chapter is concerned with the analysis of categorical data on change. But, unlike those chapters and indeed earlier ones too, the analysis is not based on the general linear model, the statistical model which includes multiple regression and log-linear models. Instead, it exploits some of the elementary theories of stochastic processes in order to describe change as transitions between, and durations in, the different categories, or 'states' of a dichotomous or polytomous variable.

There was a hint of this kind of approach in Chapter 1 when development was described as passing through a series of stages (Figure 1.3). Let us now extend that idea. Suppose individuals are measured on a polytomous variable on a number of occasions. If the variable has, say, three categories and the sample is measured on, say, five occasions, then patterns like those presented in Figure 9.1 would be observed. These are patterns in discrete time. But the pattern of states observed at particular occasions, the selection of which is often arbitrary, will not necessarily give a complete picture of all the changes which take place. Thus, individual 1 in

Individual	State at time *t*				
	0	1	2	3	4
1	1	0	2	2	1
2	2	1	1	1	0
3	0	2	1	2	0
4	1	1	1	1	1
.					
.					
.					

Figure 9.1 Examples of individual response patterns for a variable with three categories observed on five occasions

146

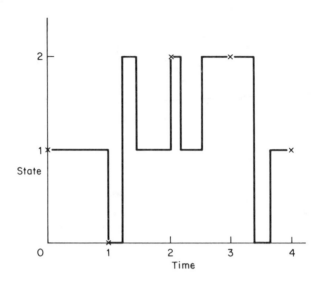

Figure 9.2 Possible path in continuous time for individual 1
in Figure 9.1

Figure 9.1 may in fact follow the path shown in Figure 9.2 in continuous time. This means, for example, that there appears to be no change in state between occasions 2 and 3 if one looks at Figure 9.1, whereas Figure 9.2 shows that the individual spends some time in state 2 after $t = 2$ and then some time in state 1 before changing again to state 2 before $t = 3$. Often, but not always, what goes on in continuous time is more interesting than the observed process in discrete time. The task of a statistical analysis is then to try to reach conclusions about this underlying process from the restricted data typically available in discrete time.

Two examples of this kind of analysis can be given. Tuma, Hannan, and Groeneveld (1979) look at the individual time paths, or event histories, of marital status for a sample of women, and go on to relate the parameters of these time paths to a number of explanatory variables. These explanatory variables include variables representing treatment and control groups because this study arose out of one of the Negative Income Tax experiments in the United States. Marital status can be treated either as a dichotomous or as an unordered polytomous variable. Plewis (1981c) analyses data collected from teachers on the classroom behaviour of a group of children on five separate occasions. Teachers used an ordered, three-point scale to rate behaviour, and the analysis attempted to make inferences about the underlying process in continuous time. Further details of this analysis are given in Sections 9.3 and 9.4.

Section 9.2 presents some elementary theory on one type of discrete-time stochastic process known as the Markov model, and this theory is applied in Section 9.3. Extensions to models in continuous time are given in Section 9.4, but with the more difficult theory placed in Appendix 9.1. The emphasis of these three sections is on description rather than on the explanation of change. But, in

Section 9.5, some of the ideas are applied to the data on mental health and worries, and mental health and loneliness, first considered in Chapter 7, and this section shows how these models can be used in causal analysis. The ideas and methods described in this chapter are developing rapidly and so the chapter ends with a brief discussion of more complex models.

9.2 DISCRETE-TIME MARKOV MODELS

For models in discrete time, one is only interested in modelling transitions between the states, or categories of a variable between the actual times of measurement. Although these models will not usually give a complete picture of the underlying process, as we have seen from the comparison of Figures 9.1 and 9.2, they are nevertheless useful. And for variables which can only change at points which are regularly spaced in time, they are all that is needed. For example, the time intervals between elections are often fixed, and governments present budgets every year.

The simplest discrete-time models are Markov models. Markov models attempt to describe, in a parsimonious way and in terms of conditional probabilities, the changes or transitions which are observed between occasions. In particular, they focus on whether the probability of moving to a new category or state at occasion $t + 1$ depends only on the state occupied at t or whether states occupied at $t - 1, t - 2, \ldots$, also influence the transition probability between t and $t + 1$. 'Transition' is a slightly misleading word in this context as it implies that the states occupied at consecutive occasions must be different, but in fact this is not necessary. Markov modelling is also concerned with the question of whether the transition probabilities vary over time or whether they are independent of time.

The simplest Markov model is the time-homogeneous, or stationary, first-order Markov chain. For the data to fit this model, the following conditions must hold for each member of the sample (Cox and Miller, 1965):

$$\text{Prob} (X_{t+1} = j | X_0 = h, \ldots, X_t = i) = \text{Prob} (X_{t+1} = j | X_t = i) \quad (9.1)$$

$$\text{Prob} (X_{t+1} = j | X_t = i) = p_{ij} \text{ does not depend on } t \quad (9.2)$$

X_t is a polytomous variable with I categories or states such as h, i, and j; $t = 0, 1, 2, \ldots, T$ is the index of measurement occasions; and the expressions in equations (9.1) and (9.2) are conditional probabilities for the population. Define $n_{ij}(t, t + 1)$ as the number of observations in state i at occasion t and in state j at occasion $t + 1$, and define $n_i.(t, t + 1)$ as $\sum_j n_{ij}(t, t + 1)$, the number of observations in state i at occasion t and in any state at occasion $t + 1$. Define n_{ij1} as $\sum_t n_{ij}(t, t + 1)$, all the observations in states i and j, one occasion apart, and $n_{i.1}$ as $\sum_t n_i.(t, t + 1)$, all the observations in state i which were measured one occasion later. If the data were generated by a time-homogeneous, first-order Markov chain, then observed or sample transition probabilities, $\hat{p}_{ij}$, can be estimated by dividing each n_{ij1} by $n_{i.1}$. Definitions of $n_{ij}(t, t + s), n_i.(t, t + s), n_{ijs}, n_{i.s}$, and $\hat{p}_{ij}(s)$ follow in an obvious way.

Bishop, Fienberg, and Holland (1975, Ch. 7) show how conditions (9.1) and (9.2) can be tested by fitting various log-linear models to data. Consider a three-way contingency table whose cells are defined by n_{ijk}^* where $n_{ijk}^* = \sum_t n_{ijk} (t-x, t, t+y)$ and $n_{ijk} (t-x, t, t+y)$ is the number of observations in state i at occasion $t-x$ and in state j at occasion t and in state k at occasion $t+y$. Refer to the variables of the contingency table as A, B, and C which, for equally spaced observations, will be X_{t-1}, X_t, and X_{t+1}, and treat C as a response and A and B as factors. The usual full or saturated model for this table is (see equation (A6.5) in Appendix 6.1):

$$\log N_{ijk}^* = \lambda + \lambda_i^A + \lambda_j^B + \lambda_k^C + \lambda_{ij}^{AB} + \lambda_{ik}^{AC} + \lambda_{jk}^{BC} + \lambda_{ijk}^{ABC} \qquad (9.3)$$

where N_{ijk}^* is the expected value of n_{ijk}^*, and this will reproduce the observed cell frequencies. A test of the first-order Markov condition (i.e. equation (9.1)) is given by testing, in the usual way (see Appendix 6.1), whether the omission of λ_{ijk}^{ABC} and λ_{ik}^{AC} from equation (9.3) significantly reduces the goodness of fit. In other words, after allowing for the effect of B on C (X_t on X_{t+1}), does A affect C (X_{t-1} affect X_{t+1}) either directly or together with B? If A does not affect C, then the Markovian hypothesis would not be rejected. But if it does, then either the process is second-order (or greater), or it is not Markovian, or it is not time-homogeneous, or possibly more than one of these. In the previous chapter (Section 8.6), we found that voting in the February 1974 election predicted voting in the 1979 election after allowing for the effects of October 1974 voting on 1979. Hence, voting behaviour cannot always be modelled by a first-order, time-homogeneous Markov chain.

It is possible that neither A nor B affects C, and that A does not affect B so, in equation (9.1), the conditional probability $[\text{Prob}(X_{t+1} = i | X_t = j)]$ equals the unconditional probability $[\text{Prob}(X_{t+1} = i)]$ and, in equation (9.3), $\lambda_{jk}^{BC} = \lambda_{ij}^{AB} = 0$. This can happen if the measurement occasions are widely spaced in time, and the data cannot then tell us anything about the underlying process.

If the sample is observed on several occasions which are not equally spaced then it might be possible to do a series of tests of equation (9.1) for those sets of occasions which are equally spaced. When the sample is large and observed on several occasions then four-way (and larger) contingency tables can be constructed to test for order. However, if the data do not conform to a first-order model then it will usually be more profitable to look to population heterogeneity—different sub-groups having different transition probabilities—as a reason for this, rather than trying to fit higher-order models.

To test time-homogeneity, which is the independence of transition probabilities and time, Bishop, Fienberg, and Holland suggest forming an $I \times I \times T$ contingency table by layering all those two-way tables of transitions which are equally spaced. Call the cells n_{pqr}^* and refer to the variables in the table as D, E, and F. Now we want to know whether the response, E (the variable at occasion $t+1$), can be predicted from D (the variable at occasion t) without knowing F (i.e. calendar time), and so we want to know whether the model

$$\log N_{pqr}^* = \lambda + \lambda_p^D + \lambda_q^E + \lambda_r^F + \lambda_{pq}^{DE} + \lambda_{pr}^{DF} \qquad (9.4)$$

fits the data adequately. Equation (9.4) is the saturated model minus λ_{qr}^{EF} and λ_{pqr}^{DEF}. Again, a number of tests of equation (9.4) can be carried out for samples observed on several, irregularly spaced occasions by considering the sets of occasions which are equally spaced. It is also possible, but only with a lot of data, to construct models for testing the time-homogeneity of higher-order Markov chains. We now illustrate some of these ideas with data mentioned in the introduction to this chapter.

9.3 AN EXAMPLE

Behaviour ratings were obtained from infant school teachers at five occasions. There was an interval of approximately six months between each of these occasions. Complete data were collected on 75 children on a scale having three categories: 'well adjusted', 'no significant problems', 'somewhat or very disturbed'. More details of the study which provided these data can be found in Chazan, Cox, Jackson, and Laing (1977) and Cox (1978). Much of the analysis presented by Cox focuses on the stability of the children's behaviour, but an approach based on Markov models offers the possibility of further insights into the data.

Consider first an analysis in discrete time. It is often observed that there is less movement out of a category over two or more time periods than would be predicted by a time-homogeneous, first-order Markov model. This means that the expected probabilities $\hat{p}_{ii}^{(s)}$ (calculated by raising the matrix of observed transition probabilities to the sth power) are often less than the observed probabilities $\hat{p}_{ii}(s)$, where $\hat{p}_{ii}(s)$ equals $n_{iis}/n_{i \cdot s}$. Table 9.1 compares $\hat{p}_{ii}(2)$ and $\hat{p}_{ii}(3)$ with $\hat{p}_{ii}^{(2)}$ and $\hat{p}_{ii}^{(3)}$ and shows that the observed probabilities are indeed consistently higher. This finding is reinforced when the reduced version of equation (9.3) is fitted to Table 9.2, which is the $3 \times 3 \times 3$ table relating X_{t+1} to X_t and X_{t-1}. (Note that, although there are no observations in state 3 at occasion $t + 1$ which were in state 1 at occasion $t - 1$ for this sample, there could be for the population.) When λ_{ijk}^{ABC} and λ_{ik}^{AC} are omitted from equation (9.3), the resulting likelihood ratio test statistic has a value of 29.0 which can be taken to be distributed as χ^2 with 12 df, so either the Markovian hypothesis or the hypothesis of time-homogeneity or both look unlikely ($p < 0.01$).

This consistent failure of observed transition probabilities to satisfy the Markov condition was first noticed by Blumen, Kogan, and McCarthy (1955).

Table 9.1 Observed and expected probabilities of remaining in the same category over time. (Reproduced from Plewis (1981c) by permission of the American Educational Research Association, Washington, DC, copyright 1981)

i	$\hat{p}_{ii}(1)$	$\hat{p}_{ii}(2)$	$\hat{p}_{ii}^{(2)}$	$\hat{p}_{ii}(3)$	$\hat{p}_{ii}^{(3)}$
1	0.71	0.70	0.55	0.78	0.47
2	0.60	0.53	0.47	0.46	0.44
3	0.63	0.49	0.46	0.42	0.37

Table 9.2 Behaviour ratings of children measured on three consecutive occasions. (Reproduced from Plewis (1981c) by permission of the American Educational Research Association, Washington, DC, copyright 1981)

Rating, $t-1$	Rating, t	Rating, $t+1$			
		1	2	3	Total
	1	43	6	0	49
1	2	5	14	0	19
	3	1	1	0	2
	1	13	7	2	22
2	2	16	42	7	65
	3	0	8	13	21
	1	1	2	0	3
3	2	3	10	5	18
	3	1	7	18	26

They postulated that it arises from transition probabilities which are not constant for all individuals or for all social groups. Instead, they suggested a 'mover–stayer' model with a proportion of any population tending not to change categories over time (the 'stayers') and the rest (the 'movers') changing according to a first-order Markov model. A number of modifications have since been made to the basic mover–stayer model (e.g. Singer and Spilerman, 1978) but, for these data, there is an alternative explanation. These children divide into two groups—the study was concerned with comparing a 'deprived' group of children from culturally disadvantaged homes with a 'control' group of children from educationally more supportive homes—and the observed differences between the transition probabilities of the two groups might account for the apparent non-Markovian behaviour of the sample as a whole. In principle, the above test (i.e. using equation (9.3)) could be carried out separately on the two groups but, with these data, the cell numbers become so small as to cast doubt on the validity of the χ^2 values. However, some progress can be made by calculating the sum of the differences between the observed and expected probabilities of staying in the same category over three occasions, i.e. $\sum_i (\hat{p}_{ii}(2) - \hat{p}_{ii}^{(2)})$. For the complete sample, Table 9.1 shows that this sum equals 0.24, whereas for the deprived and control groups, the corresponding values are 0.18 and 0.07 and these are closer to the value of zero, which would be expected under the Markov assumption.

Singer (1981) points out that $\sum_i (\hat{p}_{ii}(2) - \hat{p}_{ii}^{(2)})$ can be greater than zero when the data are generated by the same first-order Markov model for all the population but when the process is not time-homogeneous. Instead, he suggests calculating, for equally spaced measures, $\sum_i (\hat{p}_{ii}(1.3) - (\sum_j (\hat{p}_{ij}(1, 2)\hat{p}_{ji}(2, 3))))$. If this is positive then this indicates that no one first-order Markov model of any kind is consistent with the data. ($\hat{p}_{ii}(1, 3)$ is the observed probability of being in the same category at occasions 1 and 3; $\hat{p}_{ij}(1, 2)$ and $\hat{p}_{ji}(2, 3)$ are the observed transition probabilities between occasions 1 and 2 and occasions 2 and 3 respectively.) For the data in Table 9.2, $\sum_i \hat{p}_{ii}(1, 3)$ is 1.72 and $\sum_i (\sum_j (\hat{p}_{ij}(1, 2)\hat{p}_{ji}(2, 3)))$ is 1.49; the difference between them is positive and this reinforces the evidence against a single Markov model.

In view of the above results on the Markov assumption, an overall test of time-homogeneity is not useful, but separate tests for the two groups give test statistics, each with 18 df, of 19.5 ($p > 0.30$) and 22.9 ($p > 0.10$) for the deprived and control groups respectively. These results, together with the earlier ones on the Markov assumption, suggest that it is not unreasonable to suppose that there are two time-homogeneous, first-order Markov chains for the infant school period, one for the deprived group and the other for the control group. The corresponding estimated transition matrices are given in Tables 9.3(a) and (b). They show that

Table 9.3 Estimated transition probabilities (cell sizes in brackets). (Reproduced from Plewis (1981c) by permission of the American Educational Research Association, Washington, DC, copyright 1981)

(a) Deprived group

X_{t-1} \ X_t	1	2	3	Total
1	0.54 (13)	0.38 (9)	0.08 (2)	(24)
2	0.16 (13)	0.60 (48)	0.24 (19)	(80)
3	0.06 (3)	0.25 (12)	0.69 (33)	(48)
Total	(29)	(69)	(54)	(152)

(b) Control group

X_{t-1} \ X_t	1	2	3	Total
1	0.77 (59)	0.22 (17)	0.01 (1)	(77)
2	0.28 (17)	0.60 (36)	0.12 (7)	(60)
3	0 (0)	0.64 (7)	0.36 (4)	(11)
Total	(76)	(60)	(12)	(148)

children in the deprived group who are well-adjusted at occasion $t - 1$ are less likely than children in the control group to be well-adjusted at occasion t, but children in the deprived group who are rated disturbed at occasion $t - 1$ are more likely to be disturbed at occasion t. A test of the identity of these two transition matrices gives a test statistic of 17.1 (6 df, $p < 0.01$) so that hypothesis is therefore rejected by the data.

9.4 CONTINUOUS-TIME MARKOV MODELS

We now turn to continuous time models and we want, if possible, to use the data collected in discrete time to model the process in continuous time.

Markov models in continuous time are known as Markov processes. The fundamental parameters of Markov processes are not now the transition probabilities but the rate or intensity parameters, q_{ij}. These q_{ij} $(i \neq j)$ are defined as the limit, as Δt tends to zero, of the conditional probability of a transition from i to j in an interval Δt divided by Δt. (This definition of a rate is rather like the definition of velocity as the amount of distance covered in a very small time interval, divided by that time interval.) The q_{ij} are rates and not probabilities; they cannot be negative but they can be greater than one. (Also, $\sum_j q_{ij} = 0$ so $q_{ii} < 0$.) The rate of leaving state i is $\sum_{j, j \neq i} q_{ij}$ and this is known as the *hazard function*; for a time-homogeneous Markov process, the hazard function is constant and equal to $-q_{ii}$. A constant hazard function (one which does not vary with time) means that individuals are just as likely to leave any state after a short time as they are after a long time, and the Markov property means that length of time in a state is not influenced by previous states occupied.

The length of time spent by an individual in state i before moving to a different state, j, is known as the 'waiting time'. A constant hazard function implies that waiting times are exponentially distributed with parameter $-q_{ii}$ so that the mean or expected waiting time is $-1/q_{ii}$. The conditional probability of moving from state i to state j given that a move occurs is defined as $-q_{ij}/q_{ii}$ and this does not depend on waiting time. This probability is unobservable and is not the same as p_{ij}.

The assumption of a constant hazard function or, equivalently, exponentially distributed waiting times, is clearly unrealistic for many social processes. Markov processes are rather restrictive and more general models do exist, but they are much more difficult to estimate, a point to which we return in Section 9.6.

Observed data which do not conform to a Markov model in discrete time will not do so in continuous time. There is no guarantee, however, that data which are consistent with a time-homogeneous Markov chain can also be modelled as a time-homogeneous Markov process. It is possible that measures taken on the same sample at other occasions and with different intervals between occasions would have produced data inconsistent with the Markov property. There are two problems which have to be faced when moving from models in discrete time to models in continuous time, and these are referred to as 'embeddability' and 'identification' by Singer and Spilerman (1976a, b) and discussed in detail by them. Embeddability refers to the question of whether *any* Markov process is compatible with the observed data, while identification is concerned with *which* parameters, q_{ij}, are consistent with the data. The relationship between observed transition probabilities and unobserved rates is given in the first part of Appendix 9.1.

The method outlined in the first part of Appendix 9.1 shows how data in discrete time might be able to provide information about the underlying dynamic process. This is clearly valuable, but it does not provide a way of testing the goodness of fit of the model to the observed data. Also, it assumes that the rate parameters, q_{ij}, are unconstrained (except that $q_{ii} < 0$, $q_{ij} \geqslant 0$ and $\sum_j q_{ij} = 0$). However, there are sometimes theoretical grounds for supposing that some q_{ij} must be zero. Coleman (1964b), for example, when discussing the relationship of two attitudes over time, does not allow both attitudes to change simultaneously, and Cohen and Singer (1979) consider a similar situation when discussing the transmission of two types of malaria. Cohen and Singer also consider linear constraints on the q_{ij}. In the example described in the previous section, the behaviour variable is ordered and so it is reasonable to suppose that individuals can only move between adjacent categories in continuous time. Hence, q_{13} and q_{31} are fixed at zero although the corresponding transition probabilities p_{13} and p_{31} will not be zero.

Imposing constraints on the rate parameters is not only substantively sensible, it also releases degrees of freedom which can be used to test whether the cell numbers predicted by the model are sufficiently close to the cell numbers in tables of observed transitions. A method of estimating the q_{ij} given certain constraints is outlined in the second part of Appendix 9.1.

When the methods described in Appendix 9.1 are applied to the sets of transitions probabilities given in Table 9.3, the estimated rates are plausible and the models fit well. The results—the q_{ij}, the expected waiting times $(-1/q_{ii})$ and the probabilities of moving $(-q_{ij}/q_{ii})$—are given in Table 9.4. Table 9.4 shows that the children in the control group spend, on average, longest periods in the well-adjusted category; as the unit for the expected waiting time is the same as the interval between measurements (i.e. 6 months), this figure is about 18 months compared with an average of around 5 months in the disturbed category. However, children in the deprived group spend, on average, about 8 months in the well-adjusted category and about 13 months in the disturbed category. It can also be seen from Table 9.4 that if the control group children move from the middle category, they are more likely to become better adjusted, whereas the reverse is true for the deprived group.

The results of this analysis in continuous time are probably more useful than the discrete-time analysis, given that the times of measurement do not correspond to significant points in the children's school life. On the other hand, teachers' perceptions of children's behaviour probably do not change continuously but rather are formed over a period of time. If the teachers' reference period were 6 months then the results in discrete time are all that is needed, but if, as one might suppose, the reference period is shorter then the value of the continuous-time

Table 9.4 Final values of q_{ij} with waiting times and probabilities of moving in brackets. (Reproduced from Plewis (1981c) by permission of the American Educational Research Association, Washington, DC, copyright 1981)

(a) Deprived group

i	1	2	3
1	−0.75 (1.33)	0.75 (1)	0 (0)
2	0.34 (0.46)	−0.74 (1.35)	0.40 (0.54)
3	0 (0)	0.46 (1)	−0.46 (2.17)

(b) Control group

i	1	2	3
1	−0.32 (3.10)	0.32 (1)	0 (0)
2	0.40 (0.63)	−0.64 (1.57)	0.24 (0.37)
3	0 (0)	1.10 (1)	−1.10 (0.91)

analysis is strengthened. The information in Table 9.4 can in fact be combined with the properties of the exponential distribution and the fact that successive waiting times are independently distributed, to determine an interval within which more than one transition would be unlikely. For instance, the probability of observing more than one transition within a month of a previous measurement varies between 0.01 and 0.02 depending on the category and group.

A weakness of both types of analysis is that they take no account of measurement error. This is a difficult subject which was first raised in Chapter 6 (Section 6.7). One of the few attempts to link Markov models with measurement error is given by Wiggins (1973), but these models can only be estimated under very restrictive assumptions. It would be foolish to suppose that none of the transitions in Table 9.2 are due to measurement error; clearly, ratings of teacher perceptions are unreliable. It is not a lot more plausible to suppose that whatever errors there are compensate for each other, although this is essentially what has been assumed, *faute de mieux*.

9.5 ANOTHER LOOK AT THE 2^4 TABLE

In Chapter 7 (Sections 7.3 and 7.4), ways were presented of estimating causal influences from data on two occasions for two dichotomous variables. These methods all follow from the log-linear model although a number of specifications of this basic model are considered. Section 7.4 ended by pointing out that when the causal direction is unknown, the method can provide at best only a partial understanding of any causal processes.

Let us now look, not at a 2^4 or sixteen-fold table like Table 7.4, but at a 4^2 table constructed from the same data. Thus, Table 7.4 is rewritten as Table 9.5 and there is then just one composite variable at each occasion. Let us suppose that the time path of this composite variable can be represented as a time-homogeneous Markov process. This is clearly a strong assumption to make; if the sample had been observed on three or more occasions then tests like those described in Section 9.2 could have been carried out. But three occasions would have created 64 (i.e. 4^3) cells and so the sample would have needed to have been a good deal larger than 195 to have avoided the problems of estimation and testing associated with many very small cells.

Table 9.5 Mental health and worries: alternative version of Table 7.4 with transition probabilities in brackets

Occasion 1 \ Occasion 2	+ +	+ −	− +	− −	Total
No worries, good MH (+ +)	53 (.69)	1 (.01)	20 (.26)	3 (.04)	77
No worries, poor MH (+ −)	6 (.35)	2 (.12)	6 (.35)	3 (.18)	17
Worries, good MH (− +)	13 (.29)	1 (.02)	20 (.44)	11 (.25)	45
Worries, poor MH (− −)	11 (.20)	4 (.07)	8 (.14)	33 (.59)	56
Total	83	8	54	50	195

The set of rates corresponding to tables like Table 9.5 has the following form:

$$\begin{array}{cccc} q_{11} & q_{12} & q_{13} & 0 \\ q_{21} & q_{22} & 0 & q_{24} \\ q_{31} & 0 & q_{33} & q_{34} \\ 0 & q_{42} & q_{43} & q_{44} \end{array}$$

This means that individuals are not allowed to change states for both variables simultaneously. It is possible to illustrate these rates as in Figure 9.3.

If the model for the 4×4 table is a reasonable one, being both properly specified so that no important 'third variables' are omitted, and with the Markov assumptions satisfied, then the q_{ij} can be interpreted in the following way. We know that the worries and mental health variables are positively related—mothers without worries tend to have better mental health. Consequently, state 2 (no worries, poor mental health) and state 3 (worries, good mental health) can be called 'dissonant' states, whereas state 1 (no worries, good mental health) and

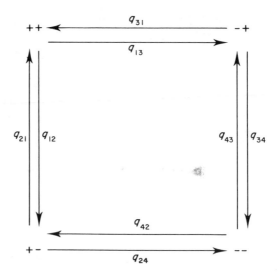

Figure 9.3 Illustration of q_{ij} from Table 9.5

state 4 (worries, poor mental health) are 'consonant' states. We believe that the causal direction runs from worries (W) to mental health (H) and so we would expect that when a move takes place the probability of moving from state 2 to state 1 ($-q_{21}/q_{22}$) would be greater than the probability of moving from state 2 to state 4 ($-q_{24}/q_{22}$), or $q_{21} > q_{24}$. Similarly, we would expect the probability of moving from state 3 to state 4 would be greater than the probability of moving from state 3 to state 1, or $q_{34} > q_{31}$. Together, these two inequalities suggest that W 'generates' H, and they indicate whether it is the absence of worries which leads to good mental health ($q_{21} > q_{24}$), or the presence of worries which leads to poor mental health ($q_{34} > q_{31}$), or both. The relative values of q_{13} and q_{12}, and of q_{42} and q_{43}, are also informative in that they show whether, when the two variables are in consonant states, changes in W are more likely than changes in H. If $q_{13} > q_{12}$ and $q_{42} > q_{43}$ then, if there is a change, a change in worries is more likely and this suggests that the worries variable 'preserves' the mental health variable.

The notions of generation and preservation were first introduced by Lazarsfeld (1972a, b) although he used them a little differently. He constructed indices of generation (which he called relative concurrence) and preservation (relative attachment) and he then combined these two indices to create an overall index of 'mutual effect'. However, the derivation of these indices is not entirely clear and, anyway, it is perhaps more useful to consider the relevant pairs of q_{ij} separately. For example, there may be situations for which variable A generates variable B, but B preserves or reinforces A, and this would be rather like the feedback models for continuous variables in Chapter 4.

The ideas of generation and preservation might also be tentatively couched in terms of prevention and cure. Thus, if A and B represent dichotomous variables which can be perceived as problem/no problem and A generates B, then one might want to intervene to eliminate problem A in order to prevent problem B developing. But if the two problems seem to go together over time regardless of initial state, and if B preserves A, then one might choose to try to eliminate problem B hoping that this would then eliminate problem A.

Applying the methods of Appendix 9.1 to Table 9.5 produces a set of rates which fit the observed data well ($X^2 = 5.24$, 4 df, $p > 0.2$). There are 4 degrees of freedom because q_{14}, q_{23}, q_{32}, and q_{41} are all fixed at zero. Figure 9.4 gives the final values of $\hat{q}_{ij}$. We see that $\hat{q}_{21}$ is substantially greater than $\hat{q}_{24}$ but, contradictorily, that $\hat{q}_{31}$ is slightly larger than $\hat{q}_{34}$. Nevertheless, on balance, the worries variable would seem to generate the mental health variable, with the emphasis on the absence of worries leading to good mental health rather than the presence of worries leading to poor mental health. Also, W appears to preserve H because $\hat{q}_{13} > \hat{q}_{12}$ and $\hat{q}_{42} > \hat{q}_{43}$. The values in brackets in Figure 9.4 are the $-q_{ii}$ so we see that the order, from longest to shortest, of mean waiting times: is first state 1; then state 4; then state 3; and shortest state 2. As one would expect, the mean waiting times in the two consonant states (1 and 4) are greater than in the two dissonants states (2 and 3).

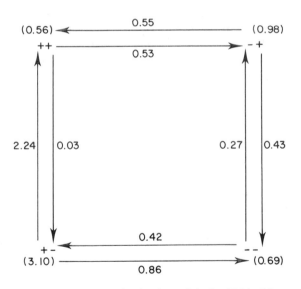

Figure 9.4 Constrained values of $\hat{q}_{ij}$ for Table 9.5

Given that W causes H, one might expect that q_{12}, q_{24}, q_{31}, and q_{43} would also be zero, so that instead of Figure 9.3 we would have Figure 9.5. However, this model does not fit well ($X^2 = 35.3$, 8 df, $p < 0.001$). The difference between the two test statistics is 30.1, which is approximately distributed as χ^2 with 4 df and clearly q_{12}, q_{24}, q_{31}, and q_{43} are not all zero.

Let us now turn to the data on mental health (H), and loneliness (L), first

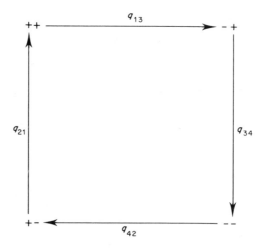

Figure 9.5 Restricted version of Figure 9.3

presented in Table 7.6. When we apply the methods of Appendix 9.1, we find that these transition probabilities are not embeddable in a Markov process. (One of the eigenvalues of the transition matrix P is negative, perhaps because of sampling error.) However, it is possible to make some progress by using an alternative rating of mental health which gives Table 9.6. This table is well-behaved and the estimated values of q_{ij} fit the observed data well ($X^2 = 6.55$, 4 df, $p < 0.20$). The $\hat{q}_{ij}$ are given in Figure 9.6 and this shows that $\hat{q}_{31} > \hat{q}_{34}$ but $\hat{q}_{24}$ is slightly less than $\hat{q}_{21}$ with the balance of the evidence favouring the generation of L by H. However, $\hat{q}_{13} > \hat{q}_{12}$ and $\hat{q}_{42} > \hat{q}_{43}$ and so L appears to preserve H. This pattern is different from the one found earlier, where the worries variable both generated and preserved the mental health variable. The order of the expected waiting times is also different, with more time spent in state 2 than in state 4. This analysis both

Table 9.6 Mental health and loneliness

Occasion 1 \ Occasion 2	+ +	+ −	− +	− −	Total
Not lonely, good MH (+ +)	85 (.80)	4 (.04)	13 (.12)	4 (.04)	106
Not lonely, poor MH (+ −)	7 (.33)	9 (.43)	0 (0)	5 (.24)	21
Lonely, good MH (− +)	17 (.43)	1 (.03)	14 (.35)	8 (.20)	40
Lonely, poor MH (− −)	7 (.30)	4 (.17)	5 (.22)	7 (.30)	23
Total	116	18	32	24	190

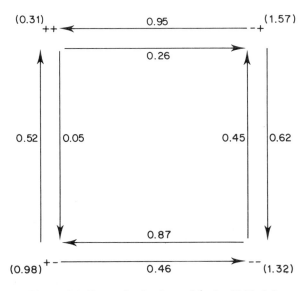

Figure 9.6 Constrained values of $\hat{q}_{ij}$ for Table 9.6

enhances and contradicts the findings in Chapter 7 (Section 7.4), which point to H causing L, but it does so at the expense of extra assumptions—that the time path of the composite variable follows a time-homogeneous Markov process. These assumptions could not be tested fully and may not be justified. We might tentatively conclude from this analysis that attempts to reduce the loneliness felt by mothers of pre-school children will not prevent them becoming depressed, but might help them to get out of a depressed state.

In theory, it is possible to extend the methods of this section to 3^4 and other tables and if the categories of these variables are ordered, restrictions can be placed on the q_{ij} as before. However, the analysis and interpretation of even a 9×9 table, as it would then be, is unwieldy. It is also possible to analyse a $3^2 2^2$ table, like Table 7.7, as a 6×6 table, but comparisons of the resulting q_{ij} are not easy to interpret in terms of generation and preservation when one variable is an ordered polytomy and the other is just a dichotomy. Hence, this method is really only suitable for dichotomous variables. Even for these variables, the various comparisons between the q_{ij} do not take into account sampling error and so any conclusions are bound to be tentative.

9.6 EXTENSIONS AND DEVELOPMENTS

This chapter has concentrated on data analysis for what is the most common longitudinal design—measurements which are taken about two or more occasions which are often equally spaced, but with incomplete information on what happens between measurements. A much more satisfactory design, for the class of models considered here, is one which collects data on the number, sequence, and timing of changes for the variable or variables of interest. These data are known as *event history data* and, for some variables, can be obtained with a combination of longitudinal and retrospective methods of data collection. Marital status and employment status are two of the variables for which event history data have been collected, and analysed in some detail, particularly in the United States. However, it is a relatively easy task to collect accurate retrospective information on variables like these because changes are infrequent and easy to remember and to date. It is much more diffficult to see how event history data could be collected for the variables analysed in earlier sections. For example, one would have to take very frequent measures in order to be sure of picking up all the changes in mental health and, as well as being intrusive and expensive, it is possible that repeated measurement in this area would lead to reporting bias.

Researchers with event history data have a much wider range of models to choose from when analysing their data. Those with incomplete, or 'gappy' data, are forced to rely much more on the crucial and often unrealistic assumption of constant hazard functions so that the probabilities of moving out of particular states do not depend on the length of time spent in them. There are often good reasons for supposing that a hazard function either increases or decreases with time, and this is known as 'duration dependence'. For example, some economists have argued that there is positive duration dependence for spells of unemployment—the longer a person is unemployed, the more likely he or she is to accept work at a lower wage. But other economists have postulated negative duration dependence—the longer someone is unemployed, the less attractive he or she becomes to potential employers. Processes with hazard functions which vary with time or, equivalently, with waiting times which are not exponentially distributed, but where change of state does not depend on history, are known as semi-Markov processes. Singer and Spilerman (1976b) give one method of discriminating between Markov and semi-Markov processes when information on transitions which take place between measurements is available. It is of course possible for there to be not only duration dependence but also 'occurrence dependence' which means, for example, that people are more likely to experience unemployment in the future if they have experienced it in the past and so have become stigmatized. But, as we have seen in Section 9.2, apparent occurrence dependence can sometimes be explained by population heterogeneity—see Heckman and Borjas (1980) for a more detailed discussion of these points.

Rather than imposing a specific model on event history data, Tuma (1982), building on work by Cox (1972), presents what she calls 'nonparametric' and 'partially parametric' methods of analysis. These make no assumptions about the form of the hazard function nor about whether or not there is state dependence. Instead, they use information just on the order of changes, and not on their timing, to obtain estimates of hazard functions and rates, q_{ij}. Earlier work (Tuma, Hannan, and Groeneveld, 1979) had shown how to relate the rates to explanatory variables of interest but made the assumption that the data were generated by a Markov process although not necessarily a time-homogeneous one. The partially parametric approach can tackle the same problem but makes fewer assumptions.

This is a promising area of analysis but one which is at present more fully developed for single, unrepeated events which are common in the medical sciences (particularly death in drug trials) than for the multiple, repeated events which are common in the social sciences (and illustrated by Figure 9.2).

9.7 SUMMARY

This chapter has shown how various kinds of Markov models can be used to answer some of the questions posed by particular kinds of social science data. With extensive longitudinal data, it is possible to test assumptions about the irrelevance of history for understanding change—the Markov condition—and about the independence of calendar time and changes in state. It is unusual for the Markov condition to hold for the population as a whole but, with large samples, it is possible to test whether it holds within sub-groups of the population. This was done in a limited way in Section 9.3, although that sample was rather small. However, when data are available for just two occasions, then these assumptions have to be taken on trust and results such as those presented in Section 9.5, although potentially interesting and insightful, must be treated with great caution. The method described in Appendix 9.1 and illustrated in Section 9.4 shows how data in discrete time can be used to make inferences about a process in continuous time, but here too, any results must be examined with more scepticism than usual. The final section does little more than hint at the progress which is being made to create models which are statistically more rigorous, and more widely applicable both to incomplete data and to event histories.

APPENDIX 9.1 EMBEDDABILITY AND IDENTIFICATION

Let P be an $(r \times r)$ matrix of transition probabilities p_{ij}, $\sum_j p_{ij} = 1$. Necessary and sufficient conditions for a first-order, time-homogeneous Markov chain with transition matrix P to be embeddable in a time-homogeneous Markov process are not known. However, one necessary condition is that the determinant of P must be positive. Suppose the eigenvalues of P are real and positive and distinct. If this is so, then

$$P = e^Q \tag{A9.1}$$

where Q is the corresponding matrix of rates and also

$$P = H\Lambda H^{-1} \tag{A9.2}$$

so

$$Q = \log P = H \log\Lambda H^{-1} \tag{A9.3}$$

where

$$\log \Lambda = \begin{bmatrix} \log \lambda_1 & & \\ & \ddots & 0 \\ & & \ddots \\ 0 & & \log \lambda_r \end{bmatrix}$$

and λ_i $(i = 1, 2, \ldots, r)$ are the eigenvalues of P and H is the $(r \times r)$ matrix of eigenvectors of P. (The largest eigenvalue of P will always be 1.)

It follows from equation (A9.1) that $P(t)$, the transition matrix for occasions t units apart, equals P^t, which in turn equals e^{Qt}.

If the observed transition matrix $\hat{P}$ has real and positive and distinct equations then $\hat{Q} = \log \hat{P}$, and if the resulting q_{ij} $(i \neq j)$ are not negative, then $\hat{Q}$ is the only rate matrix corresponding to $\hat{P}$. In other words, it is possible to identify a unique rate matrix, $\hat{Q}$.

If one or more of the eigenvalues of P are negative and distinct then there is no Markov process compatible with P. If some of the eigenvalues are repeated, or if they occur as complex conjugates (i.e. $a + bi$ and $a - bi$), then P will sometimes be embeddable and sometimes not and Q will sometimes be unique and sometimes not. Singer and Spilerman (1976a) discuss these conditions in some detail.

When constraints are placed on some of the rates, Cohen and Singer (1979) propose an iterative routine to calculate those estimates of q_{ij} which minimize the likelihood ratio test statistic, G:

$$G = -2 \sum_i \sum_j n_{ijl} \log \frac{N_{ijl}}{n_{ijl}} \qquad (A9.4)$$

The N_{ijl} in equation (A9.4) are the expected cell numbers at each iteration in the table of transitions obtained from the $\hat{q}_{ij}$ first by calculating $\hat{P}$ using equation (A9.1) and then multiplying these transition probabilities by the corresponding row totals, $n_{i.l}$. To start the iteration, Cohen and Singer suggest calculating those values of $\hat{q}_{ij}$ which minimize F, where

$$F = \sum_i \sum_j (\hat{c}_{ij} - \hat{q}_{ij})^2 \qquad (A9.5)$$

subject to the chosen constraints. The $\hat{c}_{ij}$ in equation (A9.5) are the unconstrained versions of $\hat{q}_{ij}$ from equation (A9.3) (but $\sum_j \hat{c}_{ij} = 0$). If the values of $\hat{q}_{ij}$ obtained by minimizing F are negative then $\hat{q}_{ij}$ is set to zero. For reasonably large samples, G is distributed as χ^2 with degrees of freedom equal to the number of extra constraints (2 in Section 9.4), and if G is significantly large then the dynamic process is not embeddable within the reduced class of time-homogeneous Markov processes.

The value of being able to test the fit of the model is exemplified by Singer and Spilerman (1976a), in which two 4×4 transition matrices, the elements of which differ by no more than 0.006, give very different off-diagonal terms in their respective Q matrices. Little seems to be known about the sampling distribution of unconstrained Q matrices beyond the work by Singer and Cohen (1980) for 2×2 matrices. Indeed, sampling error raises difficult problems when thinking about embeddability because it would be possible for an observed transition matrix, $\hat{P}$, to appear not to be embeddable when the population matrix P is in fact embeddable, and vice versa. This suggests that the cells defining $\hat{P}$ need to be quite large before inferences about Q, including inferences about its existence, can be made with confidence.

This appendix only gives an outline of the issues surrounding embeddability and identification and ways of dealing with them. Readers are urged to consult the cited references for more detail and they should realize that this is a new area of research which, although full of promise, still lacks a watertight base.

CHAPTER 10

Miscellaneous Topics and Conclusions

10.1 INTRODUCTION

In this final chapter, brief introductions are given to two topics which have not been considered up to now. The first of these—missing data (Section 10.2)—really merits a more detailed discussion than can be given here. Certainly there is great interest in methods for adjusting for missing data and these are particularly relevant for longitudinal data. And then, in Section 10.3, we consider data processing and computing. The chapter ends with an overview of statistical and causal modelling, one which aims to temper some of the enthusiasm which may have been generated by earlier chapters with an awareness that the models make assumptions and demands which will not always be reasonable.

10.2 MISSING DATA

Perhaps the criticism voiced most often about longitudinal studies is that they suffer from such serious problems of sample loss over time as to make any results almost worthless. The failure to trace sample members over time certainly can be a problem, both because those who are lost to the study tend to have different characteristics from those who remain, and because attrition can result in samples which are too small for detailed analyses of change. But high attrition rates, although common, are not inevitable in longitudinal work. For example, the National Child Development Study started with a cohort of over 17,000 births and obtained total response rates of 91 % when the children were 7 and 11, and 87 % when they were 16. Clarridge, Sheehy, and Hauser (1978) further illustrate the high response rates that can be achieved. And attrition in longitudinal studies of social groups will not usually be a problem. Undoubtedly, successful tracing of individuals can be expensive, but it is possible.

Having said that, it is true that all the examples presented in Chapters 3 to 9 come from studies with missing data. No attempt has been made to take account of this in the analyses, all of which are based on cases with complete data. A thorough examination of the effects of missing data on analyses of change is beyond the scope of this book, but a few comments can be made.

Data can be missing from longitudinal data sets in two ways. First, all members of the sample can be measured on every occasion (assuming that is the chosen design) but there can be non-response at the item level at each occasion. Second, some sample members can be missed completely at some occasions, as will happen when there is attrition. Item non-response does, of course, crop up frequently in cross-sectional studies, but attrition is peculiar to longitudinal studies. Similar techniques of correction can, however, be applied in both situations.

Suppose data are collected on two occasions and assume that the missing data at the second occasion are a random sub-sample of all the data, observed and unobserved, at occasion 2. Then, all the parameters estimated from the complete data will be unbiased and some of the techniques described in Plewis (1981a) can be used to improve the efficiency of these estimates, by taking account of the relationships between the variables measured at both occasions. However, there is a good deal of evidence (e.g. Goldstein, 1976) to show that this assumption is not generally tenable. A less stringent assumption is that the data are 'missing at random' (Rubin, 1976b). This means that cases with missing data at the second occasion do not differ systematically from those observed at the second occasion providing they shared the same characteristics at the first occasion. This implies that cases with the same characteristics at occasion 1 change in the same way after occasion 1 regardless of whether or not they are observed at occasion 2. It also implies that relationships between variables measured at occasion 2 and the set of variables defining the characteristics at occasion 1 are unaffected by missing data. However, means and variances at occasion 2 are affected and therefore correlations between variables at occasion 2 will be too. Another implication of the assumption is that, if true, conditional models for change are less likely to be affected by missing data than unconditional models because the conditional estimates come from regression coefficients, whereas the unconditional estimates come from means.

Williams and Mallows (1970) show how the apparently sensible procedure of basing measures of net change on only those sample members seen on both occasions can lead to biases. They focus on the dichotomous variable 'employed/unemployed' and show that, for a population where true net change is zero, a net change not equal to zero can be observed. In particular, only if 'the ratio of the probability of interviewing an unemployed person to the probability of interviewing an employed person at time T_1 (P_u/P_e) is the same as the ratio of the corresponding probabilities at T_2 for persons who were observed at T_1 and whose employment status has changed between T_1 to T_2 $(P_{eu}/P_{ue})'$, will the observed and true net changes in employment both be zero.

It is possible to obtain predicted values of the missing data from regression models estimated with the complete data, but if these predicted values are combined with the observed data, the estimated standard errors of the regression coefficients are then too low. Beale and Little (1975) propose an iterative routine which gets round this problem. An alternative iterative approach using maximum likelihood and the so-called EM algorithm is suggested by Dempster, Laird, and Rubin (1977) and this can be used for categorical as well as for continuous variables. A non-iterative version of the EM algorithm is given by Marini, Olsen, and Rubin (1979) for use with longitudinal data. This can be used when the pattern of missing data is such that if a case is missing at occasion t then it is assumed to be missing at all future measurements, $t + 1, t + 2, \ldots$ Marini *et al.* call this a 'nested' structure. Although some longitudinal studies will have a good approximation to this pattern of missing data, many will not and this limits the applicability of the method. For example, only 20% of the missing data in the EPA study discussed in Chapter 8 follow a nested pattern. Several other methods of imputation and weighting have been proposed to deal with missing data—see US National Academy of Sciences (1980).

10.3 DATA PROCESSING AND COMPUTING

This is not the right place to give an extended discussion of data processing methods for longitudinal and other studies of change. Indeed, it is not easy to make useful general statements, as each study has its own idiosyncracies for which solutions have to be found. But it is true to say that many of the tedious data processing problems which beset early longitudinal studies have been overcome, and a major reason for this has been the development of database management systems such as SIR (Robinson *et al.*, 1980). A package like SIR (Scientific Information Retrieval) makes it easy to link data on sample cases over time and simplifies the conflation of data from different sources on the same cases. It also simplifies the handling of 'hierarchical' data sets such as are obtained in a study of schools, classrooms, and pupils, for example. Checking, editing, and processing longitudinal data can still be time consuming and expensive, but there is no longer any justification for not collecting longitudinal data because it is too difficult to process.

It is clear from the previous chapters that there is no one method for analysing change; rather that there are several methods which draw on existing statistical techniques and adapt them to the particular characteristics of change data. Consequently, there is no one computer program which is suitable for all analyses. Several programs and statistical packages have been used for the analyses given in earlier chapters. Most of the regression analyses in Chapters 3 and 4 used the GLM procedures in the SAS package (SAS, 1982). There are, however, a number of other satisfactory regression packages. The corrections for measurement error in Chapter 5 used SUPER CARP (Hidiroglou, Fuller, and Hickman, 1980) and LISREL V (Jöreskog and Sörbom, 1981); SUPER CARP was also used in Chapter 8. The categorical data analyses of Chapters 6, 7, and 8 used GENCAT (Landis, Stanish, Freeman, and Koch, 1976) and GLIM (Baker and Nelder, 1978), with GLIM also being used, together with some specially written programs, in Chapter 9. GENCAT has the advantage of flexibility when specifying response functions, but GLIM uses the statistically more efficient method of maximum likelihood and can deal with a wider range of assumptions about underlying distributions of data. The growth curve, or unconditional models for several occasions described in Chapter 8 were estimated using the ANOVA procedure in SAS, which can be combined with the powerful matrix procedures in SAS to analyse a wide range of models.

10.4 STATISTICAL AND CAUSAL MODELS

The core of each of Chapters 3 to 9 is provided by a basic statistical model: sometimes a multiple regression model, sometimes a log-linear model and, in Chapter 9, a time-homogeneous Markov model. These models are used to give not only descriptions but also causal explanations of the social and psychological processes being studied. And so I want to end this book with some general comments about the use and utility of statistical and causal models in analyses of change.

Statistical models are powerful tools which can give researchers who use them an enriched understanding of the issues confronting them. But they are also specialized tools; they should not be used until certain kinds of preparatory work have been done and they have built-in assumptions which will not always be appropriate. Moreover, they are liable to produce results which appear robust but are in fact extremely delicate.

Throughout the book, I have stressed the importance of choosing a statistical model which matches the substantive question being posed and suits the measures which have been obtained. This has come out most clearly when contrasting the unconditional (or time-related or growth curve) approach with the conditional approach to change. Sophisticated statistical models have been developed for the analysis of longitudinal data on height and other biological variables. But they are not appropriate for most of the measures used by social scientists and will remain inappropriate unless social scientists are able to surmount seemingly intractable problems and develop measures which can be used with a much wider age range, or over a much longer period, than is generally the case at present. Moreover, unconditional models, which are models for differences for data collected about two occasions, are usually not the appropriate models when looking for causal statements.

Model specification is, however, a critical issue when estimating conditional models. Clearly it is unreasonable to suppose that social scientists know enough about the processess they are studying to be sure of specifying the correct model, but it is vital that they draw on all the available theory either to eliminate known confounding variables in their design, or to control for them in their analyses, or both. Inevitably, and properly, their findings will be criticized, but it is to be hoped that a combination of careful model specification and responsible criticism will lead to models which more clearly reflect the reality of change.

I have shown how to use statistical models in different ways in earlier chapters. There are, however, a number of things which users of these models should do before they estimate the models. They need to examine their variables, one by one, to check for obviously wrong or dubious values, or outliers, and to see whether any of the variables have unusual distributions. For example, the dependent variable could have a bimodal distribution and this might suggest that it would be better to split the sample and analyse the two parts separately. Also, especially when using multiple regression, users need to look at bivariate plots which again might reveal outliers, and would also show whether there are non-linear relationships which need to be allowed for. And it is always essential to look at the residuals from models to see if they indicate whether there is a better model for the data. This kind of advice applies of course to all who analyse data; it is difficult to make it systematic, but it is probably true to say that those who immerse themselves in their data for some time early on are less likely to drown in the computer output later.

Another pertinent issue in analyses of change is sample size. There is some tension between those researchers who advocate small-scale longitudinal studies which can collect detailed, good-quality data on rather few cases, and those who believe that coarser, incomplete information on large samples is more useful. In fact, both types of study are useful and could be especially valuable if used in tandem. But it is fair to say that the methods of analysis proposed here are better suited to samples of reasonable size–hundreds rather than tens. We have seen that it is impossible to carry out detailed analyses of longitudinal categorical data when samples are small. Also, analyses of non-randomized studies can only cope properly with more than one or two confounding variables when the sample is reasonably large.

I have made no attempt to avoid using the word 'cause' in this book because I do think social scientists should try not only to describe the world but also to explain it. But I do recognize that the notion of causality does raise problems for social scientists, who, on the whole, have to work with non-experimental data, and so any causal inferences are bound to be tentative. I have focused mostly on the causal relationship of two variables, but often more complex systems will be more realistic; not so much changes in variable A causing changes in variable B $(A \rightarrow B)$, as changes in A leading to changes in B which in turn lead to changes in C and then to another change in A $(A \rightarrow B \rightarrow C \rightarrow A)$. But it does make sense to start with a fairly simple model and then to introduce more complexity if the data are available to do so. Nevertheless, it has to be said that even a causal effect which is sound from a statistical point of view is unlikely, on its own, to provide a complete understanding of the underlying process. Epidemiological studies have established that it is very likely that cigarette smoking causes lung cancer, but they do not explain exactly what it is in cigarettes, or in smoking, which leads to cancer. Using statistical methods to establish causal effects does, however, represent real progress.

Analysing change presents a number of methodological and statistical problems for social scientists. Nevertheless, longitudinal data do offer opportunities, and are often essential, for a better understanding of social and behavioural processes. This book does, I hope, demonstrate at least some of these opportunities.

References

Aitkin, M. A. (1973) Fixed-width confidence intervals in linear regression with applications to the Johnson–Neyman technique. *Brit. J. Math. Statist. Psychology*, **26**, 261–269.

Anderson, E. M., and Plewis, I. (1977) Impairment of a motor skill in children with spina bifida cystica and hydrocephalus: an exploratory study. *Brit. J. Psychology*, **68**, 61–70.

Anderson, S., Auquier, A., Hauck, W. W., Oakes, D., Vandaele, W., and Weisberg, H. I. (1980) *Statistical Methods for Comparative Studies*. John Wiley, New York.

Assakul, K., and Proctor, C. H. (1967) Testing independence in two-way contingency tables with data subject to misclassification. *Psychometrika*, **32**, 67–76.

Baker, R. J., and Nelder, J. A. (1978) *The Glim System Release 3*, National Algorithms Group (NAG), Oxford.

Baltes, P. B. (1968) Longitudinal and cross-sectional sequences in the study of age and generation effects. *Human Development*, **11**, 145–171.

Baltes, P. B., and Nesselroade, J. R. (1979) History and rationale of longitudinal research. In Nesselroade, J. R., and Baltes, P. B. (Eds), *Longitudinal Research in the Study of Behavior and Development*. Academic Press, New York.

Barnow, B. S., Cain, G. G., and Goldberger, A. S. (1980) Issues in the analysis of selectivity bias. In Stromsdorfer, E. W., and Farkas, G. (Eds), *Evaluation Studies Review Annual*, Vol. 5. Sage, Beverly Hills.

Bartholomew, D. J. (1982) *Stochastic Models for Social Processes* (3rd edn). John Wiley, Chichester.

Beale, E. M. L., and Little, R. J. A. (1975) Missing values in multivariate analysis. *J. Roy. Statist. Soc., B*, **37**, 129–145.

Bereiter, C. (1963) Some persisting dilemmas in the measurement of change. In Harris, C. W. (Ed.), *Problems in Measuring Change*. Univ. of Wisconsin Press, Madison.

Berk, R. A., and Rauma, D. (1983) Capitalizing on nonrandom assignment to treatments: a regression-discontinuity evaluation of a crime-control program. *J. Amer. Statist. Assoc.*, **78**, 21–27.

Bishop, Y. M. M., Fienberg, S. E., and Holland, P. W. (1975) *Discrete Multivariate Analysis*. M.I.T. Press, Cambridge, Mass.

Blalock, H. M., Jr. (1981) *Social Statistics* (3rd edn). McGraw-Hill, New York.

Blumen, I., Kogan, M., and McCarthy, P. J. (1955) *The Industrial Mobility of Labor as a Probability Process*. Cornell University Press, Ithaca.

Bock, R. D. (1963) Multivariate analysis of variance of repeated measurements. In Harris, C. W. (Ed.), *Problems in Measuring Change*. Univ. of Wisconsin Press, Madison.

Bock, R. D. (1975) *Multivariate Statistical Methods in Behavioral Research*. McGraw-Hill, New York.

Bock, R. D. (1979) Univariate and multivariate analysis of variance of time-structured data. In Nesselroade, J. R., and Baltes, P. B. (Eds), *Longitudinal Research in the Study of Behavior and Development*. Academic Press, New York.

Bohrnstedt, G. W., and Marwell, G. (1978) The reliability of products of two random variables. In Schuessler, K. F. (Ed.), *Sociological Methodology 1978*. Jossey-Bass, San Francisco.

Bowker, A. H. (1948) A test for symmetry in contingency tables. *J. Amer. Statist. Assoc.*, **43**, 572–574.

170

Bross, I. (1954) Misclassification in 2×2 tables. *Biometrics*, **10**, 478–486.

Brown, G. W., Bhrolchain, M. N., and Harris, T. (1975) Social class and psychiatric disturbance among women in an urban population. *Sociology*, **9**, 225–254.

Bryk, A. S., and Weisberg, H. I. (1976) Value-added analysis: a dynamic approach to the estimation of treatment effects. *J. Educational Statistics*, **1**, 127–155.

Campbell, D. T. (1963) From description to experimentation: Interpreting trends as quasi-experiments. In Harris, C. W. (Ed.), *Problems in Measuring Change*. Univ. of Wisconsin Press, Madison.

Campbell, D. T., and Boruch, R. F. (1975) Making the case for randomized assignment to treatments by considering the alternatives: six ways in which quasi-experimental evaluations tend to underestimate effects. In Bennett, C. A., and Lumsdaine, A. A. (Eds), *Evaluation and Experiment*. Academic Press, New York.

Campbell, D. T., and Stanley, J. C. (1966) *Experimental and Quasi-Experimental Designs for Research*. Rand McNally, Chicago.

Chatfield, C. (1980) *The Analysis of Time Series* (2nd edn). Chapman and Hall, London.

Chazan, M., Cox, T., Jackson, S., and Laing, A. F. (1977) *Studies of Infant School Children*. Volume 2: *Deprivation and Development*. Basil Blackwell, Oxford.

Clarke-Stewart, K. A. (1973) Interactions between mothers and their young children: Characteristrics and consequences. *Monograph of the Society for Research in Child Development*, 38.

Clarridge, B. R., Sheehy, L. L., and Hauser, T. S. (1978) Tracing members of a panel: A 17-year follow-up. In Schuessler, K. F. (Ed.), *Sociological Methodology 1978*. Jossey-Bass, San Francisco.

Cochran, W. G. (1977) *Sampling Techniques* (3rd edn). John Wiley, New York.

Cochran, W. G., and Rubin, D. B. (1973) Controlling bias in observational studies: a review. *Sankhya, A*, **35**, 417–446.

Cohen, J., and Cohen, P. (1975) *Applied Multiple Regression/Correlation Analysis for the Behavioral Sciences*. Erlbaum, Hillsdale, New Jersey.

Cohen, J. E., and Singer, B. (1979) Malaria in Nigeria: constrained continuous-time Markov models for discrete-time longitudinal data on human mixed-species infections. In Levin, S. (Ed.), *Mathematical Models in Biology*, Vol. 12. American Mathematical Society, Providence, R. I.

Coleman, J. S. (1964a) *Models of Change and Response Uncertainty*. Prentice-Hall, Englewood Cliffs, N.J.

Coleman, J. S. (1964b) *Introduction to Mathematical Sociology*. Free Press, New York.

Coleman, J. S. (1968) The mathematical study of change. In Blalock, H. M., Jr., and Blalock A. B. (Eds), *Methodology in Social Research*. McGraw-Hill, New York.

Cook, T. D., and Campbell, D. T. (1979) *Quasi-Experimentation*. Rand McNally, Chicago.

Cox, D. R. (1972) Regression models and life-tables. *J. Roy. Statist. Soc., B*, **34**, 187–202.

Cox, D. R., and Miller, H. D. (1965) *The Theory of Stochastic Processes*. Chapman and Hall, London.

Cox, T. (1978) Children's adjustment to school over six years. *J. Child Psychology Psychiatry*, **19**, 363–371.

Cronbach, L. J. and Furby, L. (1970) How should we measure 'change' – or should we? *Psychological Bull.*, **74**, 68–80.

Cronbach, L. J., Gleser, G. C., Nanda, H., and Rajaratnam, N. (1972) *The Dependability of Behavioral Measurements*. John Wiley, New York.

Degracie, J. S., and Fuller, W. A. (1972) Estimation of the slope and analysis of covariance when the concomitant variable is measured with error. *J. Amer. Statist. Assoc.*, **67**, 930–937.

Dempster, A. P., Laird, N. M., and Rubin, D. B. (1977) Maximum likelihood from incomplete data via the EM algorithm (with Discussion). *J. Roy. Statist. Soc., B*, **39**, 1–38.

Dixon, W. J., and Brown, M. B. (Eds) (1979) *BMDP-79*. Univ. of California Press, Berkeley.

Draper, N. R., and Smith, H. (1981) *Applied Regression Analysis* (2nd edn). John Wiley, New York.

Duncan, O. D. (1980) Testing key hypotheses in panel analysis. In Schuessler, K. F. (Ed.), *Sociological Methodology 1980*. Jossey-Bass, San Francisco.

Ecob, R., and Goldstein, H. (1983) Instrumental variables methods for the estimation of test score reliability. *J. Educational Statistics*, **8**, 223–241.

Everitt, B. S. (1977) *The Analysis of Contingency Tables*. Chapman and Hall, London.

Fienberg, S. E. (1980) *The Analysis of Cross-Classified Categorical Data* (2nd edn). M.I.T. Press, Cambridge, Mass.

Fienberg, S. E., and Mason, W. M. (1978) Identification and estimation for age-period-cohort models in the analysis of discrete archival data. In Schuessler, K. F. (Ed.), *Sociological Methodology 1979*. Jossey-Bass, San Francisco.

Finney, D. J. (1971) *Probit Analysis* (3rd edn). C.U.P., Cambridge.

Fisher, F. M. (1966) *The Identification Problems in Econometrics*. McGraw-Hill, New York.

Fisher, R. A. (1932) *Statistical Methods for Research Workers* (4th edn). Oliver and Boyd, Edinburgh.

Fogelman, K., and Goldstein, H. (1976) Social factors associated with change in educational attainment between 7 and 11 years of age. *Educational Studies*, **2**, 95–109.

Fuller, W. A. (1980) Properties of some estimators for the errors-in-variables model. *Ann. Statist.*, **8**, 407–422.

Fuller, W. A., and Hidiroglou, M. A. (1978) Regression estimation after correction for attenuation. *J. Amer. Statist. Assoc.*, **73**, 99–104.

Gilbert, J. P., Light, R. J., and Mosteller, F. (1975) Assessing social innovations: an empirical base for policy. In Bennett, C. A., and Lumsdaine, A. A. (Eds), *Evaluation and Experiment*. Academic Press, New York.

Goldberger, A. S. (1964) *Econometric Theory*. John Wiley, New York.

Goldberger, A. S. (1971) Econometrics and psychometrics: A survey of communalities. *Psychometrika*, **36**, 83–107.

Goldblatt, P., and Fox, A. J. (1978) Household mortality from the OPCS Longitudinal Study. *Population Trends*, **14**, 20–27.

Goldstein, H. (1976) A study of the response rates of sixteen-year-olds in the National Child Development Study. In Fogelman, K. (Ed.), *Britain's Sixteen-year Olds*. National Children's Bureau, London.

Goldstein, H. (1979a) *The Design and Analysis of Longitudinal Studies*. Academic Press, London.

Goldstein, H. (1979b) Age, period and cohort effects: A confounded confusion. *BIAS*, **6**, 19–24.

Goldstein, H. (1979c) Some models for analysing longitudinal data on educational attainment (with Discussion). *J. Roy. Statist. Soc., A*, **142**, 407–442.

Goldthorpe, J. H. (1980) *Social Mobility and Class Structure in Modern Britain*. Clarendon Press, Oxford.

Goodman, L. A. (1973) The analysis of multidimensional contingency tables when some variables are posterior to others: a modified path analysis approach. *Biometrika*, **60**, 179–192.

Goodman, L. A. (1979) Simple models for the analysis of association in cross-classifications having ordered categories. *J. Amer. Statist. Assoc.*, **74**, 537–552.

Goodman, L. A. and Fay, R. (1973) *Everyman's Contingency Table Analysis: Program Documentation*. Univ. of Chicago Press, Chicago.

Grizzle, J. E., Starmer, C. F., and Koch, G. G. (1969) Analysis of categorical data by linear models. *Biometrics*, **25**, 489–504.

Guire, K. E., and Kowalski, C. J. (1979) Mathematical description and representation of developmental change functions on the intra- and interindividual levels. In Nesselroade, J. R., and Baltes, P. B. (Eds), *Longitudinal Research in the Study of Behavior and Development*. Academic Press, New York.

Hauser, R. M. (1980) Some exploratory methods for modelling mobility tables and other cross-classified data. In Schuessler, K. F. (Ed.), *Sociological Methodology 1980*. Jossey-Bass, San Francisco.

Healy, M. J. R., and Goldstein, H. (1978) Regression to the mean. *Ann. Human Biology*, **5**, 277–280.

Heckman, J. J. (1979) Sample selection bias as a specification error. *Econometrica*, **47**, 153–161.

Heckman, J. J., and Borjas, G. (1980) Does unemployment cause future unemployment? Definitions, questions and answers from a continuous time model of heterogeneity and state dependence. *Economica*, **47**, 247–283.

Heise, D. R. (1970) Causal inferences from panel data. In Borgatta, E. F., and Bohrnstedt, G. W. (Eds), *Sociological Methodology 1970*. Jossey-Bass, San Francisco.

Hersen, M., and Barlow, D. H. (1976) *Single Case Experimental Designs: Strategies for Studying Behavioral Change*. Pergamon, New York.

Hidiroglou, M. A., Fuller, W. A., and Hickman, R. D. (1980) *SUPER CARP* (6th edn). Statistical Laboratory, Iowa State University.

Hindley, C. B., and Owen, C. F. (1978) The extent of individual changes in I.Q. for ages between 6 months and 17 years in a British longitudinal sample. *J. Child Psychology Psychiatry*, **19**, 329–350.

Hindley, C. B., and Owen, C. F. (1979) An analysis of individual patterns of DQ and IQ curves from 6 months to 17 years. *Brit. J. Psychology*, **70**, 273–293.

Janson, C.-G. (1978) *Project Metropolitan Research Report No. 9*. Stockholm University.

Jencks, C., *et al.* (1973) *Inequality*. Allen Lane, London.

Johnston, J. (1972) *Econometric Methods* (2nd edn). McGraw-Hill, London.

Jöreskog, K. G. (1970) A general method for analysis of covariance structures. *Biometrika*, **57**, 239–251.

Jöreskog, K. G. (1971) Statistical analysis of sets of congeneric tests. *Psychometrika*, **36**, 109–133.

Jöreskog, K. G., and Sörbom, D. (1977) Statistical models and methods for analysis of longitudinal data. In Aigner, D. J., and Goldberger, A. S. (Eds), *Latent Variables in Socio-Economic Models*. North Holland, Amsterdam.

Jöreskog, K. G., and Sörbom, D. (1981) Lisrel V: Analysis of linear structural relationships by maximum likelihood and least squares methods. *Research report 81–8*, University of Uppsala.

Kenny, D. A. (1975a) A quasi-experimental approach to assessing treatment effects in the nonequivalent control group design. *Psychological Bull.*, **82**, 345–362.

Kenny, D. A. (1975b) Cross-lagged panel correlation: A test for spuriousness. *Psychological Bull.*, **82**, 887–903.

Kershner, R. P., and Chao, G. C. (1976) A comparison of some categorical analysis programs. *Proc. Statist. Computing Sect., Amer. Statist. Assoc.*, **2**, 178–183.

Kessler, R. C., and Greenberg, D. F. (1981) *Linear Panel Analysis*. Academic Press, New York.

Koch, G. G., Landis, J. R., Freeman, J. L., Freeman, D. H., Jr., and Lehnen, R. G. (1977) A general methodology for the analysis of experiments with repeated measures of categorical data. *Biometrics*, **33**, 133–158.

Korn, E. L. (1981) Hierarchical log-linear models not preserved by classification error. *J. Amer. Statist. Assoc.*, **76**, 110–113.

Kratochwill, T. R. (Ed.) (1978) *Single Subject Research: Strategies for Evaluating Change*. Academic Press, New York.

Landis, J. R., and Koch, G. G. (1979) The analysis of categorical data in longitudinal studies of behavioral development. In Nesselroade, J. R., and Baltes, P. B. (Eds), *Longitudinal Research in the Study of Behavior and Development*. Academic Press, New York.

Landis, J. R., Stanish, W. M., Freeman, J. L., and Koch, G. G. (1976) A computer program for the generalized chi-square analysis of categorical data using weighted least squares (GENCAT). *Computer Programs in Biomedicine*, **6**, 196–231.

Larntz, K. (1978) Small sample comparisons of exact levels for chi-squared goodness-of-fit-statistics. *J. Amer. Statist. Assoc.*, **73**, 253–263.

Lazarsfeld, P. F. (1972a) Mutual effects of statistical variables. In Lazarsfeld, P. F., Pasanella, A. K., and Rosenberg, M. (Eds), *Continuities in the Language of Social Research*. Free Press, New York.

Lazarsfeld, P. F. (1972b) Mutual relations over time of two attributes: A review and integration of various approaches. In Hammer, M., Salzinger, K., and Sutton, S. (Eds), *Psychopathology*. John Wiley, New York.

Lazarsfeld, P. F., Berelson, B. R., and Gaudet, H. (1944) *The People's Choice*. Duell, Sloan and Pearce, New York.

Lefkowitz, M. M., Eron, L. D., Walder, L. O., and Huesmann, L. R. (1977) *Growing up to the Violent: A Longitudinal Study of the Development of Aggression*. Pergamon, New York.

Lord, F. M. (1967) A paradox in the interpretation of group comparisons. *Psychological Bull.*, **68**, 304–305.

Lord, F. M., and Novick, M. R. (1968) *Statistical Theories of Mental Test Scores*. Addison-Wesley, Reading, Mass.

McCullagh, P. (1980) Regression models for ordinal data (with Discussion). *J. Roy. Statist. Soc. B*, **42**, 109–142.

McDonald, R. P. (1978) A simple comprehensive model for the analysis of covariance structures. *Brit. J. Math. Statist. Psychology*, **31**, 59–72.

McDonald, R. P. (1980) A simple comprehensive model for the analysis of covariance structures: some remarks on applications. *Brit. J. Math. Statist. Psychology*, **33**, 161–183.

Marascuilo, L. A., and Serlin, R. C. (1979) Tests and contrasts for comparing change parameters for a multiple McNemar data model. *Brit. J. Math. Statist. Psychology*, **32**, 105–112.

Marini, M. M., Olsen, A. R., and Rubin, D. B. (1979) Maximum likelihood estimation in panel studies with missing data. In Schuessler, K. F. (Ed.), *Sociological Methodology 1980*. Jossey-Bass, San Francisco.

Markus, G. B., and Converse, P. E. (1979) A dynamic simultaneous equation model of electoral choice. *Amer. Pol. Sci. Rev.*, **73**, 1055–1070.

Maxwell, A. E. (1961) *Analysing Qualitative Data*. Methuen, London.

Meehl, P. E. (1970) Nuisance variables and the ex post facto design. In Radner, M., and Winokur, S. (Eds), *Analyses of Theories and Methods of Physics and Psychology*. Minnesota Studies in the Philosophy of Science, Vol. IV, Univ. of Minnesota Press, Minneapolis.

Merrell, M. (1931) The relationship of individual growth to average growth. *Human Biology*, **3**, 37–70.

Morris, C. N., Newhouse, J. P., and Archibald, R. W. (1980) On the theory and practice of obtaining unbiased and efficient samples in social surveys. In Stromsdorfer, E. W., and Farkas, G. (Eds), *Evaluation Studies Review Annual*, Vol. 5. Sage, Beverly Hills.

Moss, L., and Goldstein, H. (Eds) (1979) *The Recall Method in Social Surveys*. University of London Institute of Education, London.

Moss, P., and Plewis, I. (1977) Mental distress of mothers of preschool children in inner London. *Psychological Medicine*, **7**, 641–652.

Moss, P., Plewis, I., and Bax, M. C. O. (1979) *The Pre-School Project*. Thomas Coram Research Unit, London.

Nelder, J. A., and Wedderburn, R. W. M. (1972) Generalized linear models. *J. Roy. Statist. Soc., A*, **135**, 370–384.

Nickell, S. (1982) The determinants of occupational success in Britain. *Rev. Economic Studies*, **49**, 43–53.

Olsson, U., and Bergman, L. R. (1977) A longitudinal factor model for studying change in ability structure. *Multivariate Behavioral Research*, **12**, 221–242.

Payne, J. (1974) *Educational Priority*, Vol. 2. HMSO, London.

Plackett, R. L. (1981) *The Analysis of Categorical Data* (2nd edn). Griffin, London.

Plewis, I. (1978) Planning pre-school services: a socio-demographic analysis. *Socio-Economic Planning Sciences*, **12**, 303–311.

Plewis, I. (1981a) *Analysing Change: Using Longitudinal Data for the Measurement and Explanation of Change in the Social and Behavioural Sciences*. Final report to SSRC.

Plewis, I. (1981b) A comparison of approaches to the analysis of longitudinal categoric data. *Brit. J. Math. Statist. Psychology*, **34**, 118–123.

Plewis, I. (1981c) Using longitudinal data to model teachers' ratings of classroom behavior as a dynamic process. *J. Educational Statistics*, **6**, 237–255.

Radical Statistics Education Group (1982) *Reading Between the Numbers*. BSSRS Publications, London.

Robins, L. N. (1980) Longitudinal methods in the study of normal and pathological development. In Earls, F. (Ed.), *Studies of Children*. Prodist, New York.

Robinson, B. N., Anderson, G. D., Cohen, E., Gazdzik, W. F., Karpel, L. C., Miller, A. H., and Stein, J. R. (1980) *SIR User's Manual, Version 2*. SIR Inc., Evanston, Illinois.

Rogosa, D. (1979) Causal models in longitudinal research: Rationale, formulation and interpretation. In Nesselroade, J. R., and Baltes, P. B. (Eds), *Longitudinal Research in the Study of Behavior and Development*. Academic Press, New York.

Rogosa, D., Brandt, D., and Zimowski, M. (1982) A growth curve approach to the measurement of change. *Psychological Bull.*, **92**, 726–748.

Rosenbaum, P. R., and Rubin, D. B. (1983) The central role of the propensity score in observational studies for causal effects. *Biometrika*, **70**, 41–55.

Rozelle, R. M., and Campbell, D. T. (1969) More plausible rival hypotheses in the cross-lagged panel correlation technique. *Psychological Bull.*, **71**, 74–80.

Rubin, D. B. (1976a) Multivariate matching methods that are equal percent bias reducing, I: some examples. *Biometrics*, **32**, 109–120.

Rubin, D. B. (1976b) Inference and missing data. *Biometrika*, **63**, 581–592.

Rubin, D. B. (1977) Assignment to treatment group on the basis of a covariate. *J. Educational Statistics*, **2**, 1–26.

Rutter, M., Tizard, J., and Whitmore, K. (1970) *Education, Health and Behaviour*. Longman, London.

Särlvik, B., and Crewe, I. (1983) *Decade of Dealignment*. Cambridge University Press, Cambridge.

SAS (1982) *SAS User's Guide*, 1982 edn. SAS Institute, Cary, N.C.

Schaie, K. W. (1965) A general model for the study of development problems. *Psychological Bull.*, **64**, 92–107.

Singer, B. (1981) Estimation of non stationary Markov chains from panel data. In Leinhardt, S. (Ed.), *Sociological Methodology 1981*. Jossey-Bass, San Francisco.

Singer, B., and Cohen, J. E. (1980) Estimating malaria incidence and recovery rates from panel surveys. *Math. Biosciences*, **49**, 273–305.

Singer, B., and Spilerman, S. (1976a) The representation of social processes by Markov models. *Amer. J. Soc.*, **82**, 1–54.

Singer, B., and Spilerman, S. (1976b) Some methodological issues in the analysis of longitudinal studies. *Ann. Economic Social Measurement*, **5**, 447–474.

Singer, B., and Spilerman, S. (1978) Clustering on the main diagonal in mobility matrices. In Schuessler, K. F. (Ed.), *Sociological Methodology 1979*. Jossey-Bass, San Francisco.

Singer, B., and Spilerman, S. (1979) Mathematical representations of development theories. In Nesselroade, J. R., and Baltes, P. B. (Eds), *Longitudinal Research in the Study of Behavior and Development*. Academic Press, New York.

Smith, G., and James, T. (1975) The effects of pre-school education: Some American and British evidence. *Oxford Rev. Educ.*, **1**, 223–240.

Sörbom, D. (1976) A statistical model for the measurement of change in true scores. In de Gruijter, D. N. M., van der Kamp, L. J. Th., and Crombag, H. F. (Eds), *Advances in Psychological and Educational Measurement*. John Wiley, New York.

Sörbom, D. (1978) An alternative to the methodology for analysis of covariance. *Psychometrika*, **43**, 381–396.

Steedman, J. (1980) *Progress in Secondary Schools*. National Children's Bureau, London.

Stevenson, J., and Payne, J. (1972) Study of the reliability and validity of the pre-school version of the English Picture Vocabulary Test and the Reynell Developmental Language Scales (unpublished).

Thorndike, E. L. (1924) The influence of chance imperfections of measures upon the relation of initial score to gain or loss. *J. Experimental Psychology*, **7**, 225–232.

Tuma, N. B. (1982) Nonparametric and partially parametric approaches to event-history analysis. In Leinhardt, S. (Ed.), *Sociological Methodology 1982*. Jossey-Bass, San Francisco.

Tuma, N. B., Hannan, M. T., and Groeneveld, L. P. (1979) Dynamic analysis of event histories. *Amer. J. Soc.*, **84**, 820–854.

US National Academy of Sciences (1980) Panel on incomplete data. National Academy of Sciences, Washington DC.

Wall, W. D., and Williams, H. L. (1970) *Longitudinal Studies and the Social Sciences*. Heinemann, London.

Warren, R. D., White, J. K., and Fuller, W. A. (1974) An errors-in-variables analysis of managerial role performance. *J. Amer. Statist. Assoc.*, **69**, 886–893.

Weisberg, S. (1980) *Applied Linear Regression*. John Wiley, New York.

Wheaton, B., Muthen, B., Alwin, D. F., and Summers, G. F. (1977) Assessing reliability and stability in panel models. In Heise, D. R. (Ed.), *Sociological Methodology 1977*. Jossey-Bass, San Francisco.

Wiggins, L. M. (1973) *Panel Analysis*. Elsevier, Amsterdam.

Williams, W. H., and Mallows, C. L. (1970) Systematic biases in panel surveys due to differential non-response. *J. Amer. Statist. Assoc.*, **65**, 1338–1349.

Winer, B. J. (1971) *Statistical Principles in Experimental Design*. McGraw-Hill, New York.

Wohlwill, J. F. (1973) *The Study of Behavioral Development*. Academic Press, New York.

Zellner, A. (1979) Causality and econometrics. In Brunner, K., and Meltzer, A. H. (Eds), *Three Aspects of Policy and Policymaking: Knowledge, Data and Institutions*. North-Holland, Amsterdam.

Zigler, E., and Valentine, J. (Eds) (1979) *Project Head Start*. Free Press, New York.

Author Index

Subject Index